Rape of the Sleeping Woman

Alejandro if you
look you will
find su nombre
en esto gran libro —
a mi querido amigo
Torres
8/15/95

Not poppy nor mandragora
nor all the drowsy syrups of the world
shall ever medicine thee to that sweet sleep.

Othello 111, 3

D.K. TOTERAS

Rape of the Sleeping Woman

&

The practice of hypnagogic sex

The Nine Muses Press 1995
Occidental, California

Printed in the U.S.A. by Braun-Brumfield
First Edition: The Nine Muses Press

Library of Congress Cataloging-in-Publication Data

Toteras, D. K., date
Rape of the sleeping woman & the practice of hypnagogic sex / D.K. Toteras.
p. cm.
Title on added t.p. : Rape of the sleeping woman.
ISBN 0-9644122-0-9
I. Title. II. Title: Rape of the sleeping woman.
III. Title: Rape of the sleeping woman and the practice of hypnagogic sex.
PS3570.0757R3 1995
813'.54--dc20 94-43091

Acknowledgments:
David Bromige, editor
Nikodemos Konstan, designer
Richard Ward, cover artist

The Nine Muses Press
P.O. Box 1138
Occidental, CA 95465

Contents

Contents

Contents

Contents

Contents

Contents

Contents

Contents

Contents

Narrator's Note

Previous to my arrest, I lived a life where excitement was performing on a stage. My greatest fear was that my musical concentration would be off during a concert, or that I would break a string on my guitar in the middle of a performance. I was a musician earning my respect on a concert stage, but as my audience and repertoire grew, so did my seclusion. I lived a musician's life...a life of necessary seclusion...endless study of musical phrasing and intonations, daily forays into the ever mysterious areas of rhythms. A lifetime spent in the study of musical perfection.

The life of an artist requires a different reality than the measurable reality of the external world. Music, like all art, requires an internal, emotional view of existence. A view composed of sympathy, empathy, pathos...human qualities that are religiously guarded in the soul of an artist.

I tried to explain this to the police and to the District Attorney. They turned a deaf ear to me. I tried to convince them that I didn't have the aggressive personality, the hatred, the indifference to commit rape, nor for that matter, any violent act.

Narrator's Note

I was being portrayed as a soulless creature who lives on a tormented landscape, identified by a number, a fingerprint, a photograph, a urine test. A creature whose essence has been robbed by the logic of indifference and the mechanical view of present life. Unfortunately my story of the events that led to my arrest was too involved, and the more I tried to explain it, the more confusing it became. I realized that reality requires repetition to be understood, and no one had time to hear it as it dislodged itself from my exhausted mind.

My feelings, my intuitions, my inner world needs love to exist. I cannot create music in a spiritual tundra...a note can't leave my fingertips, a phrase won't emanate from those six strings. Without love I knew I would die destitute on the street. I told the police I had, like a reasonable man, tried everything I could to explain my wife's insensibilities. I spent over a year and thousands of dollars trying to solve the problem of why my wife was so detached, so cold, so uncaring towards me. Her total indifference turned my soul into a cauldron of sour suspicion.

For months I tortured myself with suspicious thoughts and fears, imagining the woman I loved in the arms of another lover. In the eye of my imagination I saw her in the back seat of a car, in a motel room, in the lover's apartment, partially dressed, at times totally naked. I tried every reasonable avenue to bring some sanity back to my life. Everything I tried ended in failure.

I accused myself of being too preoccupied with my music and therefore neglecting my wife. I have to admit my interests outside of my music were meager. My existence was Spartan. I had never cultivated the social bearing or the expressions of a womanizer. Though my world was filled with women, they were all part of the paying audience. The thought of being a recreational lover was a cold reflection. It was devoid of delicate sensitivities and passionate words that seemed so necessary to my existence.

I went to a sex counselor and confessed my fears. She told me my sex techniques were at fault, and charged me $4,500 for instruction in the new ways of sexuality. I went to the wife of a friend who instructed me in the arts of duplicity and the erotic pleasure of betrayal. With all this instruction I still lost all hope of salvaging our love until Edgar, the ex-priest, introduced me to hypnagogic sex and the work of Dr. Panukla on *The Lost Art of Dreams and Hypnagogic Sex*.

Panukla's book dealt with a simple love, a natural unpolluted love, a love without effort, without endless preparation, without rejection. A love without pain, a love that took place while both of us slept, a love coated with endorphins...we would meet in our dreams in pure ecstasy and refresh our thirsty souls.

Instinctively I knew there was a need for this type of lovemaking. I, along with everyone else, was caught in an historical moment which requires a different way for man and woman to experience the beauty of love with each other.

Life has become too stressful, too fast, too demanding, too intellectual, too reasonable. Lovers have become performers who have to study for their parts. The demands of the modern lover are impossible to meet. Sexual performance requires energy. Lovemaking and its pleasure require time, and time is what the present person doesn't have. The old physical way of making love just doesn't work anymore.

I knew I was getting involved in something far more encompassing than I had ever tried before. Every step I took would be a new one, through unknown stories, unknown events, unknown explanations. I loved her. I loved her enough to take a chance on finding a new way to express my love.

I loved her, and the unknown forces of sexual attraction, patterns that took eons to create, were working on me, and at the same moment she thwarted me, rejected me. She abandoned me when I needed her the most. I was swimming in a sea of fear, the worst kind of fear, fear disguised as hope. I was terrified that my hopes would never see the lite of day. That for the rest of my life I would approach her only to have her yawn in my face. I had the desperate urge of a convict...to escape...to run and never look back again. Instead I stayed and became like the dog who chases a bone. This is the dog's misery to forever chase the bone. With what devotion he watches it, guards it from all others and spends endless hours breaking it open to suck on the marrow of pleasure.

Following the dog's example of diligence, devotion, affection, and fervor, I decided to stay and to love her in the darkness of the nite. I decided to remain anonymous to her conscious world and not offend her nor burden her with my needs. I would try to share with her the bliss of loving in our dreams, but as is the fate of all beginners...failure is the first step to mastery.

Unknown to me at the time, I made a mistake in the preparation and in the dosage of the ayahuasca elixir. The ayahuasca was necessary to open the oneiritic dream channels in the execution of this new method of hypnagogic lovemaking.

The consequences were catastrophic. Apparently the authorities saw my errors of dosage magnified beyond my human view. Whatever the degree of error, someone found it serious enough or interesting enough to make it a legal issue, to have me arrested and accused of raping my wife while she slept. It seems that fate stays hidden until the very last moment…then makes its appearance disguised as luck, either good or bad.

James Tadley

Rape

The lockup

My inner voice sounded pitiful

The terror of the law

The wife-rapist

The monster waiting

Politeness in the bed

My contribution to the civilized, objective community

When your luck runs bad, a feeling of aloneness begins to fall on you...the thought that some mysterious force has selected you by random chance, out of all the people on this earth, to be punished.
The thought that keeps banging in my head is...why me? It must be the same feeling that a sick patient gets when the doctor tells him, "You have only a short time to live." Somewhere within me I keep hearing a voice that whimpers...why me?

The fear that I had been selected, by some mysterious process, to become a martyr, a witness to my own demise, engulfed me as though a black hood had been placed over my head. A feeling of suffocation pressed on my lungs. My legs trembled and I felt the cold sweat of terror down the center of my back. A feeling of utter loss drained the blood from my head. I felt dizzy and wanted to vomit.

I sat down on the hard bench in the holding cell where I had been placed. I had never experienced fear like this before, as if some insane sick mind was at the helm of my life and had decided to cast me in the role of the modern depraved, lascivious, criminally insensitive man, who would, to satisfy some perverse feeling, rape a woman.

I was told later, by the District Attorney, rape is not sexual intercourse between two people but a violent act of subjugation. A conquering of the sexual will of another by force and intimidation.

The lockup

"What the man hang on you?" a big black man in the lockup asked me.

"Rape."

"That's big shit now days," the black man told me. "How'd you get nailed?"

"My wife called the cops to tell them that I had raped her. I screamed at her to put the phone down. She told the cops to hurry, that I had lost my mind and would probably kill her. Two squad cars pulled up with their lites lit up, sirens wailing, guns drawn."

Fate had chosen to elevate me to new heights of notoriety and my miserable, cowardly disposition trembled at the thought of it. The terror of my imagination brought me to my knees. I wanted to beg, to lick the boot of authority, to do something that would convince them that I was, by my very nature, a gentle, sensitive person…innocent of the charge of raping my wife while she slept.

"They put a gun to my head...hard cuffs on my wrists...the Miranda prayer was read to me and off I went, while the curious neighbors looked from behind the corners of their drawn drapes."

My problems were just beginning, and like all problems, they started with a pain. A small pain at first then it grew till I was overcome, not only by the pain itself, but by the pain of terror as I saw the inevitability of it all.

I was a virgin to the legal system...I was in the lockup and didn't know what to do about it.
"Shit little brother...yo ass need a lawyer," the black man told me, "and you gona need loot for yo bail my good man, or yo ass gona stay right where you at...till you old and gray."

I knew two lawyers, both of them were old friends. Howard, who was a trust attorney for a local bank, and Peter, who was an entertainment attorney.

I called Peter and talked to his wife Sissy who told me he was out of town for a week. I didn't tell her the reason for my call. Then I called Howard at the bank.
"Where you at?" he asked me.
"In the lockup at the Bryant Street jail."
"What's the charge?"
"Rape."
"Who'd you rape?"
"My wife."
A long pause..."What?" I could hear in his voice the tone of surprise at the accusation.
"I guess they haven't set bail yet. When did they arrest you?"
"Around 4 A.M. this morning."
"When were you booked?"
"Around 9 A.M. I'm sick," I told Howard, "this is more than my nerves can take."
"Take it easy," he told me. "As soon as they set bail I'll get ahold of Puccini, the bail bondsman, and have you out."

The judge set bail at $50,000, and by 2 o'clock in the afternoon I was having lunch with Howard at Tommy's Place on Van Ness Avenue. This was all part of the new social order. You need an attorney just like you need a counselor, a therapist, a tax accountant...people trained to keep you out of trouble.

"Look!" Howard told me. "I don't know how far this is going to go. The bail is a mite steep, being that it was your wife and not some unknown hapless Sunday-school teenager.

"It's the mood of the times Pal. When I was in law school 30 years ago, I had a professor who had written our textbook on criminal law. Being that criminal law was given to us in our first year, our legal reasoning wasn't up to par and the questions we raised needed the support of the professor to see the lite of day. But what was interesting, when we got to the crime of rape, the class seemed to come alive with questions. One question in particular annoyed the old professor. The question was...can a man rape his wife? That question came up more than once. And the usual answer from the old prof was that rape is a social, psychological, physical, and legal phenomenon. A complicated crime, especially if the word husband is introduced. Maybe 30 years ago was far enough back in time that the crime of raping your wife was as bizarre as trying to explain astronomy to a blind man.

"If the substantive criminal law hasn't changed, since I became a lawyer, rape still requires 'unlawful penetration' as the essential part of the definition of rape, and what is defined as 'unlawful' is that which is 'not authorized by law.' But since you are 'lawfully' married to your wife, it creates a difficult argument of culpability. Somehow the District Attorney has to construct an argument that you, the husband, did an 'unlawful act' in having sexual intercourse with your wife. The distinction between rapist and husband is important.

"The rapist hides in the dark shadows waiting. The sound of high heels walking in the distance lites his lust as he hears the steps getting closer. A woman coming home with a bag of groceries. He leaps at her throat with a knife. 'I want your hole,' he whispers to her. Reaching under her dress, he rips off her silken panties. He bends her over and bones her once, twice, three times. She groans. She picks up her groceries from the street and limps home. She never saw his face but she knows it's his unwanted fluid drooling down between her thighs. That is the classic example of rape," Howard says, "a Neanderthal man let loose in a civilized world.

"Though a husband might be disgusting to his wife, to the point that she doesn't want him touching her with a 10-foot pole, she is, as far as the law is concerned, lawfully married to him, and if she doesn't want him touching her, the law has provided a remedy...she can legally separate or legally divorce him.

"You need a criminal attorney, someone who is really up on this sort of thing. It's not my field. I'm a trust attorney, old friend." While Howard was talking to me about the elements of the crime of rape, my mind wandered off again to the same thought that kept circulating through my emotions. I had the depressing feeling that I was being picked by the chaotic combinations of chance to be paraded into the arena for the final show of human reason gone berserk. My guilt would be as arbitrary as thumbs up or thumbs down, and would depend on whether the judge and jury liked my face, if they had slept well that nite, had eaten well that morning, or felt that justice would be better served if they left the bedroom arguments to be solved by its occupants. If the crowd saw me as a loving husband, carried away by my wife's beauty, so that I caressed her and fondled her in a way that the gods would approve, I'd be home free. But if I was portrayed as a fucken nite ghoul, seeking with malice and violent force to have this hapless creature who couldn't stand me because of bad breath, or for whatever reason, then I'd be in trouble. Being a husband might not save me, since the word husband had about as much validity now as a dodo bird in a shooting gallery.

I felt betrayed, and not so much by my wife, but by my own actions. I had betrayed myself by my own needs, by my own fears. Now I felt alone. All the grains of sand had fallen from the hourglass. The time had come. I had let my desires for a woman bring me to this untimely end. My crime might make some lawyer his fame and fortune defending me. I might ascend to the same level of fame as all the rest of the historical figures who had their wives when the wife was sleeping. Didn't God visit Mary in her sleep? Didn't Zeus, posing as a swan, visit Leda as she lay in front of him sleeping, waiting to be had?

I'd be scared to say this to someone. They would take it as outrageous, as advocating that, because the gods raped their women, I could do likewise, or that I was placing myself in the same position as a god.

I wanted to fall on my knees and start praying that my end be swift…quick…and that I wouldn't be left to linger...in the hell-holes of prison.

"I'm scared," I told Howard.

The magic was gone and I didn't have sense enough to see it. You can't dictate love and passion. It comes when it comes... something lets loose inside of you and it happens. Being able to control it gets you through the day, but passion is hard to control when you're lying in a bed with a woman you love.

"What did you do?" Howard asked me.

At this point I had to decide if I was going to tell Howard the whole story. But how could I? The story was so involved and complicated that no one would believe it.

"Did she ever tell you not to touch her?" Howard asked me.

"No…but she might as well have said that. She ignored me day in and day out. How many nites I just lay there next to her, staring at her, in the darkness of the nite, passing my Nifty Pocket Lite over her still body, wanting to taste that bitter fruit while she slept. I felt she had put a 'No Trespass' sign on her ass. It was like some dark road to my passions with a blinking red lite to warn me of danger and not to get any closer. It was a warning with a threat that I didn't understand."

"It seems almost ungrateful that you should complain," Howard told me. "Your infamous introduction to history will change totally the way couples go to bed at nite, and infamy, like fame, has a price to pay.

"Now this is what she says happened to her on the nite of the 28 of November."

He read the charges to me slowly, with every word emphasized so it would sink deep into my soul…like a dagger that would never be withdrawn.

> ***The defendant, James Tadley, without any legal consent from the plaintiff, Nomi Tadley, his lawful wedded wife, did willfully and unlawfully sexually penetrate one Nomi Tadley.***
>
> ***Awakening, Mrs. Tadley found her husband, the defendant James Tadley, on top of her thrashing her in a wild manner. He proceeded to batter her about the face with his penis, which he referred to as his 'Tool.'***
>
> ***The defendant then proceeded to ravish her with abandonment and total disregard of her personal desires. With his teeth he bit her on the face, breast and buttocks.***
>
> ***When the plaintiff screamed, he willfully and with disregard to his wife's well-being, did wrongfully and unlawfully enter her with his 'Tool,' forcing upon her his uncontrolled desire, whereupon she begged him to stop, but he continued till he had exhausted himself.***
>
> ***Thereupon he ceased. Falling off her, he lay on the bed next to the plaintiff, in total disregard of the injuries that he had inflicted upon her person. Whereby Mrs. Tadley, attempting to report this incident to the proper authorities, was screamed at and threatened with bodily harm.***

"You're on the stage now my dear friend," Howard told me, but the tone in his voice sounded like the doors of doom opening for me to glimpse into. "It's the great American truth show, Pal…the person who can testify to the worst or hardest luck at the hands of a woman will win the first prize. I can see it, in the eye of my mind. Generations to come will know your name and the facts of the case, and as with all infamous and famous men, the moment has made you, so learn to enjoy the excitement of notoriety."

My inner voice sounded pitiful to me

Gone were my objectivity and rationality. How could anyone know what I'd been through since I married her? I found myself pleading with unknown faces, trying to get them to pity me. Only through pity could I ever hope to escape this awfulness that was growing bigger around me by the day. I was starting to acquire the voice of the betrayed and the condemned…of the man walking up to the gallows while the crowd cheers the hangman on.

I found myself creating mental scenarios, constructed out of shadows and faceless accusers, dressed in the black robes of the present Inquisition. I was pleading with my unknown condemners for pity, rehearsing my speech before the tribunal as they deliberated prison or freedom…life or death.

Babbling to myself for hours, I practiced long soliloquies as to my innocence. I had worked out, for my imaginary audience, one long oration concerning my life as a good citizen, a good man, a reasonable man, a sensitive man, a man who loved his mother and his sisters, womanhood, family, marriage, monogamy, children. I was sensitive, I wrote poetry and played the guitar. I had taken the road that all reasonable men do…the road of reasonable avoidance. I became the reasonable man...the man that the law bases its standards on...the man who should be able to foresee the final result of all his actions. I failed, for the first time in my life. I knew I had failed.

The terror of the law

I had tried to live a life without social guilt, but not because I was more honest than the next guy. It was my fear of authority and the blindness of the law that brought me to the decision to stay legally good. The power and the indifference of the law terrifies me. It's eating me up by the hour. Every time the phone rings, I think it's the police telling me not to try and run away, because they are coming to get me. I hear them yelling at me, "Wait right where you're at. We're coming to get you. Any resistance, and we'll blow you apart with hot lead."

The wife-rapist

Now I was placed in the same category as the man who waits, in the shadows of a doorway, for his female victim.

I was on my way to becoming the first of the new type of felon who, for some primal reason, desired the sleeping flesh of his wife as she lay next to him.

As the days passed, I added more fear and terror to the ever-growing scenarios my imagination was creating. Depressing thoughts evolved out of my head, like a culture of pathogenic bacteria left by some fiend to eat me up alive.

I could see my condemner sitting on a bench, dressed in a black robe, the legal mind that was ready to make comment, all perfectly reasonable, on the case at bar. Then he would send me to prison, to the hell-holes of San Quentin or Soledad for the rest of my life, or be merciful to me and give me a choice, prison or amputation.

I can hear my condemner whispering in my ear as I try to sleep.

> ***Womankind cannot survive with nite crawlers chasing them between the bedsheets. Womanhood is entitled to a full nite's rest without the thought of having to be awoken in the middle of the nite to entertain. Not only is a woman's health in jeopardy because of this constant violation, but her dignity and her rights as a person are violated...and outraged. A husband can commit an unlawful act with his wife. Yes a man can rape his wife, and worse yet, rape her when she's asleep.***
>
> ***There is an implied understanding between people who are to sleep together, that certain laws of civilized behavior must be adhered to while sleeping. There are limits as to what you may do and not do to someone who is sleeping next to you.***

> ***One will not fuck one...***
> ***Shit upon one...***
> ***Piss on one...***
> ***Steal from or beat the other***
> ***while he or she is asleep.***

My blasphemy wasn't towards God, it was to the law. I was in the hands of the law, not the supernatural powers that created it all.

> ***Your hardon has trespassed...in the middle of the nite, across the imaginary close that surrounded her body while she slept, a common law right given to all free persons holding a proprietary right over their bodies, that no one will trespass.***

"My hardon appeared, your Honor, from the unknowable. It appeared from what the ancient poets call the Apiron, from the Void. It appeared in the middle of the nite, hooded like a medieval monk. It took command of all my existence, and crashed me through the imaginary line of privacy, dragging me into her like a dog drags its tail into the bowl of plenty. It was man's aggressive impulse, the mystery of the universe against the innocent soul of the woman. I'm guilty of desire and bad judgement your Honor, but not a crime of such insensitivity as rape."

The monster waiting

"I wake up and the monster is there, waiting for me. The bedsheets are lifted up high, like a Bedouin tent celebrating the coming of the Lord...'Go forward and multiply.' It was programmed in me when the whole thing was put together. I have no control over it being there, hard as the will of God. Once I see it get hard, I have to tend to it. I have to find some way to make it go down. I can shove it in ice-cold water. I can hit it with my fingers, or I can jack it off, or hopefully put it in a warm waiting hole. That's why I got married. I wanted to love and propagate, and let it come down naturally with satisfaction, with the strength of its existence, with health and dignity."

I would plead with the District Attorney, hoping to appeal to his humanism or empathy or that thing in us that says...this man is innocent of any crime. I tried to reason with my accuser. Rape was not part of my character, but how could the D.A. understand? His education was the law. The law is not interested in people, it is interested in legal issues. Had he been a poet, he would have hugged me and cried with me, and commiserated with me in the loss of my love.

In loss of affection
comfort
security
self-esteem
pride
love
passion
tenderness
all of it gone down the drain of legal accusation.
Pity for me would sound like the following.

> ***This man is a husband, a lover, a male human***
> ***who wanted to make love to***
> ***his wife,***
> ***his sweetheart,***
> ***his loveress...call her what you want...it was his***
> ***woman, not a stranger in the nite.***

"There are legal issues involved," Howard told me, "that will make their appearance quickly, once the groundwork has been laid to have you prosecuted."

I had already committed an assault on her decency, assaulting her with my eyes, staring at her when she didn't want to be stared at. She was sleeping, I knocked on the door. No one answered, I entered her without permission. "Kissing a woman without her consent can constitute a battery," Howard told me.

I could be portrayed as Quasimodo, drooling, masticating, salivating and involving himself in the dance of the mad... carrying off the beautiful Esmeralda to the belltower. A despicable, insensitive male, a mongoloid idiot who, when he becomes aware of his hardon, can't keep his hands off it. I was the perpetrator of a crime and she the innocent victim. The scene of the crime was our king-size bed. I was accused of callousness and indifference. A swollen battering ram had been put in a dry well. A groan and a fart had broken the silence of the nite.

The days passed slowly as I waited to see if the D.A. would bring charges against me. I called Howard daily. He was a friend, and kept telling me to take it easy, not to think about it. That it was a difficult case to bring to trial. Maybe the dear lady would take pity on me and forgive me for my trespass.

The thought of my criminality was hard to accept. Did I really commit a crime? Howard told me that a crime was any social harm defined and made punishable by law. Was it unlawful to love up my wife? Did I steal her love? All of this was circulating through my head like a cyclical storm. I was accused of using "it" without permission from its owner. I was told that if I called her, or went near her house, or tried to make contact with her, I would be arrested and dealt with severely at the hands of the law.

Politeness in the bed

I recognized the definite limits of politeness. Even though it's polite to ask "if I can have some," and polite and correct to recognize the rights of another person's body not to be violated, you just don't wake up your woman and ask her in the middle of the nite, *Please can I put it in?* and wait for the answer. It ruins the magic of the moment. The asking seems so disgusting... *Please can you wake up? I have to unload.*

What the hell's the use of sleeping with a woman, if not to give it to her when nature raises the Hardon? If God gives man a hardon, when and how is man to use it? And to what extent does the law have the right to dictate when a man is to use his rod? Day or nite? Awake or asleep? Wife, lover, stranger, all of it can't be the same?

My contribution to the civilized, objective community

I don't know if Howard was trying to console me...trying to make me feel that my life was not wasted...when he told me that I did contribute something to the civilized, objective, community I lived in.

"If this ever went to trial," Howard said, "it might be a landmark case dealing with the human condition. Somehow the laws of nature have been disturbed by the indifference and the objectivity of the legal system. The Court has its back to the wall. Eventually the court must decide on the issue...if desire is more compelling than reason in the mating process of the human being. We have gotten to the point that we feel we can subpoena God for his testimony and place the question right in his lap, 'Is desire stronger than reason?'"

But a Godly deposition might be hard to get, and God might be a reluctant witness, being that his two first creations proved that a serpent in the hand was better than an apple in the tree. Even the evolutionist would have to agree that somehow desire has played a great part in the evolution of mankind from a paramecium to a primate.

Maybe we ought to change the question and subpoena God to answer...what was his intent when he put desire into Adam and Eve? It seems that without desire there would have been a quick end to the great human experiment.

"Don't look so glum," Howard told me. "We are now in the land of the absurd, just like Alice-In-Wonderland hoping to find a land of imaginary solutions. Your wife's desire and your desire are a lot different than the legal desire to keep public order. You want her and she doesn't want you. Desire, my dear friend, is what might be the key issue in this battle that is being fought on a bed by two great opposing armies."

I knew Howard was right. It was as simple as that. Her desires and mine weren't the same anymore and what happened from here on was anyone's guess.

"I'm sure it will all work out somehow," I remember Howard telling me, as if he knew that my ordeals were just beginning.

Getting a Lawyer

The District Attorney
The bed devoured me
I contacted a woman lawyer
The logoretics of love
Ms. Cynthia Trumble, Attorney-at-Law
A painted face
The sleeping woman and hypnagogic sex
A blind dog in a meat shop

The District Attorney
had Nomi's deposition in front of him. "She claims your constant hardon, which you kept trying to put in her, was having a deleterious effect on her nervous system. You spent months driving her crazy. One nite in particular, she claimed, she woke up and saw your 'tool' in your hand heading for her face…I quote her…'he was in a sexual frenzy.' She was afraid that you would ram it down her throat and choke her to death with it. Is this correct Mr. Tadley?"

"That's a lie!" I told the D.A. in an aggravated voice. "She was never awake, she probably dreamt it."

I assured my interrogator that I would answer all his questions with honesty, but by the same accord he must, if he was married, try to understand the circumstances of my acts.

"I'm not interested as to why you did it Mr. Tadley...I'm just interested in the fact that you did do it. The jury will have to determine the truth of it all. Now why don't you answer the questions as I pose them?" His voice was deliberate, accurate, and to the point. "Did you, at any time, try to or have intercourse with your wife while she was sleeping?"

I was afraid to answer. I hesitated, and he noticed the hesitation. He was a professional. His ears flicked like a dog's do. His nose twitched. He smelt my fear. He was looking for something. I needed someone here who would tell me what to say.

"She wasn't a stranger, she was my wife. I didn't think I needed nitely permission."

"Please answer...Yes or No...to the questions I ask you."

"Yes sir," I said, in a very servile tone. "I got tired of just looking at her under the covers. I got tired of rubbing up to her while she snored. Jesus man!" I said, "What did you want me to do? Don't all people do that with their wives?"

"Do what with their wives Mr. Tadley?"

"Look at them, touch them, feel them, kiss them, when they are asleep."

"Please refrain from wandering away. Answer only my questions. You're charged with raping your wife and not just kissing her while she slept."

I could feel my blood boil and my eyes becoming blurred. I was afraid he might feel the anger coming out of me was directed towards him. If I could only share one intimate thought with him, maybe we could become brothers.

"Excuse me," I said in the most polite voice I had in my arsenal of hypocritical attitudes. "You must get hardons, don't you?"

He looked at me. I had to continue. If I stopped now he would see me as vulgar, a man capable of rape, as a man who intended to insult, but if I continued it would be man talking to man, like woman talking to woman about their monthly cycles. We could talk to each other about our daily hardons and their meaning.

I wanted to yell out, as loud as I could, so the world could hear me. A morning hardon was different than a hardon at nite. A morning hardon was filled with hot piss. A nite hardon was filled with hot love-potions, with life-creating juices. A hardon appearing while you sleep can be like a storm at sea. It's filled with piss and spunk. It is the lava that Vesuvius spewed on Pompeii. But I was afraid. I was frightened by the coldness of my interrogator's logic and his determination to have me hung. In a humble voice I said, "I'm just another male, married and living with a woman who says she is too tired to have me."

The bed devoured me

The District Attorney told me it was the first case he had had of a husband being charged for raping his wife while she was soundly sleeping in a bed they both shared. And with a look of concern, and maybe brotherly love, he admitted to me that he wasn't looking forward to prosecuting it.

The bed, sanctioned by love, money or marriage, once the playground of Eros and Aphrodite, had now become a Venus plant waiting to devour the unsuspecting husband. I was sure of it. I could see women's groups, dedicated to woman's dignity, pressing for my speedy trial and my ultimate conviction.

It could be that I was gaining the D.A.'s sympathy. I told him that poetry and deep affection were at stake, that the 20th century would see the end of male and female sleeping in the same bed. Poetic phrases such as

I shared the same bed with her for 30 years

would be a statement of dangerous implications as to how many times you raped her while she was sleeping. And she didn't know it until her hypnotist informed her.

The District Attorney said, "You'd better get a lawyer."

I told Howard about the advice the D.A. gave me and Howard suggested that I contact a good criminal attorney that he knew, who was, by the way, a woman.

I contacted a woman lawyer

At first the thought of having a woman lawyer defend me sounded crazy, but Howard assured me that my defense would be viewed differently if I had a woman lawyer plead and argue my case. I couldn't see any reason why a woman lawyer would refuse me, even though I was accused of raping one of her kind. To a lawyer a dollar is a dollar and it's a known fact that most lawyers would sue their mother if life went sour for them.

The more I thought of it the more reasonable it sounded. If a woman advocated my cause, other women would believe in my innocence, and if not my innocence, then at least my intent to be or become my wife's lover and not a felon hell-bent on raping her. "She's like an animal in the courtroom," Howard told me. "The judges are scared of her. She looks like she'd claw the eyes out of a tiger."

I called her secretary and made an appointment for the following day. She didn't waste any time, and my nerves began the ordeal of anticipation. How would I describe the facts to her? I had only a day to prepare my tale of woe.

How do I tell another woman that my troubles with my wife began by her falling asleep, before I could get her? She wasn't available to me when she was awake, so I got her when she was asleep. It doesn't sound innocent. It sounds contrived, planned-out, malicious, embarrassing. Staring at her with a flashlite. We were both innocent as I lay there watching her touch herself, rub herself, listening to her farts, her snoring, slurping, teeth-grinding, all of this while she was innocently asleep.

The logoretics of love

It was her innocent indifference that caused such a turmoil in my life and brought me to this point of having to find a lawyer to defend me. A world so legalized, a world so artificial, so contrived, so rational that the natural activities of marriage could now be constructed as rape.

I was caught in the logoretics of civilized savagery
in the cock-and-bullshit stories of modern times
where a person sifts out his thoughts to such an extent that he becomes stupefied by his own daydreams. I was sure some

lawyer would make his fame and fortune defending me from the logoretics of love. Words seeking out some meaning, words squeezed and shaved like loaded dice to make prosecution possible.

Slowly a feeling started developing in the bottom of my stomach. A feeling that somehow I might be doing the wrong thing in using a woman lawyer. Why would a woman sympathize with me? How could a woman ever feel what I had to go through? How could I ever explain the deviousness, duplicity and cunning I had to develop in order to have my own wife?

Ms. Cynthia Trumble, Attorney-at-Law

I drove my car to her office which was on Union and Fillmore, parked at a lot across from her office and walked over. I was looking for Ms. Cynthia Trumble...Attorney-at-Law.

There it was, her name in beautiful gold Gothic lettering, done on an imposing black-enameled door. A brass bell waiting to be pressed.

I was ushered into the waiting room by a small woman with straight yellow hair. I can't even remember what she looked like, but I remember that she scared me as I heard her voice tell me, "Ms. Trumble will see you right away."

I didn't know exactly how to introduce myself other than by name. I stuck my hand out and she did the same. We touched, showing each other that we had no hidden weapons in our hands. She told me to "sit down," and pointed to a straight-back chair in front of her desk.

"Mr....what's your name?...Oh yes!...James Tadley...What's your problem Mr. Tadley?"

Introducing myself to my new lawyer was a difficult ordeal. I wanted her sympathy and I became painfully aware of my face and if I was wearing the right expression. The look should fit the occasion. But how do I portray a face that tells the viewer that I'm scared, hurt, depressed? What does a face look like that needs sympathy? I was afraid that my face would not reveal the pain that was in me. Ready or not...here I was...hoping to get her sympathy?

She put a yellow legal tablet in front of her, and with a golden pen in her left hand she asked me, quietly and without a trace of anxiety in her voice, to tell her my story. She was left-handed. We had something in common. I felt more at ease and like a fool, instead of starting from the beginning of my tale, I started from the very end of the story.

"The law is charging me with rape for having my wife without her consent...while she was asleep."

"Having your wife? What the hell's that supposed to mean?"

"I am, as of 2 weeks ago, a suspected wife-rapist. If I don't clear myself, I will, from hereon in, add this to my introductions. I'm Jim, a wife-rapist. The world will know me as the first mortal to be tried for raping his wife when she was snoring."

A painted face

The creature must have taken a great dislike to me from the first moment she met me. I saw a glint in her fishlike eyes. A small twist of those hardened lips. I don't know what it really was, but I could feel her dislike more than I could see it. I was fascinated by the awfulness of her painted face. It belonged to a billboard advertisement with a smile painted on it. There was no movement on it. I must have looked like John the Baptist searching the desert for a well with fresh water, but finding nothing in that desolation.

Her face gave the appearance that it had been vacuum-formed out of plastic. There wasn't one flaw on her face, not a pore, a pimple, a wrinkle, a scar, hair or a mole, visible to the human eye. She lived with a face done with an air brush, in a pale white with no color on the cheeks. Her eyes had been outlined in a Prussian blue. Her eyelids in a rose pastel. Her hair was blonde and long and was parted in the middle of her head. She disguised herself with a smile that was drawn in with lipstick. Her voice had that crackling sound of ice.

"I want the facts and nothing else, do you understand?"

"Yes Ma'am."

"Get off that Ma'am crap."

I gave her all the facts as neat as I could. I told my tale in a tone that you'd use to talk with your sister.

"I'm in a jam," I told her. "If you can't help me, I'm afraid I'll become a future convict. I'll have a label of depravity stuck on me that only a jail and heavy counseling could correct."

In a pleading voice I told her how I was filled with consideration for my wife's tiredness. I told her of my need for my wife's love. This male thing I did, having my wife when she was sleeping, seemed to be a natural desire in a man.

I told her bits and pieces of my story, moulding the pieces so I wouldn't be abrupt. I told her of the days and nites filled with deep respect for my wife's sleeping, and added that a saint could turn into a thief if starved long enough.

The sleeping woman and hypnagogic sex

I kept the stories of the aphrodisiacs to myself. The nectar of the ayahuasca vine, of Edgar the ex-priest, of elixirs I had slipped to her that had made no visible change in her sex desire or in her sleep. I mentioned Dr. Panukla's book, which advocated that a new revolution in sex was necessary, and I felt the time had arrived.

"What's this Panukla crap all about?" she asked me.

"It's about having sex with the woman while both of you are asleep. It's in Dr. Panukla's book called *The Sleeping Woman and Hypnagogic Sex*. It's about the sexual revolution of modern times."

She wrote it all down on her yellow pad, but as I extended and magnified the event, I realized that I was talking to the wrong person.

She put her golden pen down, raised her painted face and looked at me like the executioner does his client, with eyes as empty as piss holes in the snow. There was no pity in them. There was no look of human recognition, only a painted smile with cold fishlike eyes.

Each color on her face was drawn in for its own purpose and effects. It had the look of speed. The colors were applied in upward strokes, giving her the look of a fast-moving cheetah cat on the prowl for a victim.

A blind dog in a meat shop

"I find your activities at nite, while your wife sleeps, disgusting. As a lawyer I'm supposed to leave out my emotions and just look at the facts and the rules of law that apply, but I can't. I could defend a murderer. I could defend a person who I know is guilty. But a slime-ball like you, a creep that would sit up at nite staring at his wife with a flashlite, masturbating and spilling his fuck over her, is more than I can take. Only you know what you did to that poor woman while she slept, in what she thought was the safety of her home and bed. You're more than just a rapist, you're a terrorist, a persecutor, a depraved person, something so foul that I can't deal with it."

There probably were many words in the woman's dictionaries describing various types of male behavior, but according to her, there weren't any to describe me. I don't know what got that legal hag that pissed off. I told her all the necessary facts so she could, as she said, evaluate my legal position. But the lunatic used the information I gave her to get angry at me. She continued, unabated, like a blind dog in a meat shop, growling, snarling, barking, gulping, hissing. I was afraid she would leap up on her desk, pull up her skirt and piss in my face. Her voice now escalated to a threat.

"I find it disgusting that a woman has to keep the male at bay throughout the whole nite. It's encouraging to see the development of female individualism and self-esteem. To be able to turn her husband in for violating her when she doesn't want to be touched. This is a great advance in a woman's thinking." She stared at me, wanting to say more, but holding herself in check like a cocked pistol pointed at my head.

She continued with her prognosis of women's future.
"If something isn't done soon, the 21st century will find women wearing electronic chastity-monitors to make sure that the bastards they live with don't screw them while they're sleeping. A laser beam, triggered by the bastard's prick, will burn his prick off his slimy body. It's a pity that we have to cover ourselves with

gadgets in order to protect ourselves from you bastards. Do you understand?" she screamed at me.

"Yes Ma'am I do." My legs were shaking in a cesspool of fear. I was afraid that she would accuse me of some other crime while in her office. I got up and left like I was running to the toilet, before the painted monster came unglued. Anyone who painted their face like she did was to be taken seriously.

I ran across the street to get my car. I gave the parking attendant a fiver and didn't bother to pick up the change. I looked at my pants and they were wet. The painted bitch had so terrorized me that I had pissed in my pants like a child being scolded. How could someone scare me or upset me so much that I would allow myself to become so uncontrolled? If this was the beginning, what would the rest of it be like? Nothing was worth this. No woman's love was worth this pain, and yet I let myself become just another clot for the sake of that love hole.

A Dream in the Park

La Machina de Dios

It all started out one beautiful sun-filled day.
Louie, my agent, woke me up in the morning and asked me if I wanted to play a recital in a few weeks. I looked out the window. It was such a beautiful spring day that the thought of talking to him or having to think about a recital would ruin my whole day.
"You want to play?" he asked me again.
I thought for a moment. I hadn't played for over a month. I really needed the money, but I had a new book I wanted to read that day. My mind was made up and having to make a decision about anything else bothered me.
"Can you call me the day after tomorrow?"
"You're not making sense."

I had received a book in the mail the day before from Charlie B, an old poet I had met some years before, who always wrote about women he'd known in and around the bars of L.A. His poems had the smell of beer and wine, cheap perfume and sweaty bodies. It was so different from the world I knew that I read his work with the fascination of a child. I also had an ounce of good Mendocino sensimillan that a friend of mine left me for a guitar lesson I gave him. It was all a very beautiful coincidence that needed only this beautiful day to make it happen, and any thought about anything else would ruin the day for me.

"It does make sense to me Louie," I said.

I was on my way with Charlie's book under my arm and the indica, rolled in fine French paper, in my special pocket.

Charlie knew who he was. He was what he felt and he liked what he felt. He liked drinking and being seen. I hid away and smoked the delights of good cannabis. He liked bars and I liked green grass and hideaway parks. He liked women that were out front with their habits, women who meowed like alley cats and never bothered to wash it out after making it with a friend of his. Women who soused it up and pissed in their pants. He had a wonderful way of not getting along with anyone. I could read his latest exploits, smell the bars and stale smoke-filled rooms, the smell of stale beer on the breath of his women. Dirty sinks and unmade beds. A world that frightened me. A world I could never be part of, other than through the pages he wrote.

I was going to spend a day at Shakespeare's Glen, a little patch of grass behind the Natural Science Museum in Golden Gate Park. It would be a day of lying on the grass, smoking industrial-grade bud and poeticizing myself in the grand salon of the master-poet's book. My afternoon was now booked solid, not one more person or event could squeeze in.

"No Louie," I said, "I can't think today. I sprained my fingers opening up a bottle of Kerns Apricot Nectar, and I don't know how long it's going to take me to get ready for a performance."

I wanted to spend the day away from the guitar and the thought of a recital.

"Call me up next week, Louie."

"Too bad," he tells me. "No more than 3-hours' worth of work, good money for a solo act."

"I'd have to use my feet to do it, Louie, thanks." I hung up the phone, grabbed Charlie, and headed for that corny place where all things beautiful could happen in the flash of one picosecond.

It was a place that the street movers somehow missed. You could fall asleep amongst the flowers and wake up with your pants still hanging on your hips, your wallet where you left it, your zipper still up.

I liked this little place. With a few hits on my solo joint, the glen turned into a little dream world. The rest of humanity was missing. They didn't belong in here, they were stuck in the afternoon traffic with half-eaten peanut butter and jelly sandwiches sitting next to them in brown paper bags.

It was a little garden dedicated to love, lovers and flowers. All the flowers mentioned by Shakespeare in his plays were supposedly planted in this little garden by various groups of thoughtful people who donated this paradise in Golden Gate Park to lovers of poetry, music and the life of quiet dreams without grief. It made San Francisco a cultured city, a sensitive city, a place where one could go, smoke a good joint, read some verse and fall asleep.

I woke up, my cheek pressed on the green grass and my eyes looking at a sandaled foot that belonged to a set of beautiful long legs standing over me.

I stared, just a few inches away from my face, at a pair of beautiful feet with their toenails painted like rose petals.
I lay there looking, trying to figure out if the toes really belonged to a beautiful female or to one of the bull daggerts who roam the park and stand naked over a sleeping poet, whacking themselves off. For a moment I felt I had been selected by one of those purple lilies leering from behind one of Shakespeare's poetic plaques, waiting to unload his spunk and then piss on me to clear the barrel.

A hunch...maybe an intuitive feeling, an energy that draws male and female together...was fondling my brain. I felt it was a female waiting to be looked at, admired and lusted for.
The toes were feminine. They lay next to each other in a quiet way, the way female toes lie waiting for someone to enshrine them with little jewels, then kiss them with the devotion of a monk wanting to enter heaven.

A feeling of utter bliss had come over me. These weren't the boots of a cop, nor the dirty feet of a mop of shit looking for a handout. They were feet that had been cared for and had walked on the quilts of heaven. I knew the rest of her would be just as beautiful.

My eyes couldn't wait to begin their long journey upward, past the knees, the thighs and the tits. I was heading for her head, but I would take my time getting there.

I raised my eyes slowly up to her calves, where I rested before traveling any further. Then up to the hem of her dress, which hung like a curtain just above her knees.
Why was she standing over me?
Did I know her?

My desire to stick my head under her dress and kiss her hidden thighs, overcame all my fears of who she was and what she wanted.

My eyes wanted to see the rest of her so I began the long journey up to her breasts, and crossed over the gentle slopes. From there my eyes were ready to ascend to heaven. They stopped at her face, and I looked at her.

A pair of soft red lips were waiting for me. They parted with a soft smile, and a soft voice lilting asked me,
"Why are you reading Bukowski in Shakespeare's garden?"
I rang a bell in her head. She knew of Charlie and maybe she knew of me, but what was important was the sound of her voice. It turned me on. The key of the tone, the vibrato and timber of the voice made my ears salivate…they were drooling to hear her talk to me. I wanted to hear her voice again, asking me that strange question one more time. But a fear of answering came over me.

I don't know what comes out of my mouth when I'm asked a question. Even someone asking me my name makes me stumble. I never knew why this was part of my nature, but being a musician meant being lost in a nonmusical world where everyone knows each other through words and astrology charts.

Music was a sound through a faceless electronic box...keeping someone company while they washed the dishes or their underwear in the kitchen sink. Music comes from a black box sitting next to a cornflake carton. I was part of an electronic signal across the maze of wires. I was a micro dot on a magnetic tape, an impulse that can be replayed, thrown away, given away. It seemed I had no real expectations of myself other than pressing myself onto a record spinning on a record player, a sleeve photograph of me on a chair with a guitar cradled in my arms. Even if I knew who I was, and where on this earth you could find me, I would have to be able to abbreviate my existence between the mumble, stumble, hem and haw coming from my head...

I still had to find a quicker way to explain...Me...my past, present and future, so I wouldn't be thrown in the trash basket. Quick explanations tell people you're not lost in a world of confusion. You're moving around, you're visible, available and hopeful, you're ambitious and willing to take on responsibilities in a junkyard that is moving as fast as the lites blink.

If something fails, it's because it took too long to make its move. You weren't fast enough. You only get one chance with anyone. If you don't make it the first time, no one has the time to look at you, to understand what it is you're trying to say.

I had to be careful. If the wrong words came out of my mouth, she might walk off. But all events start out with the wrong introduction, yet they keep finding their way.

"Bukowski reminds me," I tell her, "that things have a smell to them, and if you get up close they usually stink."
She found it funny. I made her laugh. She sat down next to me on the grass. I offered her some weed and hoped she wasn't working for the D.E.A. or the locals, hell-bent on clearing the park of all the leftover dopers from the 60's. I knew she wanted to make conversation. Maybe she was lonely. Maybe she just had a fight with her lover and needed another male to comfort her through the separation. She must have seen that I was half-awake and dreamy-eyed with weed, that I was a park doper afraid that the

"Scooter Cops" were waiting in the bushes dressed in their blue jumpers, white helmets, black leather utility belts, pistols, radios, handcuffs...whistles, mace, pencils, paper, bullets, waiting for her to give the high sign. They would crash out of the bush into the glade to make the big raid, the super-bust, another park doper caught by a beautiful undercover narc.
She felt my apprehension. I offered her a hit on my roach. She took it and pulled a beautiful feminine draw on it.

She took another hit. We spent the afternoon talking about nothing. Most of the time my eyes enjoyed looking up her dress at a pair of cute little panties.
"You like them?" she asked me, with a voice that carried a promise of a dark room with a candle flickering on a bare wall, and the voice asking me if I like it. I was too old to be embarrassed and too young to give a shit.
"Yes I do."

La Machina de Dios

"I've figured it all out," I told her. "There is only one thing that makes life worth living and that is a good woman to look at, to lie next to, to get on top of and lay it into her. The rest of it, all the conversations and courtesies are merely preparations to do just that. It's the grand design,
La Machina De Dios.
It's the way of the Tao. It's male and female.
It's courtship a la mode."
She smiled as if she agreed with what I was telling her.
It was safe. I was in the harbor and after two or three hours of being with her, all I knew about her was that her name was Nomi, that she came from Bismarck, North Dakota. She said she really had enjoyed our afternoon together, gave me her phone number and told me to call her when I got around to it.

I thought it was a dream that I had shared with a beautiful woman in the little dreamy glen. A dream offered to me by the little drops of resin that the little buds carried, or it might be the spirit of that great poet...that made all things possible.

I thought about her that nite.
The next day I went back to the glen, but she wasn't there.

Waiting for something to happen is hard painful work. You're all lit up, every minute is an eternity, every second pounds in your ear like a bell in a church tower...pounding out over and over...
Where are you?
Why aren't you here?

I hate calling a woman up. It's so much easier if it happens by chance, but chance had played its hand…a dream in the park. Now it was effort.

I called her that nite and told her I had been thinking of her all day. She told me she had been waiting for me to call. She would see me tomorrow at the glen at noon.

I got there at eleven, lay on the grass and lit up, and by noon, when she showed up, I was well on my way to a state of calm reflection. A feeling of calm unconcern, a world dominated by fate rather than design...the clock had stopped. I had stepped into eternity. She made it easy for me to call her, to smoke with her, to touch her. Being with her made me high. I felt like an exaggerated thought, blown bigger by the winds of desire. I carved out my character with exaggerated words, slowly telling her I was a dreamer and the only way I could enjoy life was by playing my guitar and doing as little else as possible.
I got closer to her and as my courage grew, so did my newly created confessions.

Days passed as if they were drops of water on a rainy window sill. Then one nite thunder hit my ears. She cried out, just as she was ready to tear my back open, that she loved me. The magic word had been uttered...my hardon emptied its cargo and left for the barn. I had finally climbed the mountain in the back seat of my car. I Swam the Mississippi. I Dove off the Golden Gate Bridge. I Was the Grand Marshal of the Chinese New Year's Parade. I had finally conquered her feelings. She was mine, meaning that when my hardon came, she would be there to love. And along with that magic word...LOVE...came the free lunch.

She didn't care if I was a nobody,
a loser,
a feather merchant,
a dreamer, a doper, a man who lacked the virtue of ambition considered as essential to the modern man, the man who has it. We *were in love.* I lacked ambition and aggressiveness. I confessed to her, like one would to a priest, and she loved me for it. I told her of all my faults so she wouldn't think I was shortchanging her. I definitely was not a leader of men. I didn't have enough charisma to sell water to a person dying of thirst. I had no ideas, plans, nor did I ever look any further into the future than the very moment I lived in. Whatever displeased me, I avoided. I lived by the guide of pleasure. Pleasure was my only criterion to life's ultimate purpose. Simple pleasures. The pleasure of silence. The pleasure of good weed. Lying in the shade of a tree, daydreaming. I loved daydreaming more than any other activity. I daydreamed so often that daydreaming was an automatic response to being awake. I told her all the feelings I had Identified and had accepted as being the essential me. I was an open book. I was afraid of secrets...they drained my energy. I presented myself as a stripped-down version of a human being who wanted nothing more in life than love. The rest of it, whatever it was, was waiting somewhere in the future, and rather than trying to figure it out, I would avoid it. *We were in love.* And all my characteristics, shortcomings and failures were virtues to her. I told her the world was running on the slogan

DO NOT REPAIR....REPLACE

She agreed. I told her that finding yourself is not an easy feeling to live with, discovering that your existence is mostly being a nothing, is anti-something...anti-modern...anti-thankful...during a time when you could have been something. Everyone should be something, even if he's something that is vulgar, a liar, a cheat, a feather merchant, a soft shoe con man...or face the accusation that he is a person who lacks the last moral fiber left to modern man, a will to be something. And according to the smart money, a man with no will is like a mannequin in a store window, dressed but lifeless.

She said she loved my honesty and humble character. She promised to treat me with sensitivity. She would kiss me, hug me, stroke my head, unbutton my pants, kiss my balls. She would be my woman through thick or thin. She would make me so dependent on her lovemaking that all the women on earth would be a glob of
faceless
tit-less
shit-less...hags.

All my dreams begin in isolation, but this dream was different. It had hooks on it, hooking it up with other dreams. It just grew, step by step, like a chain with links tied to each other, until it became something that no one could ever imagine. She opened Bacchus's silken purse and I propelled myself into her. My ass quivered at the thought of a billion lite years existing between us, and yet we were coming together like two comets on a collision course. I spent a lot of time with her. I played music for her. She said she had never heard the Gypsy guitar of Andalucia. I told her of the years I lived with the Gypsies playing the guitar in the Cuevas de Granada. I told her of the Alhambra, of a full moon on the Daro River. I told her of the world of a musician, the stages that I sat on alone, in a chair with a guitar in my hands. I touched her soul...I touched her. I let my hands know her like they knew the strings of my guitar. *She said she loved me.* The greatest gift to man, the most thought-about, the most sought-after ingredient to life and all its infinite elements had been put on the celestial speedmobile, and sent flying through the universe. Grab it when and however you can, as you go by each other in opposite directions at the speed of lite! One day it was just ready and waiting. All the necessary things had been done. The instrument had been tuned and was in place. All the necessary words had been said. All the private places had been touched, fondled and kissed, and now I placed my pants and her panties together, next to us, on the floor of her small apartment at 2230 Bush Street. I found it funny, I told her, that our shorts were entangled in the same position that our bodies were on the bed.

We had embarked, like two adventurers, on the road to the holy city where everything is disclosed to the searching eye. Where the tongue strokes the flesh and the fingers caress the nipples and the scent of a magical garden engulfs you. Both of us naked and exposed like two gleaming knives lying on a bed...only one purpose to our existence. We groaned and moaned, huffed and puffed, sweated and exaggerated and held each other as we slept. I was on the road of love, and nothing else was important to me anymore.

Agreements are Necessary

Living together

You are...The one

The perfect (O)

Picking a place to live

We decided to get closer to each other, and the most important consideration and the litmus test of our love would be if we could live with each other.

Living together

I felt it would be safe and secure. But like everything else, one never knows what's comfortable or irritating, what's good or bad, what's sweet or sour, until it enters your world. One never knows what waits for him or what fate has in store until he shuts the door behind him.

We decided, out of a need to be closer to each other, that we would live like man and woman or husband and wife or as lovers under the same roof, eating out of the same pot, using the same toilet seat, sharing the same roll of toilet paper, tub, soap, and most important, sharing the same bed.

Sharing the same bed is a very spiritual encounter. You find yourself sprawling between the bedsheets. One bed two people. One wall with a painting on it...four eyes looking. One radio, four ears listening, and both dealing with each other's dreams. All of it must be in sync, like an orchestrated piece of metaphysical music. We would both be exposed to the silence of sleep and the vagaries of the dreams that come along with it.

In the bed is where man first discovered another world. A world that could be visited with the closing of his eyes. Another world, sometimes so terrifying that your heart is still pounding long after your eyes have popped the theater doors wide open. Waking up, your eyes focus on her open mouth. You have to have a neat lady to live this close. Something nice has to lie next to you. The person you take to bed might not be the person you wake up with.

What the problems of living together would be or what we would be looking for or adjusting to, neither knew. What we knew for certain was…nite people don't look or act the same in the daytime. In the morning they sit and stare, gulping cups of black coffee to help bring them back to daytime life. Day people don't like the nite nor the people who inhabit the dark.
I knew the best way to solve any problem was to erase it and start over. If it got difficult, we would both evaporate into the universal swill...along with the rest of the disgruntled lovers. We could walk out. The door was swinging both ways, like a fan in the hands of a Gypsy dancer.

The need to meet someone was gone. Having to do the Friday or Saturday nite thing was gone. Putting on your hunting clothes and drifting down to the Single Mingles…with its special clientele of asses to rub…the reason for that was gone. I was in love. I didn't need to look for the Celestial Woman twisting around somewhere out there, waiting for me to come and find her under some street lamp.

The slapping of the tongues, the meaningless exaggerated words that flow through the nite…of who you are. The polish and luster you've laid on yourself. One would be a fool not to make himself the hero of his own story. She tells you that you're all those things that make up the perfect person. She tells you it's all according to the stars and the signs of the zodiac, tarot cards, palmistry, phrenology, numerology. The spinning of the Ouija board lets it all be known to the whole world.

On a solo piece of cardboard written in big letters:
You are...The one
To be "The one," in a world that is filled with "The ones" who have it, isn't easy. To be "The one" you have to beat out "The guy" who has it. The more beautiful the female, the more "Ones" are sniffing about, looking, leering, salivating, bulges in their pants, like a double-barrel shotgun waiting to go off in her or in your face. "Has it" means He has it, and you wish you had it. "Has it" means you want it. He has it. You lost it or you never had it. He's always ahead of the crowd. He's ready to come through the door with that little skip in his walk. That little extra inch of personality and sensitivity, that little bit more than you have. A jingle in the pocket...a lilt to the voice. A story about mom, love and devotion. He says it...a different way...different than you. It sounds new, fresh, sincere.

The phone rings at 2:00 A.M. in the morning and she answers it in a soft, barely audible voice. The Saturday-nite revolving doors are swinging. Everyone, known and unknown, is going through them. I hear her whispering the following words. "Hi...how are you? Haven't heard from you in a long time.
Sure...aha...maybe...why not?"
Hushed tones, the one who has it is near. His voice has penetrated the locked door. He is in the bedroom whispering in her ear. I'm not supposed to hear. If I ask her, "Who was it?" she'll say it was her brother, he just got into town. You know he's calling because his cock is hard, and yours has turned into a nite prick, sleepy, drowsy, filled with piss. His cock...hard from denial...need...want...is lusting for her and she can hear the heat and passion spilling into the phone. Any minute now he'll bust the door open with his steel rod. If you're in the way, he'll ram it straight up your ass. To try for one more nite is difficult, impossible, you're finished. You have to get the hell out of there quick.

The perfect (O)
It's time to leave, 2:00 in the morning is as good a time as 2:00 in the afternoon. One is leaving and the other is just coming. The thought of it makes me cold. I'll leave him a spermal note, down deep in her perfect (O). A token of my appreciation, letting him know...it was good, and not to get too excited, because he's just the next guy in line. Then he can do the same for the next guy, and so on to the next guy, and the next guy. Standing in the doorway, I put my hat on and ram it into her for the last time. So quick, so neat that my flat top-hat never moved an inch on my head. She must have been so happy I was leaving without too many questions and all the "how comes?"

She gives me a long passionate kiss for being polite, sensitive and just a good guy. "Call me sometime," she tells me as the gooey spunk runs down her leg and on to the floor. The word "sometime" means never. "Call me…never." I feel stupid. Another week from now and she won't remember my name.

Now, I had arrived…in grand style. I had a woman all of my own. I didn't have to look anymore. I didn't have to get up at 2:00 A.M. and beat it out the door while she's telling me
"Honey don't forget your hat."
Like the guy who has it, I had arrived in style. Whatever it was, I had it, and it came together the way things come together, by luck and by fate.

Picking a place to live
Nomi decided that we should find a new place to make love and both of us move in. I had gotten used to her bed, and she couldn't get used to mine. We wanted to combine our habits in a new place, a new bed, and a new life. We could leave all our bad habits behind, along with the dirt on the floor, and all the stories that had accumulated during the sleepless nites. We held hands and agreed to share the same bed somewhere. The finding of a new place would leave us to create new bad habits together…new stories, new pleasures. It was important that we find the right branch of the tree to lie under…the right patch of grass to kiss

on, to love, to dream, to hurt from so much pleasure. We had to agree as to the tiger's lair.

Life was unfolding its precious mystery…the reason for man and woman. A mysterious energy that pissed rogues and frazzled old hags knew nothing about. My prick became my thermometer to life. If it was up, I was healthy, hungry, wanting, power, energy. If it was down, I was out, depressed, hungover, my stomach hurt, my back ached, my tongue was white, my eyes red.

Nomi gave me power and strength. It was a woman that lit the fires of life in me. She whispered…she'd be friend and confidante, wouldn't nag or yell, would leave me alone to play my guitar. If I smoked good sinsemilla, she would share it with me. Then she promised to heaven above not to get hot for anyone else, nor to do the forbidden…screw the bastard in the same bed we shared together and leave his drippings behind. She wouldn't leave her kotex where I could see it. She would flush the toilet when she finished. She would not fart in bed.

If we got out of line, we would both sit down and tell each other stories about things we wanted to hear, putting ourselves back on the main line again. If we found it necessary, we could use the most current terms, words or thoughts, in our conversation, to bind things, firm things up or dissolve things. There were books and lectures, counselors and advisors using new words to tell me that living together would have an obvious benefit.

All this seemed like a lot of work, but love looks for a way to verify itself, to prove its willingness to be giving…to sacrifice…to destroy yourself if need be…for love. "All we have to do," she said, "is to be honest and clear with each other." The rest of it was pure love.
I could hear it.
She told me.
I believed her.
She loved me.

New Habits

One day it all came to an end
Sleep as a pastime
Conversations concerning why
Bed-racing
I was taking on the realities of a child
Social/Time/Motion/Complex/Syndrome
Work-numb

After a month of looking, thinking, talking, walking, parking, we found a new place with a garden and a beautiful view overlooking San Francisco Bay, Oakland, Fruitvale, Hayward, the sky, the Trans-American Building, the clouds, the heavens, the sun coming up in the morning.

At nite you could see the City, boiling in electrical soup. Market Street, Mission Street, Howard, Folsom, looked like black stripes painted in this lit-up cake. There was a big pyramid built for a modern Pharaoh. A dozen more of them all lit up, reaching like cathedrals for the sky and a peek at the almightiness of God.

We were on the top of the world at the very center of existence...we were on Twin Peaks on the very top of the city. The view was so beautiful we thought buying drapes would close that beauty out of our love life.

But San Francisco, like Rome, is a city of seven hills. No matter where you live in San Francisco, there is always a hill somewhere nearby where one can look up, across or down, into someone else's window. With a good telescope you can become a guest, a brother, a lover, the third person on the couch, on the floor, or crawl into the bed with them. It is a city for all professional pie hawkers and peeping toms to congregate, salivate, masturbate and exchange information. It is a city of two loves, the love of loving and the love of looking.

The City was plagued with pie hawkers, pud beaters, peeping toms, gorps and fence jumpers, sliding their eyeballs through your windows with high-powered telescopes that could see an ingrown hair or a dingleberry hanging on your ass, from a mile away.

San Francisco is a city where maps are sold of windows, along with the time and place of activities. Nothing remains a secret in a city that was dedicated to the truth, honesty and the clarity of a Saint. The secret must remain a mystery or it becomes a joke. A secret must be forgotten for it to remain a secret. If you remember a secret you will tell it to someone, sell it, or show your friendship by sharing it.

We bought drapes so we could keep our lovemaking hidden, mysterious, and a secret from those eyes that searched for the midnite sun.
We bought rugs to keep our asses warm on the floor. A big beautiful circular bed, like an Aztec altar. A bed that you could lie on crosswise and never have your legs dangle over the sides. A bed you couldn't fall off as you rolled around on top of it.

Life was ready. The nest was prepared. All that was necessary was for the lovebirds to enter the little cage and start chirping. The beginning was like all beginnings, filled with curiosities and questions. The breaking of old habits and the creation of new ones.
I had two big water pipes I smoked my hash in. A big Moroccan argilla and a Persian hookah.
I asked her if I could put them next to the bed for decorative purposes until I could get more hash to smoke.
"No problem," she said.

Working together like geographers, cartographers and navigators, we found a special spot on the bed where we settled our love, along with a special couch and a special chair, all donated to the making of love. We paid extra attention to the way we were to do our lovemaking.

Soft lites were important to key into the rhythm of the moment. A couch with huge stuffed pillows to lie on. All the artifacts necessary for the senses to be aroused, awakened, and blended with the unexplainable dreams of wanting.

Nomi was a beautiful woman, she was soft like a gentle breeze on a summer nite. She was easy to get along with...that was important. There was nothing about her that grated on my nerves, agitated my stomach, or created feelings of anger in me.

I loved looking at her, the way she moved her hands, the way she moved her head when she laughed.
I loved watching her get dressed. She would transform herself piece by piece from just flesh...into an adornment of beauty. She knew this, like an animal knows how to hunt.
She took her time putting on
her bra
her laced panties
her silken stockings.
My eyes searched out her curves, soft curves that make women so beautiful to the male eye. Her slow movements extended the curves into a dance of desire. At that moment love was an insipid word. I wanted to ram my way in her. I wanted to chew on her tits with my teeth. I wanted to hear her scream with pleasure. What used to cool me off was watching her put on her pantyhose.

This was the only spot in the getting-dressed process that bothered me. The jerks, the jumps that interrupted my looking at and enjoying her visual existence. It didn't look soft, smooth, graceful, and female, the way the rest of it did. She squirmed and jiggled, jumped and shoved like she was stuffing meat into a sausage casing.

I asked her to change her style of nylons to the kind that require the fingers to be delicately maneuvered as they pull the silk over the bare thigh. As she stood in front of the mirror looking at herself, I'd run my fingers over her silken dress and let my hands rest on her covered breast.

It was all hidden now. Her clothes had reshaped the tempting flesh. Her movements looked beautiful, faithful. Long legs and deep green eyes. A body that moved like a lithe panther on high heels. She was drenched in visual aphrodisiacs, parading in front of me, while my prick hardened and tempered itself into venous brute steel.

"Don't you see Mr. Simms," I said to the D.A. in a pathetic voice, "all the systems, beliefs and faith of the thinking world can't help you when a woman parades in front of you. Religious men have fallen to their knees in fear that it might happen to them one day." The words flowed from my mouth like a dam had broken.

"Saint Augustine confessed that it happened to him, his cock thumping on his breast plate…screaming to be let out to plunder a woman who paraded in front of him. He trembled when he thought of the naked flesh being dressed or undressed. Tempted to touch it, to kiss it, to hold it, finger it…to take his tongue and smear it.

"The good Saint's ears must have been filled with the delights of hearing the panting, the sighing of the woman, swimming deep in her satisfaction. His nose was being loaded with the aroma of her passion, his fingers exploring the roads leading to her sacred altar. It's the magnet that draws you to the altar, not the sacredness of the altar itself.

"If I was a rapist," I told Mr. Simms, "would I refer to her cunt in such soft tones and gentle phrases?"

The weeks passed in pure pleasure and daily escapades. We spent our days in half-a-dozen love nooks that we had developed in our love palace. She would dress herself in different-style clothes and I would undress her. Sometimes she would wear an Indian sari and my hands had to find their way to her flesh. Every style required a different way to reach her and she would patiently wait for me to undress her. We had created a temple devoted to love with altars for every mood, for every feeling.

One day all of it came to an end
The gods heard our sounds of pleasure and happiness, and like all rulers, they became jealous when their subjects enjoyed life more than they did.

There were many reasons that it had to end, but the most obvious beginning point that led to the end was when she said she should get herself a job.
"Love, pleasure, and work do not go together," I said in a voice that sounded sad even to my ears.

The drum of the moment started its regularity, like the heart that beats out the moments of your life.
She got a job.
She'd leave for work at 7:00 in the morning for an hour's commute to San Mateo. My life now changed.

I'd go back to bed and pretend that she was next to me. I'd listen to the radio, get my pipe, have a little bowlful of smoke to open up the receptors in me, a few cups of coffee, then begin my day at my guitar, and wait for her to come home at 6:00 P.M. She was always on time. She had that natural virtue of regularity that constipated people seek.

The nite would begin the same.
After eating she would lie on the couch. I would turn the TV on. She would smile at me, yawn a few times, tell me how tired she was. Her eyes would close as if she had been touched by death. I'd give her a kiss as she left this world, and like Persephone, entered the next one.
How quickly, I thought, passion turns to lukewarm dishwater, then to cold swill...then dissolves into oblivion.

Sleep as a pastime
Sleep was now becoming a favorite pastime of hers.
Tiredness was part of our conversations. Where once she waited for me to play the guitar, now she asked if I could put it away so she could sleep.

There were times she would nod off when we were eating. I'd watch her head swing from side to side, then gently roll until her head reached its apogee of tilt, and not being able to finish its cycle, her head would jerk back, so abruptly, that I was afraid she'd break her neck. Her eyes would then open in a daze, like a drunkard waking out of a deep stupor. I'd watch her staring at the floor or at the ceiling or at her feet. Sometimes she would stare at me, like I was fly-shit on the wall.

She'd yawn, get up without saying a word and head for the couch, lie on it, give out a deep sigh and fall asleep.
Since I had no one to talk to, I'd listen to the radio or study a piece on my guitar, write in my notebook and keep myself entertained until it came time for me to go to sleep. Then I would try to enter into her world, to what seemed to be utter contentment, satisfaction, security and the blessed life of togetherness just waiting for me in the bed, but she snored too loud and it was like a tourniquet strangling my desires.

At first I saw all her actions as an expression of innocence. I would sit in front of her and watch her. I had enjoyed watching her dress and undress and now I felt I could enjoy her in the most innocent of all human endeavors…sleep. The beauty of her legs crept over me like a moistness of sublime satisfaction.
Her legs were a perfect shape. Long legs, beautifully shaped calves. A beautiful thigh exposed as her dress was pulled up past her knees. I wanted to touch them. I wanted to lie inbetween them and share a closeness with her.
It might just as well have been a window, and me a pie hawker leering at her with a throbbing in me that would defy description. She was sleeping.

I was now realizing that I was becoming lonely for human contact. It was the first time I had ever experienced that feeling. I noticed that it was seeping into me by the day. I was losing my concentration. I became aware of time. I felt like leaving the house, to try to find people to be with, where before I preferred to be alone.

As time went on and the weeks turned into months, this contentment and satisfaction of hers ripened into her daily home activity. Her favorite pastime, her only recreation, her love and devotion became sleep.
The Altar that we used to make love on, now became the couch where she fell asleep. Along with her desire to sleep, her conversations became unbearable to listen to. They were about her job, about people who called on the phone. I knew that it all had some meaning to her, but I couldn't grasp it. The magic chair that once was devoted to the most divine was now used to store newspapers.

When she wasn't sleeping she would complain of her tiredness. She had trouble catching up on her sleep. She complained that the drive home from work was devastating to her. The freeways were more than she could stand. She found herself wishing for more sleep.
She kept telling me she could sleep forever, as if sleep was her salvation from life.
For some stupid reason I had thought that we would just go on in life and make love. But now something new was appearing that I had never counted on. Like a virus it crept into my life to deprive me of human contact…both physical and mental.
I thought maybe I was being selfish and wanted only my pleasures satisfied. Maybe I was being consumed with self-interest, but self-interest dictates to you what it is you want.

The newness had worn off, the exploration of each other had left no new continents to be discovered. Maybe it was time to end all this hassle before real problems appeared. But to my own self-pity, I had gotten hooked on her, sleep or no sleep. My eyes wanted to devour her. Even when she was sleeping, I found her beautiful.

I didn't want to get angry at her, so I allowed myself to wallow around feeling sorry for her. I developed a system of social, physical and psychological pity to explain all her new attitudes.

She works all day, I kept telling myself. Everything about her must be tired. Her head, her tongue, her ass, her legs, even her cunt must be tired. Name it and it was tired.

While she ate she said very little. When she did say anything, it was about her job, and the ambitious little middle-of-the-road capitalist who ran the insurance company she worked for. She talked of him daily. Nothing missed her eye. The smallest detail occasioned a torrent of anger. She was always angry at him. She always had something to compare him with. A pig, a snake, a toad, a hooked-nose vulture. He was left-handed, he weighed 145 pounds. He was 5 feet 6 inches. He had dark hair. He was dressed in tailormade suits, handmade shirts and shoes, silk socks, and a Patek Phillipe gold watch. He had square shoulders, light-blue eyes. He gave the employees pep talks, using the 1,000 gallon fish tank in his office as a point of reference.

The tank housed big Amazonian Arawanas, which he fed twice a day with cute, big-eyed goldfish. Not only to satisfy the Arawanas' appetite, but for the employees' benefit as well. "One example is worth a million words," he'd tell his employees. "The big fish always eats the little fish," and he'd throw a handful of wide-eyed goldfish into the tank...and watch them as they tried to hide while the Arawanas sniffed them out.
"All the goldfish disappear," my little darling would tell me, "while the employees stand around the tank wondering when their day will come to enter the tank and be devoured."

Evidently, Nomi didn't worry that I would get tired of this daily routine, and of her daily referral to Him...the Man who had control of her life. She never thought that neglect might drive me to the park, waiting at the glen for fate to bring me another minnow. I told Nomi I was always a one-woman man. I told her in clear 24-point-size words. I couldn't deal with two women at the same time. This thought must have given her the security she needed to neglect me. Time was too short to spend thinking about why something wasn't happening, but I found myself doing just that. I found myself wanting to know what the mental mechanism of my existence with her was becoming. She had touched me somewhere, the way she moved, the way she did things…the sound of her voice.

Somehow she must have known this or felt this, because she didn't seem disturbed over the fact that she made Morpheus her lover.

I was being drawn into a strange form of fascination.
Usually when I didn't feel right being somewhere, I would just disappear with no further conversation, no note, no letter of intent, just an empty space that I used to occupy with my guitar. Feeling comfortable was my secret. Whatever bothered that feeling was a thorn in my existence.

Conversations concerning why
Why we should be or shouldn't be together, didn't interest me. The feeling of being uncomfortable with a person was enough to make me want to leave.
The argument of happiness, to me, was based on feeling comfortable. Even leaving a person was important. I had to make my leaving as comfortable as possible, without the conversations and the bad feelings that come with the last moment of separation. In a way it's like death, so irrevocable and permanent…talking about it makes it harder.

It doesn't take long for a routine to set itself up in one's life. It seems the body is just begging for some regularity to enter into, to avoid the chaos of an unregulated existence.

An internal clock would ring around 8 P.M. and she would get up from the couch, pull her dress down and head for the bathroom, peel her clothes off, scrub her teeth, take a good strong piss and jump into the bed.
A secret button on her back touched the mattress and plugged her eyes up with steel lids.

Bed-racing
I found myself running a race to see if I could get to her before she went to sleep. Sometimes I would catch her before she hit that sleep button on her ass. But by the time I could get my pants

off, she was snoring. It was a difficult move to time properly. When you're rushing, sex becomes a chore, a burden. Its softness soon leaves, and it becomes just what it was at the beginning of time, the act of a procreating dog that has to wait for the bitch to get into heat, nail her before the rest of the dogs do, and get on about his business.

Her being gone all day, and me being alone during the day, coupled with the new torment of my life of looking at her asleep, and not being able to, as simply as I could state it, fuck her, created in me a desire which made me daydream of her constantly.

I was taking on the realities of a child
who first learns to roll the images of a girl in his head. Like moulding a piece of dough into a loaf of bread, waiting for it to become a polygon of reality with clear edges of resolution. Slowly you lift the dress up and stare at her legs. Instinctively you know that the legs are the gates that guard the portals to heaven, but in your head the gates open miraculously. It becomes so real you lunge to lie between those legs. It doesn't take long to search out that root and to start rubbing Aladdin's lamp, waiting for the genie to appear.

I would dream of lifting her dress and doing it to her. I could see myself, in the eye of my mind, going through all the moves. Slowly, over and over, from every angle, like I was watching myself through a window.
I would create an image of her in the garden where I first met her. Or I would recreate the scene in the back seat of my car, where, even though it was uncomfortable, the confinement in such a small area was erotic in its closeness.
But now we were living together and the curse of man and woman, once they are together, is to work as hard as they can, and to snore next to each other like two dogs that have gotten used to the same doghouse.

I checked out the calendar. I had marked every day I didn't put my throbbing cock into her. For 85 consecutive days my love fell

asleep before I could get my pants off. She didn't bother giving me any of the worn out excuses, about
headaches
backaches
fainting spells
periods
belly pains and general feelings of not feeling good.
Since she gave me no excuses, I made one up for her from an article I read in the paper.
Her problem was minted by the new wordmakers. She suffered the ***Social/Time/Motion/Complex/Syndrome.***
I asked her if this is why she seemed so remote, so distant. She worked so hard getting to work, working and getting back that she lacked the energy to feel…she had become
Work-numb.
"What are you talking about?" she asked me. I realized that it doesn't take long to lose your sensible abilities when you're torn between wanting and not being able to get that which you want.

I knew a girl once…the thought of her not being around me would bring me to tears.
She left one day to go to the store. It was her birthday. It was the last time we ever saw each other. On the way to the store a car ran her over, as if she was a petal from a red carnation.
I had to go to the morgue and identify her. I talked to her, but she never answered.
I kissed her, and she was cold. My tears fell on her closed eyes, which gave her a strange look, like a doll with warm tears coming from eyes that could never see me again.

A woman, Nomi, lying next to me with her legs wide open, and I have to walk away from her, rubbing my prick with the sadness of a lost dog. Even my guitar lying on my lap started to remind me of a woman. Its curved body, its long sensuous neck, its sweet tones, the fragrance of the wood. Life was becoming more and more a dream.

I started to develop two personalties, one that looked, leered, peeked and wanted. A disgusting personality that I had never really experienced before. It was ready and willing to put up with anything as long as it could get what it wanted.

The other personality felt anger, ready to throw out and get rid of that desire before it devoured me.
I was spending most of my hours in thought about her. No matter what I did, she would come into my head like an unwanted guest.
I started asking questions that had no answers.
Why did fate bring me to this?
Why did the day end in anger?
Why did she ignore me like this?
Why do I bother to think about it?
Why didn't I see it coming?
Why did I expect more than what I got?

I felt like one who is getting ready to convert himself to some religious life. I felt the exhaustion of constantly asking that despicable question—Why—knowing all along that all the whys have been given a reasonable answer.

My first personality, because of
wanting
desiring
needing,
showed pathos, concern, understanding and sensitivity. Like a hypocrite who bows his head to benefit from his servile flattery. The imposed politeness was driving me nuts. I could hear the sound of my voice, just short of begging. I was becoming a cunt lackey.

My second personality lived in
frustration
anger
dreams of escape
intolerance
depression
sleeplessness
suspicion
resentment,
with the need to do something to relieve the emotional pain.

My first personality made me appear more understanding, more tolerant, even though it was motivated with an animal instinct of waiting to be fed, and trying to be good so when food time came around, I would be the first to get fed.

I helped around the house. I swept the dogshit off the back porch, where her two favorite terriers lived. I washed dishes and clothes, cleaned the house, made the bed, as if I had been trained as a house-servant. I worked hard to join her in her tiredness, hoping that I could get it in her quickly when she didn't feel this need for sleep. But privately I found myself looking up her dress, getting hardons, wanting to get on top of her and put it where I felt it belonged.

That's an awful feeling…to want something and be unable to have it, yet it's right next to you. You can touch it and yet you can't have it. A lite year away. I can see her next to me. I can hear her pissing in the toilet, and as far as I'll ever know it again, it will be merely as a thing that pees.
A sign hung on her doorway…"Out to lunch. Be back later."

Love is a Slow Process

The vulvatic gulp
The cyclical moon-sister
Go Ye unto the world and suffer
Hope
Pathological patience
The scheming stage of wanting
Oneiritic aphrodisiac
Music and sexual arousal
Music and sexual orgasms in women
Conversations

Like the tides, love pulsates in its ebb and flow. The feelings come and go, they are ignited without any apparent reason, and when events in the lovemaking process are speeded up, feelings are hurt, hearts are confused and life becomes a bleak and quarrelsome affair. "Come on," I would shake her and listen to myself beg. "Let me have some please." "Not now! Please...can't...you...see...that I'm tired?"

Her voice was agitated. Agitating sounds are hard to define. Their tonal shapes are painful to listen to. The voice is accusing, demanding, wanting, threatening, forever threatening. "Stop!" she said. "Stop you bastard!" she yelled at me. It took me by surprise. For the first time in my life, I felt like a beggar in front of the church doors, hoping that my evident needs would create charity amongst the parishioners. But I was mistaken.

The vulvatic gulp

I lay on the bed pleading for a handout. I felt like I lost, I wanted to say my dignity, but it wasn't that. I could now be intimidated. I could be threatened. If I didn't obey I might never get any of the sacred offerings. This piss hole had taken over my life. It was on my mind continually. I felt I had lost my freedom. I thought nothing could have ever impaired my love for music, but something did. I realized that the story of Jonah and the whale was really an analogy of the power of the cunt. With one vulvatic gulp Jonah was devoured. If it could happen to Jonah…why not me?

Every day almost the same words were strung together in order to control me. The same words, with more or less the same tones and meter. "Stop!…Stop!…let go of me…can't you see I want to sleep…take your hand…off my cunt…maybe tomorrow when I'm not as tired…please don't wake me up." And she'd push my hand away, roll over and snore the nite away.

It was a lyrical poisoning of my feelings. It was like a piece of music memorized with a deadly rhythm inherent to its melody. What I just said might not make sense to you but to me it does.

My world is dominated by sounds and the way these sounds are patterned creates my reality. She said she had a reason for her resistance. My wanting her was interfering with her sleep. Her reason forced me to lie quietly next to her in bed, with my eyes closed, hoping at least to fall asleep with her.

The cyclical moon-sister

The world is full of old stories from the Homers of the bedroom. Odysseus' journey to Penelope's bed. Stories from men and about men who tied themselves up with women. They made their lives part and parcel of a woman's world. They discovered the meaning of woman as a creature of the moon. She pulsates like the plasma of life. She is a history that repeats itself over and over, a cyclical creature of monthly hormonal changes. Her moods change as the moon moves across the sky. Her eyes see your face change in the shadows of the day. Her love for you depends on the equations and distribution of these essential items during her moon cycle. Moon-sister can close the doors to her altar, like a priest closing the doors to the sanctuary…where the holy of all holies waits to be plundered by the marauding savage.

Go Ye unto the world and suffer

Biblical-sounding phrases came out of my mouth,
as if I had accepted my fate…and now I would travel down the tormented road of my imagination skipping a rope of hope.

Hope

I often wondered if hope was just one more type of perversion which belongs to a man and to some degree to all men. It is what makes Man so pathetic, so forgivable. It is what makes great operas, great music, poetry that cries for you. It is the elixir distilled from denial, that potion that Pandora left for men to suffer with…Hope…the food of the condemned, the poor and the destitute. And me the pathetic, denied, whimpering lover.

The more she denied me, the more I wanted her. Wanting her with the thirst of the devout. I was in the Nave of a great Cathedral, I could feel the presence of god in the sounds of her voice. "Tomorrow for sure," she would tell me. Tomorrow something will happen, the promised land lay there next to me. How could something so close be so far away, while days turned into months?

I became the dreamer who nourished his soul with the dreams of not-having. Not-having was stirring the cauldrons of hope, letting me inhale the essential vapors of a dream that might never happen.

Pathological patience

A bizarre pathological patience started to develop in me that was based on waiting for the woman to wake up. I had hopes that somehow I would find the secret button, the elixir, the magic word that would turn back the clock. I wanted to go back...to a time when making love was the fare for the day, and came as normally as the breathing of a healthy lung. I wanted to feel again the throbbing of a passion waiting to spill its love.

I would have to wait for tomorrow, and hope that it would be different. I began to believe that hope was a whore herself. A piece of spiritual pornography. A promise made without any way of performance, always waiting...while the sounds of a dormant life banged on my ears like a madman trying to break down the doors of my sanity.

It was 2:00 o'clock in the morning and time to leave. But hope kept me lying there, in the bed next to her. Tomorrow would be different, there was love, there was hope. Love created passages for my eyes to see, in the nite skies. I could see her face outlined with pearls. Guided by the mysterious finger of hope, I was planning my next move.

The scheming stage of wanting

Even though I slept next to her, her naked body just a few inches from me, asleep, I couldn't have her. It was a trial of endurance. I was told I was forbidden to touch her. If I touched her, she would say "please don't." But "please" was merely disguising her anger. All I could do was raise the bedsheets, like one would raise a circus tent, and shine my Nifty Pocket Lite under the covers, illuminating her body like a stage production of The Sleeping Beauty. I needed more than a circus-tent performance in the middle of the nite.

When you want something, there are various stages you have to go through in order to get it. I found myself in the scheming stage of wanting. My plan was to keep her awake, and the next move would be to turn her on at the same time.

I tried everything a reasonable man would try to keep her awake, at least long enough to touch her and see her smile. To put my hand on her flesh and feel it move toward me rather than try to escape like a trapped animal.

The first dose of hope was, that if I gave her something to keep her awake, nature would set in with healing properties and let the natural juices of desire flow between us.

My attempts were the attempts of an idiot. I thought that all I had to do was to give her some stimulus, something to mingle with her chemistry to keep her awake.

I thought of various ways of doing this. The first was lacing her up with amps, but she might buzz so fast that she'd think something was wrong. Strong coffee put her to sleep. Drinking was out, too messy. The alcohol might bring about unforeseeable problems. It is a strange phenomenon as to how knowledge of a certain thing at the right time moves you into a commanding state of existence, but at this stage of the game I had not heard of hypnagogic love and its sexual expressions. I was like most men, ignorant of anything more than expecting the woman to satisfy me when I needed satisfaction.

Oneiritic aphrodisiac

Had I only known of the Tabernanthe iboga...the hallucinogenic plant used as an oneiritic aphrodisiac by the Egyptians, and by members of the cult of Isis. A yellow-flowered bush from West Africa that has a structural relationship to beta-carbolines.

The Tabernanthe iboga was an innocent-looking bush, related to the coffee bean, that the West Africans took upon retiring in the evening in order to have dreams. Dreams which could be controlled from the outside world by stimulating certain parts of the body known to the activator, shaman, priest or holy man. Certain nerve-endings were located, allowing the chemical relations to form in the shape of sexual symbols, deep in the dream itself. But being ignorant of any way other than the way I saw the world of sex, I stumbled around like a blind dog in a packing house, sniffing the flesh, hoping I could have it by cunning or by accident.

The problem was deeper, but my ignorance wouldn't let me see it. These were complicated moves, and to make them, you have to be able to correlate needs, drives, passions, conversations. A world of fragments which required careful planning and placement to bring together.

In the months that followed, I struggled with futile attempts to keep her awake. In the process I hoped to excite her, like one would excite a wild animal, to make it growl and to bring it to a high state of agitation like a lion tamer does to the beast of the jungle he has locked in his cage.

As I was to find out later, it was in the dream world where the real pleasure of the flesh was waiting to be had. My first failure encouraged me to try something else. I did what I knew best, music.

Music and sexual arousal

Being a musician, I knew what music did for people. Music has always been part of mankind's sexual and religious stimulation. The drumbeats of the jungle. The drumbeats of the Bedouin in his tent. The drumbeats of an army marching. The Byzantine chorale with the mosaic God filling the ears of the faithful in Saint Sophia. The Gregorian chant with castrated little eunuch tenors evoking God in all His splendor. The Cantor in the synagogue praising the Lord.

The Puritans knew music stimulated the female, driving her to wild lascivious moods. Her quim would get titillated. Her wants caused her to gyrate, move around like a top spun off a cotton string. The cosmic dance of stars, moons and planets intoxicated her.

I played music for Nomi, hoping to stimulate her rhythmic cycles to awaken her sexual moods. Certain rhythms and beats allow the primitive instincts to awaken within you, to excite you, to bring you to an elevated frenzy that could resurrect the dead. I've been in churches that could swing their way up to heaven, with beats that drive the most laidback to start speaking in tongues.

Music and sexual orgasms in women

The female orgasm, and rhythm, was a theme followed to the tee by a girlfriend I had, Marcia. She was a little Jewish girl with almond-shaped eyes...coal-black hair...and a nose like a beautiful

anteater. She used to tell me every time I saw her,
"Rhythm, Baby James!...let your guitar...slide down...my street. Oooo..ah..wee...you are indeed Doctor Feel-Good."

Marcia told me that sex therapists used music to help women get orgasms. "I was really laidback," she told me. "I just couldn't get off. I went from guy to guy, thinking if I changed men, the next one would get me over the hump, but my mojo was off, I was out of touch, out of sync. So I went to a sex therapist I knew who had helped women get it off. He would put a record on, and show me how to gyrate around his office whipping myself up in a lather, like a racehorse after a 2-mile run for the Roses."

Then she'd put a record on for me and dance around the room, twisting, turning, jumping. She would be drenched in sweat, breathing hard, rubbing herself with hands that knew their way to the depths of her pleasure. She'd lie on the floor and raise her legs up and start pumping to the rhythms of African drums. "Too bad your body don't move like your fingers do," she used to tell me. She loved my guitar playing, but said my fucking had no rhythm to it.

She was the musician's sexual Muse. She only went out with musicians. She only lived with musicians. Only musicians were allowed in her fuckatorium and on her bed, the stage for her great drama. Her instrument was her body. She could create complicated rhythms with it.
She said
Jazz
Flamenco
Blues
AfroCuban drumbeats
Tibetan whistles
and Indian sitars excited her inner world, allowing her to break certain spiritual and psychological rigidities and free the feelings from her thoughts. "Get with it!" she used to yell at me. "Get with it, you motha fucka. You're crashing man...you're out of whack. This shit's going to fry you man, don't let me down."

She'd put on her record player, AfroCuban drumbeats, Flamenco juergas, Chicago blues, Indian ragas, Caribbean reggae and jiggle me like a big mama looking for the juju market to sell me. "We'll work with this one," she'd tell me, "and then get to more complicated rhythms later. I have to crest…how am I going to jam and mess if you don't get with it Mr. Maggilicuddy?"

Being on top of her required great stamina, a great body-endurance and lightning-fast reflexes…like a dancer would have. It was more than love or lovemaking, it was sexual gymnastics. She said it was sport-fucking and screw-blasting. "It's rhythm-sticking…honeeeeey boy…real hole-poking. It's when all that shit talk fizzles itself into a pile of dog crap…and a 12/12 beat hits your groin…and I'm wet."

I was like a soldier serving his General and country. It went on all nite long, with no stopping. I was hoping my prick wouldn't go down, while trying to keep it up to the rhythms of a stack of records five feet high, which kept growing like the Tower of Babel, straight up to heaven where the god Apollo was hosing down his guitar with a tumescent rod the size of a telegraph pole, which kept getting bigger with each plucking of the string.

I ran away from her after losing 25 pounds in 2 months and almost having a myocardial infarction on the stage floor of her "Fuckatorium."

There are exceptions to every law, deviations from every truth. Though music will peel the pants off most humans, there are those that music puts to sleep, or rests them enough to take a shit, or eat or think…ride an elevator or put you on hold. Music can make you pensive, cause you to cry, make you dream of glory, die for your country, see God.

Somewhere into this category my beloved Nomi seemed to fall. Music seemed to have a quieting effect on Nomi. The savage beast was tamed by the lute of Andronicus. No matter what type of music I played, it tended to quiet her down, to put her at ease, to put her to sleep faster than without it. Music, to her, was tonal valiums.

Sleep has such a peaceful look about it, and in a strange way resembles death. But the sounds that are connected with sleep can be such guttural sounds. "How can such a beautiful woman emit such ugly sounds?" the prince must have thought, as he stood over the princess, and listened to her snore, whistle, chirp, grind her teeth, fart, sigh, mumble, flutter her lips, drool and suck the spittle back up her gaping mouth.
It seems that sleep had an orchestrated sound-track in various keys and haphazard arrangements.

Conversations
I tried conversation to keep her awake. I talked to her about her job, about her health, about the fish tank in her office, about the weather. Conversations that showed I had no imaginary connection with her. Her answers were just as unimaginative. I talked to her about people making love and she'd yawn. I rented a video with lovers sprawled over each other like seals mating. She yawned and fell asleep. "Yes" or "no" was the depth of her reply along with a tired look on the face, pleading with me to shut up, followed by a great big yawn, a quiet fart, and the scratching of the chair as she would get up to do all the rituals that precede going to sleep. The long strong stream of piss, the scratching of her ass, the flipping of her tits, followed by a few short and a few long blasts of her tooter. Faithful sounds, like a locomotive coming up to a crossing.

I could tell the Honeymoon, with all its promises, was over. All that was left was to watch her take a shit and that was it. I would have seen it all, and the mystery that makes love so necessary would be gone, flushed down the sewer pipe of reality.

All I wanted to do was to keep her awake. I thought that having a conversation with her was the way to do it, but like a river that flows, a conversation has to be going somewhere, to some mysterious island in the middle of an ocean. The tongue was the messenger of happiness or sorrow, the destroyer of kingdoms. Even though the tongue had no bones, it was capable of breaking them, but her tongue did nothing but lie in her mouth semi-dead.

The words that were supposed to come from the word mills to help us get back on the track again, somehow got routed to somewhere else.

One day her mouth opened and her tongue uttered in a flash of lite, “Maybe this is why we get along,” she said to me. “Maybe if we talked too much we would find reasons to hate each other.” She yawned…smiled at me, got up and went to the couch, lay down on it, shut her eyes…and went to sleep.

The Holy Father

The requirement of modern sex

Making love with a priest

If I was going to stay with her, I had to do something, but the distance between a need to do something, and knowing what to do, can be an eternity. Nothing seemed to work. She kept giving me the excuse of being tired. But didn't all people get tired? How did humans do it before? Maybe sex wasn't as complicated or as necessary or as perfected as it is now. The working classes just rolled over, put it in, dropped a load and went to sleep. Now I had entered into the period of quality sex, the type that royalty had always enjoyed. This might be the period in history when sex for the common man had reached the point where work detracted from it.

The requirement of modern sex
Great energy
alertness
understanding
physical endurance
knowledge of female needs and wants.

I remembered an ex-priest I used to know, Edgar, who had given up the cloth for bedtime stories, dope, cognac and young women. He had the ladies read to him from "The Tales of the Lascivious Hypocrite" while he lay on his bed. He told me that he had come across "The Tales of the Hypocrite" while studying for the priesthood. He had copied the work, and was proud of the fact that the commentaries had nurtured his erotic flavor while seeking out his devoutness.

Making love with a priest

Edgar was a man in his forties. A bruiser whose face showed that he drank the wine before it got transubstantiated on the holy altar. He allowed the sacrament to fully glow in him. He would remain drunk during the high mass. "It raised me up," he said, "without any sacrificial guilt, and on into the nite I pumped the beauties till my heart felt the anguish of the strain." He said that he appealed only to women who wanted to feel the blasphemy of making it on the bed with a man who had taken vows to serve God, and wore the cloth of celibacy. "It brings the woman to another level of passion when she knows that you have broken your vows because of her beauty. It's defilement greater than merely a married man who has taken vows only to his wife…and breaks them with another woman. I had taken vows to God the Almighty. Each one of these lovely ladies, in her own way, became Eve seeking the original sin, looking for the disguised apple."

He'd get loaded and tell me that the apples were his two balls and his hardened cock was the branch that they hung from. "They swing from it, while God in his omnipotence and total presence watches. He's always watching, looking, counting." He would break out laughing. "An ex-anything is better," he'd tell me, "than a man who has secrets."

I decided that I should look him up and get some advice as to what to do. If anyone could help me it would be Edgar.

I was surprised that Edgar was so glad to hear from me. He wanted me to promise that I would come by some day and play the guitar for him and his wife. "I'm married now," he said, "and my life has changed for the better. Marriage is the way to go. One marries with God when he marries a woman. It's a natural act. You lose that self-serving need when you get married."

I told him my problems to the last word. "Marry her," he said over the phone. "Marry her…it's bound to wake her up or put you to sleep. No matter what, you'll both be one in harmony with the whole universe. Sorry I can't do the service for you, but you know they defrocked me and tried to make me into a religious eunuch. But I prevailed. I married one of the ladies who closed the Book of the Lascivious Hypocrite on me. Who knows what will take place in the future?"

I thanked Edgar for his advice, and his urgency to get me married. But I wondered if marriage was one of the hopes which were left at the bottom of Pandora's gift box? I promised him I would stop by soon and play my guitar for him and his wife.

Marriage and Pandora's Hope

The inseparable marriage
Isaiah's prophecy
The reasons for marriage
The Male Hardon
The Ceremony of It
The judge's hidden desire
A wedding nite
Ignition of the sexual mechanism
The point where holy men fall from grace

Marriage seemed to be the answer to all problems between man and woman. It's like the word that the magician uses to turn sour into sweet, iron into gold, coldness into warmth, passionless into passion.

The inseparable marriage
When things marry they become one.
Cigar-makers marry the tobacco leaves and make a good Havana.
Violin-makers marry the joints of the instrument into what seems to be an instrument with no separations.

Two become one. They create a third identity. They become married.
They acquire each other's habits.
They start looking alike.
They talk alike.
They think alike. They are into each other. They spill their fluids into each other.
They swap spit, words, laughs, tears.
They are one.
They don't need to communicate.
They have nothing to say. They just are.

Maybe Edgar was right about marriage. If any one knew anything about women it was Edgar. He knew what the woman's real desires were. I only knew what I wanted from a woman.
I wanted to kiss a woman and smell the musk on her breath.
I wanted to hear her female voice tell me things that made passion boil in the depths of my balls.

I knew very little about women, and their habits, or for that matter what the word and the thought...*female*...really meant. I knew a woman was someone you wanted when you were lonely, when you hoped to...desired to...schemed, lied, stole...in order to lift her dress up, pull her pants down and sit and marvel at the raw beauty of your conquest.
There it was, in all its naked splendor, a work of art hidden like a fig behind a silken leaf.

Maybe the woman wanted the same thing but in a mirror reflection. I wasn't sure. Did she dream of my swollen desire while I dreamt of her lubricated passion?
I on top...she on the bottom
I give...she receives
I shove...she groans
She sleeps...I watch.

The thought of her being my wife electrified me. I wanted to consume her totally. I couldn't see any other reason to get married other than to have her completely.

It was Edgar's advice that marriage would awaken in her the element of active love, something we had at the beginning. But there was always the chance that the thought of marriage, to her, might mean even more security, allowing her to do some real deep sleeping, unperturbed by what I felt or what she denied me.

Then, Edgar said, I would have to learn how to love her in my dreams. I took it to mean I would have to learn to devote more of my time to lying in bed and snoring together, like a duet in harmony with the SemiDead, and learn how to enjoy the darkness of the nite.

I was taking a gamble of the most severe kind, but I had always been a person who allowed fate to dictate my life.

Isaiah's prophecy
It was no secret amongst men of past and present that a woman can really get ugly after getting married. According to Isaiah's prophecy, "The person you marry either becomes more beautiful or more ugly during the marriage. Once you're in the basket they don't give a shit, and a woman that don't give a shit is as close as you can get to hell in this lifetime."

Desperate conditions create desperate decisions, and one day it just came out of my mouth, the words that were intended to startle her into awakeness. Maybe it was an inner desire to fully and completely destroy myself. I had no way of knowing. It just came out of my mouth. A word, sliding off a slippery tongue, was bound to fall. I was thinking out loud. The words fell out of my mouth, in parts and pieces, like parts of a puzzle that were supposed to be put together in the outside world.
"Day off."
"What?"
"Can you take a day off?"
"What are you talking about?"
It was like the wheels on a slot machine putting the cherries and plums on the same line. If the right words fell together something would make sense. "Take the day off."

"Why?" she asked me. And the word came tumbling out of my mouth like the cascading waters of a good urination.

"Marry?"

"What?"

"Let's go get married." I told her as if I had brought the sacred cow to her doorstep.

It was too late to stop. She heard what I said, up to the last incoherent word. I hesitated, wondering if that tongue of mine hadn't driven the last nail into my box of life's little postcards.

For a few moments there was silence...she said nothing. The words lay on the floor, like breadcrumbs off a kitchen table. She must have thought of marriage during the months we lived together? Even though she never said much about anything, she must have asked herself where all this was heading. But maybe she never gave it a thought. It might be that she had accepted the ancient rule of life…let tomorrow bring its own.

She looked at me. Her eyes said nothing.

"Why not?" she said in a soft voice. "We'll give it a try Jimmie." It was the first time someone called me Jimmie, other than my mother. It sounded good, my ears enjoyed the word. To hear my name in the diminutive. It was affection at its best. It was familiarity. I knew she loved me. She said "yes," as simply as if I had asked her to take a walk with me to the corner grocery store.

The reasons for marriage

I didn't know how I should introduce my real intentions to this marriage. One usually marries another for wealth, love, jealousy, possessiveness or out of general boredom, brought about by constantly being around that person and not having the energy to find someone else. But my reasons were different. Her constant yawning was my reason. As a husband I had more of a right to ask her to stop yawning in my face and stay awake, at least when I made love to her. But if she took it as a joke and laughed at me? What then? Or would she take it as an insult and leave? Or she might take it as a sign that I was nuts and she'd be better off without me. A woman this beautiful would have no trouble finding a man an hour after she left, but then again, the next guy would have the same trouble with her as I did, and he might not be as patient as I was.

The real problem was...there were too many angles, too many decisions to be made, too many possibilities that could go wrong.

The Male Hardon

I was tired of a few kisses, a few hugs and a lot of yawns. I would give her a kiss, and she'd close her eyes, and zap the ziplock went. I never had a woman that was so addicted to sleep. I wanted only one thing from her, and that was for her to stay awake long enough to handle my hardon, to love it and to cherish it. It was over her that it was getting hard and not the woman down the street. Since she was making it hard, she should do something with it, and not leave me with another excuse to give to my magnificent erection. You can have only so many hardons in a lifetime, and why waste them on a sleeping woman?

If I had maintained a count of how many hardons I had, since I was first able to have them, to be able to tell her the exact number, she would have seen the need a man has to use this god-given miracle.

If I told her, "You have made my 1 millionth-878 thousandth-665 hundreth hardon, and I hope to make it 2 million with your help and inspiration," she would immediately realize the difference between man and woman.

To a woman a hardon was a manicured piece of desire, throbbing to get in her. The harder it was, the greater her happiness, knowing she had brought it into existence.

To a Man the hardon represents many things. The effort and energy to get it up and ready requires good health, a good diet, a good thought and desire. It wasn't like the elephant's proboscis, just there. There is a process of getting it there. A task that a young boy never realizes and an old man only dreams of.

I wanted to tell her now, before we got married, that it was a tiresome act to have to stand there wearing a hardon, like a soldier at attention, waiting for the order to place his rifle in its rack. I told her that there would be a condition to our marriage vows that she would have to promise me...in front of the official performing the marriage ceremonies. I stopped for a moment. I could see in her eyes a curiosity as to what this condition was all about. I hesitated and then I let her have it. "On condition you never yawn in my face, and stay awake long enough for us to make love."

She thought I was joking because I was nervous. She smiled, as if I said something funny. Like the first day I had met her in the park. I should have taken the hint, or I should have been smart enough to know that if you get the milk free, why do you want to buy the cow? That didn't sound right either.

I got no milk
I got no joy
I got no poon-tang for my toy. All I got was a fart in the sack.
Watched her lie
watched her sleep
watched my prick
It wants to weep.

The Ceremony of It

I had never realized the myriad ways that "it" was used in identifying the sexual organs of a man and a woman and the sexual act of bringing them together. This might not seem important to my story, I told the D.A., but it did go to show that we had lost the beauty of describing those parts and either out of fear of being called rude or the desire to be polite and sensitive…all of it was called it.

We both got dressed for the occasion. I watched the bride put on her underwear. She wore silk stockings with a garter belt that had embroidered flowers on it.

"Oh let me put it in you...right now," I begged her, "just for good luck's sake."

"When have you ever heard of a bride getting it, just before she got married? Let's wait till after we get married."

A feeling of sadness came over me. She said it as if I had never touched it, loved it, kissed it or had it in her. She probably forgot that I had. Maybe she wanted to pretend that we never had it before. But the truth was, it had been so long since I had had it that she probably had forgotten, and was going to walk up to the altar with the thought of purity, virginity, and commitment. "I'll let you put it in me after I suck it good and hard. Does that make you happy?" she asked me. Those were the magic words I dreamt of, those might have been the words that made the mundane into a holy ritual.

The judge's hidden desire

I drove to the City Hall and parked. We ran up to the Marriage Licences Department, paid the 10 dollars, and stood in line for the judge to perform the rites of passage from single to double. The judge could see my pants were hanging on an oak branch. I saw a smile on his face. A wishful smile, wishing he was me, heading for the land of the big promise. There was no doubt in my mind, the judge picked out the most beautiful bride during the day, and flamed up his daydreams of being the husband that nite.

I whispered in her ear that the judge had selected her to be his mental bride that nite. He too would raise the flag of desire, and march on behalf of beautiful womanhood. Through the whole marriage ceremony my prick was hard. I put the ring on her finger. I couldn't wait for the affair to come to an end so I could get into some bed with her, or the back seat of the car, or some doorway, or a darkened movie house up in the balcony, or out in the park behind a bush. Anywhere, just as long as I could do it to her quickly.

I felt as if I was going to open her up for the first time, and look at it with the eyes of a child and the lust of a dragon. To want something so much, and not to have it, is what hell must be all about. Thirsty men, hungry men. I was a prisoner to that hole between her legs, and the judge was pronouncing sentence on me:

> ***You are now the proud owner of a beautiful cunt that is hidden in the briar patch surrounded by an army of No's and two stout legs locked until death do them part.***

Some women have a quality that every time you kiss them it feels as if it was the first time you did. You never get enough to satisfy your need. There is something to those lips that causes the wanting valve to stay open. This woman had that natural talent. She had lips that were shaped for kissing. They were soft, and fitted perfectly with mine. When she was awake her lips, with great ease and pleasure, had fitted other parts of my body like suction cups. It wasn't that she couldn't, it was that she had stopped. Had she become tired of it?

A new event was on the horizon, something I never had experienced before. It would be the first time I would be having her as my wife. The first time I had her she was a stranger, a woman I had met at the park. Now I felt as if I was being unfaithful to the one I knew before. Now I was with a person who was new to me. A wife...my wife. The thought of all this newness made bubbles come from my stomach up to my mouth, causing me to burp while I was saying..."I do."

A wedding nite

We walked out of the City Hall into the dismal fog of San Francisco. It was 11 o'clock on a Friday morning. She wore a silk print dress that had been poured over her by the hand of fate. Her shapes were round, her hips formed gentle landscapes for my eyes to rest on.

"We have all weekend," she said. "Let's go somewhere, but not back to the house."

She wanted to spend the wedding nite somewhere that we would both remember. A new place. A nite of total abandonment. She was making the plans like an architect planning the temple. She was the only one who knew what she had in store for me. She decided we would spend it at the M.G.M. in Reno, a 4-hour ride east. Nothing big, I could wait.

All the way up there, my hand was on her legs, opening them up, running up her thighs, pulling on the garter where I could feel the silk meeting the flesh. It was the beginning. The sense of touch. The feeling of softness, pliability. The feel of coldness, warmth, wetness, dryness, roughness, smoothness. Different textures meeting together in some motel room. All the senses mixed together in a moment of utter completeness. I kept asking her to let me touch it or to take my engine out for her to run her tongue on it.

"Can't you wait?" she asked me in a soft voice filled with promises for the nite. "I want to do it with all the little trimmings."

Ignition of the sexual mechanism

Hearing her soft voice telling me those gem-like words ignited my sexual mechanism. My pants were wet, and my groin started to hurt. My balls started to ache like someone had kicked me. A truck driver was looking at us as he drove by. I felt like the whole highway was getting turned-on to the long beautiful legs next to me, with a beautiful set of lips waiting for the nite to come.

The M.G.M. was lit up, waiting for me to come crashing in. We got a room on the tenth floor, and all the way up in the elevator, I had my hand in between the 2 cheeks of her ass. Touching her gave me a feeling of warmth and agitation both in the same instant. There was no one else in the elevator, and I wanted to lay her on the floor, open her legs and give it to her right then and there.

"Let's wait," she told me again, in a beautiful-sounding promise, "Till we get loaded...please."

When we got into the room, the first thing I did was take out a rolled-up number. I put the match to it, and took a long deep pull on it. I handed it to her and she took a hit, a small one. "No fooling around," she said. She made me promise to wait so our desires would reach a point of explosiveness.

I took a cold shower, but it was useless. It stood out like the bowsprit of a ship through the cold cascading waters of a storm. I had a dozen fantasies going on in my head all at the same time. Maybe I ought to jack myself off and cool down, but then I would lose the edge that was building up in me.

We got dressed and went down to the theater.

In the elevator I kept touching her with the delicacy of a blind man touching the holy altar. "Remember," she said, "you promised to behave."

We paid $35.00 apiece for the dinner and the show. It was amazing. I was looking at a hundred chorus girls cast in a 20th-century Pompeian extravaganza. Long-legged women being screwed in a simulated earthquake. Fat old ladies with dyed hair, sitting at the same table with us, giggling. A plane landed on the stage. Naked airline attendants marched off the make-believe plane. It all had the magic of lites, color, sound and flesh. The stage was set. The trumpets had blared. My love was at attention. My cock was at the ready. The multitude were wined, dined and entertained. Then sent out in a daze to stumble into the dice tables and lose a few hundred. Go back home knowing they've been somewhere. "Here...drink a little," I told Nomi, my wife of six hours, handing her a glass of red wine.

"It's our wedding nite," I said, feeling the importance of being a husband. "Let's do everything just for the nite, and if we like it we'll do it for a lifetime."

She smiled, took a drink, twisted her nose and drank more. I kept looking at her like it was the first time I had ever seen her. I wanted to take out her tits and lick them right here on the table. I dropped a fork from the table and bent over to pick it up so I could have an excuse to look up her dress.

The point where holy men fall from grace

The show was buzzing with a promise for the nite. My inner world was bubbling over, ready to spill on the table. On my way up here I had wet my pants. Up in our room she had lain on our plastic bed. Her dress had crawled up her legs. I tried getting on her. Jesus Christ, I was on fire. This is what hell must be like. This must be the exact point that holy men fall from grace. This is where the blood boils. This must be the point where Edgar took command, letting the women read to him from "The Lascivious Hypocrite." This was the burning at the stake of all those who dare to feel passion. Two bottles of wine…and a joint, rolled and in my pocket ready to lite.

The show was over. I flew through the gaming room, and headed for the elevator, with my hand gently resting on her divine ass. The heat from my hand was flowing through the silken dress. She was being fried by a burning hand reaching out from the torment of passion. I fumbled with the keys and finally got the door open. She walked in. Watching her was like looking at a beautiful mare whose nostrils flared out. Her mane flowing down her neck. The head inquisitive and defiant. The wine must have done something to her. She looked as if she was ready to command me to tear her clothes off. To eat her panties up, and begin to pump her in some uncontrollable delirium.

I was at the ready...to take any order she gave me. To execute my orders with passion and uncontrolled madness. If she ordered me to jump out the 10th story window...I would. I was ready to steal for her...lie for her...denounce god and the holy hierarchy. My love was waiting to be tested.

Philosophy and Sexual History of the Bedroom

A bedroom is a holy place. Naked...lying in the dark
waiting for the moonbeams to lite the way to her.
To feel the softness of her hair
the sweetness of her breath
the flutter of her eyelash
the beauty that exists in the dark
the beauty that exists for the nite owl
the panther
the creatures god said should love and live in darkness.

The renting of a bedroom

I was in the holiest of all holies, the temple of pleasure, forgetfulness and sleep. Even though it was a rented bedroom, a rented bed, a rented pillow to lay her head on, it symbolized the place where the most divine of man's activities take place. I was in the chamber of love, lust and the final surrender to the all-pervasive god of sleep.

A bedroom has its own language, its custom and history, but I wasn't sure if this held for a rented bedroom. All the objects in the rented room have been placed here for practical reasons, to remind you of your own bedroom and in the process of lovemaking each one has its own special usage. There is a chair to throw your pants on. A nite stand with a lamp on it. A lamp that glows, like the candle on the holy altar, to raise the mysterious to the heavens. The bed itself is where the sacrifice to the god and goddess in charge of passion is to take place. There is a quilt to cover the white bedsheets that catch the fluids of life. Pillows to place her head on, and the most important of all, the door, capable of being locked.

A woman, like a matador, has an innate sense of directing the moves of a charging beast...who is charging at her with his horn.
She made the first move.
She took her dress off slowly and folded it over the chair.
She took each piece of cloth off her body, with the gentleness of fluttering silk.
A glance, a look from her eyes, a sigh, the bull is in the center.
Another pass with the cape and the bull circles to the right. Then

the cape changes hands and the bull charges again. The cape moves closer to the matador, and the bull is drawn into the circle. She puts her hand on the horn and the bull's head is lowered for his final charge. She was totally naked.
She sat on the edge of the bed and looked at me. I felt as if I was looking at her for the first time in all her majestic beauty.
A beautiful woman who has real beauty knows how to take her pants off so it becomes a work of art.

I look at the beautiful mat of silken hair between her legs, like a garden that has a fountain hidden somewhere, and I am compelled, driven by some inner urge to find it.
She was going to stay awake. It was all worth it, even the trip here to this plastic Taj Mahal.

I took my clothes off, and her eyes admired my tumescent engine reaching out ahead of me, like a horizontal rod made of steel, waiting for a flag to be hung from it. I could hang my courage on it...my loyalty, my love. I could ram it through a wall. What is that mystery of desire that makes my manhood so hard, large and swollen?

Physiology had discovered the reason it got hard. Religion found it embarrassing. Did the rented bedroom give it all meaning? Would I have felt the same in an alley behind Sammy Chung's restaurant, sitting her ass on a garbage can, her legs folded over my shoulders? In the back seat of my Dodge Dart? Out on the beach where the wind blows sand up your ass?

Etiquette in a rented bedroom

I couldn't help noticing that there is some form of natural etiquette which takes place when two people enter a rented bedroom. I wrote it down so I would remember it.

"There is some natural law that dictates what a man and woman will do when they run off to a rented room, what moves are common. There is an etiquette that is mixed in with the natural laws of desire that has evolved through eons of time, as to who does what, and when, in a room rented for the express purpose of lovemaking.

"When man and woman use a bedroom daily, rituals and habits are created as to how to approach the bed, and the time of the day or nite that you enter and leave. You've agreed on what side of the bed you lie on. You've learned what to do with your arms and hands while you lie there during the nite. The amount of pillows under your head, the heaviness of the covers, the clothes you wear to bed.
One-piece jumpsuit
nitedress
pajamas
nitecap
blinders
nothing, naked, exposed to each other. The door is locked. You are in a capsule of protection, preparing yourself. Her red lips open and you're gone.

"The conveniences you find in a home aren't present in a rented bedroom. You don't get a chance to go from room to room, falling asleep on a couch, getting up, eating, going back to bed. Giving it to her, then turning on the radio to hear the traffic report.

"There is an honesty to a rented bedroom. You're in here with each other to use the bed. You're in the bedroom, the minute you walk in. The work bench is laid out in front of you. There is a TV to look at when you're exhausted."

Scenarios of entering a rented bedroom
A woman going into a rented room with a man performs certain moves that are more natural to the woman. Usually a woman who has been a frequent visitor to rented hotel rooms with different men, knows what procedures to follow. She might even find the reluctance or shyness of a less experienced male exciting while she guides him through the procedures.

First scenario
You give her the keys and she opens up the door. She walks in first. She walks over to the dresser and looks in the mirror. She runs her fingers through her hair, puts her purse down, walks over and sits on the edge of the bed, kicks her shoes off and lies on the bed. The man stands over her while he unbuttons his pant

flap, pulls it out, and gets ready to ram it in her mouth. She grabs it in her hand and strokes its head, like it was a pet snake. She looks at it for a moment and then takes it, like a polish sausage at a Sunday outing, and gives it a long slurpy lick with her tongue.

Second scenario
We both stand by the side of the bed and kiss each other, falling on the bed together like two birds out of the sky. Our tongues in each other's mouths.

Third scenario
We both start taking our clothes off at the same time, both becoming closer to nakedness as each second explodes. Leaving the lite lit to see what we're doing.
We sit and stare at each other, filling our eyes.
We stare at each other as we both get closer
breathing louder
sweating...wanting...hoping...nothing stops us.

The question of clothes and nakedness
Should the woman be asked to undress first, while the man lies on the rented bed and watches her? His gimlet poking through the flap of his pants, where it can be seen. The woman comes over and starts to undress the man. First she takes his shoes off, then his socks. She unbuttons his belt, unhooks the first button, pulls the zipper down, reaches in and rubs his swollen balls. Or should it be the exact opposite?

Should the woman lie on the bed while the man comes over and begins to undress the woman?
My desire for my dear Nomi was pure and simple. I was the end result of my species. She was all I wanted this very moment. Not a roaming thought nor a sound crossing my mind.

A joint in my pocket to break the ice. We both took a hit. I held her in my arms and whispered in her ear...Amore doesn't need a stable nor a stall, it needs the whisper of a dove.

The measuring-rod of manhood.
She closed her eyes.
It was so stiff and hard. Every milligram of blood in my veins was pumping dynamite into that swollen beauty that manhood is

measured by. "Oh what you've done to me," I said, boiling over with cunt heat, hoping that she would open her eyes and look at me…to see how I lusted for her, craved her, salivated, felt dizziness in my head. My eyes felt as if they would burst out of their sockets and fall on the floor.

An engine so hard should be a complement to any woman in a rented bedroom. She could swing on me, like a gymnast, and it would support her through every leap and jump. Her long legs opened a little, and I gently stared at her most private possession. That thing that was totally hers. She could touch it when she wanted to, and she could use it as she felt. She could give it to me or to Joe or to Sam. What a terrifying thought… something so pleasurable and she could use it as she felt. Her lips parted just enough to make my hardon throb with every heartbeat. Mouth and cunt became my only concern. I wanted both at the same moment. Her eyes opened a little, in that look of total passion that a woman gets when she has entered the dream world of a rented room.

Delirium in a rented room

It reminded me of the time I first nailed her. Her terriers were on the deck. The dogs somehow knew that something was going to take place. They sensed the carnal act and they got to it themselves. I looked through the glass sliding doors at Mingo, the male terrier, give it to the bitch, Bertha. Mingo looked at me, as if to tell me,

"This is the way it's done in the animal world, Buster."

Watching the dogs do it lit me on fire. "Look!" I yelled at her in a voice of total excitement, "Your dogs are stuck, that's the way nature intended us to screw, stuck in each other."

Her eyes opened wide, as she looked at the dogs going at it. She said nothing.

My prize for that nite lay on the couch, waiting to get rammed by a long-horned goat. I gave it to her like I was a bulldog, a horse, a cock on a hen. I was a barnyard creature, pumping so hard I bit my tongue. I wanted to get stuck in her. I wanted an emergency crew to come pour buckets of cold water on us, and get us unstuck.

She looked at me in our rented bedroom. Her eyes were half-closed with that look of passion overwhelming her. Eyes that tell you she is in a world of pure desire. Somehow men can't get into that state of bliss. It's so total that I find myself wishing I could experience such deep emotions with such abandonment, but my engine needs fuel. It's an active instrument. It lunges, it breaks, it's mechanical, chemical, it has magnetic fluid. It has balls, big balls like a Brahman bull. It is moving, it can't wait. If it waits it will deflate. In its place will be a soft piss-rod. You have to wait for it to come back. It might not.

The weather got cold.

There was noise in the alley. A car backfired. A wrong smell, a wrong look, a wrong word and it might go. It's here for only a minute at the most. It can't wait...it needs the moment. It is the contradiction that man carries with him.

"Oh Nomi," I yelled out. I was afraid I would come before I could put it in where it belonged. Or maybe I would get so excited, it would fall like the leaf does off the oaken branch in the winter.

Patience and hope seemed like virtues to me now. They were going to pay off. This nite would be devoted to love, the kind of love a man understands. A woman yelping like a dog to be screwed. She knew that she had taken her marriage vows in front of the judge and included in the vows were the marriage prohibitions that I had asked her to take. Not to fall asleep when we were going to play life's most beautiful duet. She looked at me. That look Phaedra had...when she saw Hippolitus pissing in the palace garden. Her eyes were glazed. She had never smelt me this hot nor tasted me so sweet, heard me so needing. I was a
total man
health
strength
desire
need
conquering
exploding. She looked at me with her dreamy eyes. Then without any warning she yawned. I was terror-struck. "I know this sounds stupid," I told the D.A. "but I felt I had been betrayed."

She yawned again and again. I had to move fast, if I was going to get her. She yawned again. Maybe the fucken wine did it to her or the goddamn weed. She was passing the critical point of no return. Yawns and passion don't mix, they detract from each other. Anger tries to protect the moment from oblivion. The hardon begs for help. If she yawns again, I'll lose it. It might take another month, another place, another look, a different word to get my piss pole this excited.

The great American woman on the cover of Cosmopolitan was yawning, tired, exhausted, wasted. What I wanted was still a million miles away, covered up, hidden under her hand. She turned her head, closed her eyes, folded her legs and fell asleep.

The wine had lifted my spirit to new highs. The joint had lessened my nervousness. Just a few moments before, I felt her breathing vapors of fire, and now everything was in a sporadic noise-chamber where different sounds are thrown together and you create an emotional image out of the noise. I watched her mouth open wider, and her lips flutter as growls, whistles, and long-winded screeching poured out of her gaping mouth. Sounds of trumpets blowing out her ass, sounding the arrival of a royal party.

There was no way I would waste such passion. To try and freeze it out in a cold shower. To sit in a corner and meditate. To give myself reasonable conversations. To try and be polite and understanding was out of the question. On our wedding nite?

It was the first time I screwed her while she was asleep. It was a very delicate moment. I didn't know what I felt. I screwed her while she snored. I had never done this before. It was my first time. I had never fucked a sleeping woman. I watched her face as I rammed her. It was in a peaceful, serene state.

I told her she was the best woman I ever had. "Do you hear me?" I asked her. "My desire to put it in you has reached some sort of mania."
She grunted a few times when I shoved my ax handle in her as deep as I could. I lifted her legs up and held them in the position of acceptance. She didn't bother to wake up. She took it all and never lost a moment's sleep.

I thanked her for the wonderful pleasure she gave me. I talked to her like a lover who has given all. She farted, she grunted, rolled over and that was it. I took a nice warm shower, and as I was soaping myself up I watched what the process of life and death was all about. Everything was in reverse. Everything went back to where it came from. A stillness, a quietness, a moment of prayer for guidance and patience as one buries the dead.

The thought about the drive back home, with my new wife sitting next to me, made me nervous. I wanted to tell her that I was damn sure I had made the biggest mistake of my life in marrying her.

Yawning and its Effects on the Male

Meditative silence

Common yawn

Polite yawns

The serious indifferent yawn

The put-off yawn

The kissing yawn

The yawn as a question

A few days after our marriage and the depressing marriage nite in our Reno hotel room, we found ourselves sitting at the table drinking coffee and looking at each other, saying nothing. I was looking at the woman I had just married and hadn't yet given her, as far as she knew, a Nuptial screw as a husband.

I sat there watching her pick up the coffee cup, put it to her mouth, take a small sip, then put it back down again and repeat the moves without ever saying a word. The only sound that came out of her mouth was the sound of her sipping the coffee. She saw me looking at her and smiled. I felt a warmth come over me, like the hand of the sun had stroked my forehead. I smiled back at her and my hand reached over and touched her hand. I squeezed it with the assurance that she was mine. She winked at me. We didn't utter a word. I knew I loved her. I felt that twinge that comes just before desire blossoms in your pants. I wanted to fuck her, just as simple as that, at 10:30 in the morning.

I tried convincing myself that the trip to Reno and her falling asleep on me on our wedding nite was just an awful coincidence of excitement, tiredness, wine and weed. She just fell asleep from exhaustion. But it also came to my mind that she could be bored with the familiarity of being with me.

In other words, the newness and the excitement of the unexpected was traded in for the predictable and the tiresome. I was either a new cock on the prowl or an old husband destined to be a cuckold. I had nothing more to offer and therefore her tiredness became the main theme, the motif of our love, the climax of our wedding nite.

While all this was rattling around in my mind, it happened again. I started to talk to her, and there in front of me at 10:30 in the morning, that goddamn yawn came over her face like a pall of smoke from an open peat-bog hearth. Patience...I told myself. All things are accomplished with the help of the Queen of all virtues, patience, but I lacked the experience...the imagination...the suaveness of a felon. I couldn't hold it back any longer, my blood was ready to burst through the membranes, the cells, the arteries of my brain. Her yawning in my face was making me sick. She yawned when I wanted to make love to her and when I wanted to talk to her. She yawned when I sat next to her. It seemed that she yawned every time I got near her. Her yawns had started to invaded my sanity. I could feel anger every time she opened up her mouth to do the yawn.

The morning could have been so beautiful, it could have been so different, but it wasn't. She yawned a few more times, took another sip of coffee and just stared out the window without saying a word. I felt like a stranger with a desire, trying to start a conversation with a woman who didn't want to talk.

Meditative silence

This shit…that silence is golden and one must learn to remain in a state of meditative silence…was not advice intended for the bedroom. While the world that I called "My Life" was passing over the icy rocks into the oblivion of sleep, I was starting to realize that words and sex go together. In a dark room the words guide you. Your ears wait to hear the right sounds moulded into cock-igniting words…words that lite up the nite. But with her I could actually hear silence. I could feel the absence of sounds and it terrified me.

She had become a silent partner in our marriage. It was a total package of yawning, indifference, and thrown in for good measure, a pair of vacuous eyes staring at me. Eyes filled with emptiness. I had a feeling that she saw emptiness in the chair I was sitting in, emptiness in my face, emptiness in my intents. A feeling as if I didn't exist, or worse yet, I didn't belong.

I was a starving man who needed a dinner for his soul, platters filled with concern, dishes overflowing with words of desire. I was being starved and my tormentor kept food constantly in front of me so I could lose my mind as my desire to eat became a frenzy.

She had created problems for me I never thought possible. I felt I had a mark on my forehead. Some sign telling the world, "This asshole will put a woman to sleep." That grotesque yawn was worst than the bite of a viper.

The implication of the yawn was painful, not only to my eyes, but to my well-being as a lover...a husband...a human. I needed the energy a woman can give a man. I needed it...the way the earth needs the sun, and when she yawned I felt the stabbing pains of her indifference. What a pity. She was so beautiful and yawning twisted her face. It made her chin wrinkle up. The mouth opened, exposing a flattened tongue which lay in her mouth like a beached whale. Had she been ugly, the yawn would have given her face a more human look...a look of needing compassion for her tiredness...a look of normality.

She yawned
when I talked to her
when I asked her a question
when I tried kissing her
when I put my hands on her
when I did what husbands or lovers do to their women.
She would stretch while I had it in her and yawn in my face.
She yawned when she ate and after she finished.
I don't know if she yawned when she was pissing or when she was taking a shit, or if she yawned in front of that hooked-nosed bastard she worked for. I could feel the anger in me simmering, the cadence of the words paralyzing me.

I started keeping track of her yawns like I was a score keeper at the great yawn-in that takes place on the 6:00 A.M. commute.

In a 5-day period she had yawned in my face, either while I was talking to her or trying to make love to her, 186 times. An average of 37.2 times a day. This doesn't seem like a lot, but when you consider that I didn't see her from 7 in the morning till 6 at nite, 37.2 yawns from 6 P.M. till 8 P.M. when she fell asleep, allows for a yawn approximately every 3.6 minutes. Enough to interrupt whatever is being said or done.

Common Yawn
The most common yawn was the yawn that came in the middle of a conversation. Her eyes became glazed, and the damn mouth would open slowly. I could see all the fillings in her teeth along with that little hanging, dangling piece of flesh, guarding the entrance to her throat.

Polite Yawns
Then there were the polite yawns, as if she was practicing how to turn her yawns off by plugging the air flow and twisting her mouth around, like a gargoyle trying to stop that yawn from exploding in the church below. This polite squiggling of the face takes about a full minute, and is followed in repeated waves until the mouth finally blows open, and the face slithers apart.

The serious indifferent yawn
All the parts that go with a yawn come into existence. The stretch, the shaking of the head, the release of the bowel tension and the upcoming blow from the backside. Naturally I felt like an intruder between her and the impending sleep. I got the feeling of being the cause of the yawn. Instead of feeling good in helping a person to reach such a relaxed state of mind, I got the feeling of being a third party, when two people want to have each other, and you're there in the way.

The put-off yawn
Sometimes I felt that she yawned just to put me off, to make me feel like I was boring and uninteresting or stupid and insipid, or that I lacked that magnetic fluid that could majouberize the panties off her ass.

The kissing yawn
Then there was the most terrifying of yawns…while kissing her she stops and yawns. I tried to be understanding, to hide my remorse and my impending depression, but I was starting to get disgusted with her for making me feel like a self-serving dog who wants the cunt at all costs, ready to take on the whole world to prove that I deserve to have it...now.

The yawn as a question
Yawns are like nose twitches that a person gets when he has smelt bad fish, foul gas, bad breath, sweaty armpits. You don't dare continue. The finger of accusation is following.
The nose says…"No."
The twitch of the face says..."No."
The Yawn says..."No."

You have been politely rejected. There is something about you that makes the woman yawn and want to fall asleep, maybe to save herself from you and your boredom.

One nite, every move in my body was going forward, led by my triumphant swollen cock, a symbol
of fertility
of religion
of man
of god
life
death
the four seasons
and she yawned underneath me, and that beautiful chiseled jaw of hers moved like a cow eating on her cud. I felt instantaneous
ashamedness
embarrassed
rejected....dead.
This ramrod...that I have been accused of bashing her with...had now shriveled back down to a pissing thread, a deflated balloon, a gland held by a pair of tweezers and tied with a piece of string. "Give me some answer," I begged her. "Tell me something, anything. Why do you keep yawning in my face?" She just looked at me. "You're forcing me to become like a prisoner, locked in a dungeon, who touches his prick to see if he is still human. You're going to cause me to start jacking myself off, and at my age." She yawned a small yawn, closed her eyes and went to sleep.

Evodiaphobia

Denials of sex and its effects

Is my scent putrid?

The compatibility of odors

The ethical duty to inform your spouse of malodors

Self-Identity through odors

Memories brought to life with odors

The delusion created by scent

The virtue of good odors

Bad smells are associated with decay

What effect did human odors have on the passage of history?

A foul-smelling beauty

Identifying my own odors

Denials of sex and its effects
As the days passed I became more aware of the disorders that sex denial can create.

The inability to close my eyes
Nervous agitation
Anger
Extreme sensitivity to lite
Constipation
Prostate inflammation
Inability to concentrate
Loss of appetite
Skin rash
Pain in the groin.

There was a coldness that was creeping over my whole existence, like the fog that crawls over the coastal hills during the early morning hours. When you feel rejected, you try to pass the thoughts off as just bad feelings. You give yourself generous servings of the most palatable explanations, until you get down to the nitty-gritty...that after six months of marriage, for some reason, she just can't stand you anymore. That depressing question unfolded in my head...why?

I needed some imaginative reason to explain her attitudes. Being tired was not enough reason to do what she was doing to me. I needed a prime reason that made sense to my poor tired brain.

A strange thought entered my head one day...as I stared out my favorite window over looking the bay. A thought that had never entered my head before suddenly appeared like a total cosmic force, as if someone turned on all the lites in a theater while the play was unfolding itself in the hands of the actors. The play stops. Every one looks at each other. I ask myself the almighty question.

Is my scent putrid?
Do I smell awful to her?
I never smelt myself. I had never been depressed nor amazed by my odors. I was never aware of them. Either I didn't care, or nothing caught my nose to make me care. My concern was

ignited one day as I read an advertisement. I read in a magazine that morning a full-page advertisement of a man with a bewildered look on his face. His girlfriend had walked off with another man who glowed with happiness. It had to do with a deodorant that claimed to

> ***Stop those odors that break people apart and keep people away. She won't tell you***

was the theme of the advertisement. Was it possible that my problem was a bad smell? Something as simple and as complex as a smell? The thought came and went, then it came and stayed. Maybe it's my smells and odors that are offensive to her. It's difficult to smell yourself, to detect a personal odor that is offensive. I've heard of cases where a change of diet created vile odors in a person. The mixing of wrong foods in the system. The creation of imbalances between the pH factors. It was complex and beyond my understanding, so I never gave it a second thought. But the fear of having an odor was becoming very real and very important. The advertisement said

> ***He didn't know that he was driving people away with bad odors. The nose of a normal person can only accept so many molecules of malodor before it sends messages to the head to shut off all systems and leave the area.***

Was it possible that I had become one of those people that smell, and my dear wife wouldn't tell me or didn't know how to tell me without destroying our love? Was she pretending to be tired just so she wouldn't have to be assaulted by my odors? What an awful thought, to feel like you're so offensive that people dread seeing you come close to them.

The compatibility of odors

One Sunday morning while the sun was filling the windows with a golden color, she sat eating her favorite breakfast of cornflakes. I raised the subject of odors carefully so I wouldn't prejudice her answer. "What fragrances do you like?" I asked her.

She looked at me as she was sticking a spoonful of the goods in her mouth. I waited patiently for her answer. Up and down and from side to side her well-chiseled jaw went. Finally she stopped chewing and took a long swallow. When she felt her mouth was clear of all the food in it, she said, while looking at the bowl of flakes in front of her, "I never gave it a thought."

"I read somewhere that people get together because of the compatibility of their odors," I told her in a poetical tone in a moment of despair, "like the scent that draws the hummingbird to the fragrance of the flower."

She shrugged her shoulders.

"Do you think that's true?" I asked her.

"I don't know," shoving another spoonful of that crap in her mouth.

"What do I smell like?" I asked her, witnessing a sense of utter fear waiting for the answer.

"Different," she said. "You smell different." And her nose twitched enough for me to see it twitching. Was it a message she was sending me?

"Did you like the new after-shave lotion that I bought?"

"I really didn't notice," she said, shrugging her shoulders, "but I'll try to keep it in mind to smell you."

The conversation felt awkward, out of balance...out of rhythm. Almost as if she was telling me something by her indifferent attitude. I had never experienced the thought of smelling bad. It's like a pain or a sound you hadn't noticed, but when you do, it seems to grow by the minute till it's ready to consume you. Eventually it became my obsession.

The ethical duty to inform your spouse of malodors

The world was becoming one great sensor, an ultimate megapowered electronic nose searching out human foulness, depraved odors from subhumans that have overpopulated this earth. A feeling, as if I had been duped, came over me. I felt that my wife had some marital duty to inform me that my odors turned her off. That I offended her. I assaulted her nose, battered her brain, caused pain and suffering. She had an ethical duty to inform me, and yet she said nothing. She acted out her disgust by deleting me from her world. If this was the case, was she building up her reservoir of disgust...to finally break the ties of matrimony without any sense of guilt?

Self-Identity through odors
All the old fears seemed trivial in the lite of the newly discovered fear. My old fears felt like part of my mental wardrobe. I had become so used to them that they seemed part of my life. This new fear was or could be catastrophic. I had no natural defenses built up. No plan of attack. If someone said I stunk, I would have no reply.

Questions of vital importance haunted me daily. An army of questions standing in line waiting to be asked. Questions that had the ring of a joke, the sound of the Ad-man's con job. Questions that sounded as if they were being asked of God. Do I stink? And if I do, tell me what to do.

Questions and answers kept popping up in my thoughts. How do I know I smell? I'd have to ask others, become sensitive to the looks on their faces when I got close. Give myself...a self check. Stick my fingers in the suspected areas and bring the malodor, smeared on my fingertips like smello Jam, straight to my nose.
What is the nature of my odor?
Acrid like urine?
Sour like an old mouth that has been guzzling beer for years?
Putrid like rotting flesh?
Gaseous like shit?

How close should I get to another, if I know I stink?
I didn't know the answer.
Do I stink more in the morning than at nite?
Again I didn't know the answer.
Are there certain foods I should avoid?
No answer.

Does the rest of the body emit odors like the mouth does?
Yes, and each one is different,

the advertisements said.
How does one disguise the various odors coming from the various parts?
No answer.

There had to be more questions, but at the moment I was running out of courage to ask them. I was caught in one of history's greatest fears, the fear that grabs anyone who is in close association with someone. The modern fear of smelling bad.

Memories brought to life with odors

Odors can bring back all kinds of memories. Copra docks...ships emptying their cargo holds of that smelly rotting copra.
The smell of a harbor
The smell of a garden
The smell of a woman
The smell of a girl...so different...so greatly different. It seems that when a woman has had a man, from then on there is a different odor about her. A sour odor, an odor of cohabitation drying up in her like cheeses in a vat. Covered over with perfumes, covered over by someone else's perfumes until it resembles a thick jungle of odors betraying that beneath it all, it does smell bad.

A man who's had a woman, does he smell of cohabitation? Then a thought came that really amazed me. I had never thought of it before. Did deceit have an odor?

The delusion created by scent

I didn't have to be a genius to realize that a world, crowded as it is, can't have someone around who terrorizes another's nose. If you stink you're thrown out of the group immediately. But luckily for human culture, the human nose has been desensitized by sprays, lotions, elixirs, and powders.
Olfactory rings that look like haloes around her sprayed hair, armpits and crotch. Powders that leave a cast of baker's bloom around her ass, feet, toes. Mouth washes, rinses, douches of various scents and flavors of strawberry, lemon lime, wild camomile, cherry. Scents cascading from the orifices like rivers from mysterious gorges.

She said I smelt different. The whole world has a manufactured odor. The odor of modern times.
All the scents are made at the same plant somewhere in New

Jersey, where lilacs are mixed with jasmines, where the smells of mimosa and rose petals mix in rivers of scents, where bottles and urns are filled and sold to the waiting nose.

The virtue of good odors
He who smells good is good, and he who smells good is healthy, wealthy and wise. Polished and perfumed, you cast your lot to the world and take your chance. If you use the right deodorants in the right places, you will be keeping up with the first rule of modern success. To smell good is to take the first step to success. A man who smells good…is good.
Virtue has a scent. Happiness has a fragrance.

Bad smells are associated with decay
death
rot
decay
garbage
throwaways
green mold...
homelessness...depravity...crooks...cheats...liars.

I started reading about diets and odors. I wanted to know which foods create acidic odors. I wanted to know the history of smells, odors, scents. I became, for the first time in my life, concerned about odors, and especially odors that people found offensive.

What effect did human odors have on the passage of history?
The odor of life and its effects on the human imagination, on cultural history, of the rise and fall of nations. The effects of odors on crime...the odor of passion, infidelity and murder. Somehow all of this must be connected to the odors that humans emit.

I often wondered what people in the past smelt like or thought of each others odors. Did Socrates enjoy the odors of Xanthippe?
Did Pericles get devoured by the odors of Aspasia?
Did the courtesan, Thais, overcome Alexander The Great with her scent, which made her even more sought after by Ptolemy?
Did Lucrece recognize the odors of her rapist?

Did Hippolitus smell the passion of Phaedra?
Could Phaedra smell the suspicions of her husband Theseus?
Could Hippolitus smell the odor of suspicion from his father, the king of Athens and the husband of Phaedra?

Daily I saw more advertisements In big bold letters pointing their insidious finger at me.

> ***There is nothing to fear when you smell good. Modern times require certain attention to your personal odors, just as it requires attention to your personal needs.***

Every magazine I opened had the message waiting for me. Important things to do before seeing your intended women. Just looking good is not enough. Looks good and smells good was the complete man. "Be careful," I read in the book. "Don't set yourself up with bad smells."

Everywhere the message was blaring loud and clear. I could hear it.

> ***There is nothing more offensive and disgusting to the modern woman than a foul-smelling man.***

It all started that awful day when she told me I didn't smell like other people do. I didn't know if that was meant to be a compliment or a caution. She didn't elaborate nor clarify it. It was only natural, having the suspicion in me already, that her words added more fuel to the fire. It seemed obvious to me now, that she fell asleep when I got near her to escape from me and the odor I was emitting. I depressed her through her nose. But why didn't she tell me, or at least put me on notice that I stunk? Maybe I didn't stink. That might not be the right word. Maybe I had developed certain odors she detected and found unbearable to be around.

A foul-smelling beauty

I remember a woman I knew, beautiful to the eyes, but deadly to the nose. The poor thing tried everything to disguise it, but it was unbearable to be around her. One day I found the strength in me to tell her. It was one of the hardest things I ever did.

As I found out later, an odor has a description to it and a number on the aromatic scale. From sweet, to sour, to putrid. The odor can be delivered through the breath or by the body. An odor can attract or repel. It can be heavenly or hellishly vile. I couldn't describe to her the number on the aromatic scale that she represented, but it was probably at the outer limits of human bearability. Breath and body ranged between sour and acrid. It pierced my nose like a knife, causing me to vomit more than once.

She tried everything to get rid of or disguise the smell, but like the poor creature in the inferno, it made no difference. Somehow her odor was connected to her genetics, to a nervous system that blew when she got excited. Every time she wanted to be fucked, this appalling odor, capable of flooring a horse, oozed out of her pores. It smelt like the open end of a public sewer that was connected to a whole historical evolution of human stink.

If only I was able to smell history, I could have understood the odors of hell coming out of that poor woman's passions. She cried and through her broken and sobbing words I could hear her telling me that no one had ever told her she stunk. I had never seen such honesty in a woman's eyes as when she swore to me...no one had ever told her such a thing. She asked me a sad question. I still remember the question. "How can I exist, when wanting someone to fuck me would only liberate the putrid odors of hell within me?"

She smelt worse than a skunk. She belonged to a species of womanhood capable of repelling a man bent on screwing her, the way a skunk does the predator. I wanted to fall on my knees and beg her forgiveness. But the nose, above all the other senses, can dominate you and is not forgiving. You can see things and still stand them.
You can hear and bear it.
You can taste and spit it out, but the nose will make you run.
The nose seems to be connected to everything,
to your stomach
to your head
to your wand.

The greater her depression, the more unbearable her smell. Even her tears stunk. Someone told me that she committed suicide. It was probably a joke, but underneath it all there was a justifiable reason to do it. I think if I smelt that bad, I would try to end it all. "Maybe it's me," I told her once in a fit of compassion.

"Maybe your chemistry, when connected to mine, emits noxious vapors."

It got to the point that I couldn't get near her any more. Every time I did, my tongue got caught in my throat. Was it me reacting to the smell, or was it a smell that 10 people out of 10 would say the same thing about? I remember her crying as I left her apartment. I was glad that I would never have to smell her again.

The fear that I might stink to someone the way she stunk to me was mentally devastating. How did I get my ass into such a predicament? Body odors were the last thing in the world I feared, and now that's all I was aware of. As the days stretched themselves out into weeks, I found more reasons to suspect that the malodor aura around me was the cause of my wife's indifference.

Identifying my own odors

I started to acquire new habits. I took at least four showers a day. It seemed that every time I went into the toilet to take a piss, I jumped into the shower. I scrubbed and washed and soaked till my skin was red from attention.

One of my more visible new habits was to raise my arm and sniff my armpit, trying to catch a stray odor. Another habit I developed was blowing through my teeth to catch the odors fuming out of my mouth. I would curl my lips, up to my nose, in order to get closer to the hidden smell. I developed a very noticeable habit of constantly sticking my hand down my pants...to grasp an odor on my fingertips and immediately transport my fingers up to my nose and smell my fingers for a telltale sign of a bad smell. I started soaking in the tub for hours.

I bought various bath oils, Spanish Nites, Indian summers, aromatic herbs, bay leaves, cinnamon sticks. Every herb I knew, that had some aroma to it, I used in the tub.

I started reading the ingredients of the deodorants. I went to health shops and asked them what diets were good for having a proper odor. They saw a sucker in need and sold me vitamins.

The Aromatologist

Fate works in strange ways. While I was concerned with this problem of odors, I read in the paper that a famous Bulgarian aromatologist had decided to make his home in San Francisco, with the notation that his "Nose" functioned better in a climate that was fog-bound 300 days of the year.

With a little imagination, I found where he lived and made a phone call. I told him on the phone that I had a need for consultation on a specific odor and left the details to take care of themselves when we met.

I guess it puzzled him enough to make an appointment with me for the following week.

I found his place up on Pacific Heights, a neighborhood that catered to the wealthy and successful. Big two- and three-story mansions lined up, side by side, with their occupants lost inside the grand monsters. My aromatologist lived in one of those beautiful houses on Lyon Street.

I parked my old '64 Dodge Dart around the corner so it wouldn't be seen, walked up to the big front door, pressed the bell and heard the chimes let go inside like a battery of cathedral bells. A few moments later a tall, beautiful woman with straight black hair, parted in the middle and pulled back, opened the big oak door. I told her who I was, and that I had an appointment with the Maestro Monsieur Zephetiries.

"Yes," she said, "he is expecting you."

He was a skinny little man wearing a dark blue suit, a white shirt and a dark necktie. I could have mistaken him for a mortician, a banker, a lawyer, but never for a man who made his fame and wealth with his nose. A man who was gifted with the nose of a dog.

When I entered the room the first thing I noticed was that the room had no odors in it. It was as if my nose had just turned off. I had entered a sterile world that had no smells.

I saw his nose twitch...like when a dog recognizes the scent of another dog. He gave me the impression that he didn't care who I was…if I had come out of the clouds…or out of the local nut-house or had just stepped out of his closet into his odorless world. His concern was my odor...my scent...my evodia...my fragrance, my aroma, my smell, my stink.

What concerned his nose concerned him. His money came from his nose...his friendships, his women. All of it was collected and identified by his nose. I wondered if that beautiful woman who opened the door for me had an odor about her that lit the fires of hell in him. After a few obvious sniffs, he proceeded to tell me who he was, with the finesse and clarity of a man seeking the highest office of the land.

"I don't smell any fragrances," I told him. "I expected to find you living in a garden of beautiful aromas."

He looked at me and told me that he had what was known in his business as "A Nose," an exceptional nose, and a few molecules of odor could unleash his imagination. He preferred to have a clean nose palette, uncluttered and unconfused. He could identify and remember over 3,000 scents. "I can identify 100 different roses, and as you know," he told me, "the best roses for the oils come from Bulgaria. But if I had to subject my nose to all the odors daily life is shrouded in, eventually I would be unable to distinguish sour from sweet. Now what can I do for you?"

I hesitated for a moment before taking the huge leap into what might seem to be the abyss of ultimate absurdity. "I have developed an abnormal fear that I, for some unknown reason, emit foul and unbearable odors. I would like to have you confirm this, and if so, advise me as to what fragrances I might use to cover the offensive smell."

He looked at me and didn't utter a word for a moment or two. I thought he didn't understand me, and I rephrased it again for him. "I would like you to smell me out."

The question seemed perfectly reasonable to me, but evidently the Maestro had never been asked to smell out a person, he merely smelt out flowers. Rather than sputter and dangle incoherent sounds of surprise such as, "Oh, uh, yes I see, hmm, tell me more," he held his composure and asked me, "What do you mean, smell you out?" trying not to show any difficulty in understanding what I was saying.

"I want to know," I asked him, "if I stink."

"All people stink, if you want to put it that way, but fragrances and aromatics are not merely for the covering of these vile human odors. Aromas in the hands of a master perfumanary have a way of altering your wants and your moods. It is more than just covering an odor. It is evoking a feeling that comes from your sense of smell." He paused for a moment, like he was looking for some book in his head to read, a memorized passage, a line from a poet, a paragraph from some philosophical work.

"A child smells its mother long before it can understand her voice. A scent can make you happy or it can bring sadness.
The scents of a funeral
The fragrances of love
The blossoms of spring
The smell of the grasses in the fall
The aroma of chestnuts in the winter
The nose never forgets.
I use my nose differently than you do," he said, looking me straight in my eyes. "My nose evokes my imagination. I use my nose to detect fragrances and to blend them into fine perfumes. Your nose creates fears in you. My art is to evoke and stimulate your thoughts and feelings with the proper scent, not to disguise bad odors. That, my friend, is the job of deodorants."

"But bad odors must be a serious condition," I told him. "I read that they have spent 32 million dollars to advertise a fragrant toilet paper that had the softness of goose down and could evoke the fragrance of spring."

I could see the pride in his face. He knew that he had made a contribution to the civilization of mankind. With pride he told his part in it and the problem he faced.
"Which fragrance do I use? There were a multitude of fragrances. The fragrance of lilacs under your arms and your crotch makes you feel elevated spiritually and psychologically. The essence of citrus blossom, the blended essence of jasmine and bergamot, helps in transcending relationship difficulties.
I had a fragrance that I had worked on for a number of years. It would alter the most devastated personality. One drop of this divine aromatic would open the doors of heaven to the most disfigured cretins. It was a strange marriage of rank odor and divine fragrance, placed on a piece of tissue paper. As far as I was concerned, the future of mankind was secure. If both extremes could be united in such a complementary fashion, all things were possible."

I realized that I had found my man, the man with the right nose. This guy could tell me in a second what I smelled like. "I believe you Maestro," I said, almost in a voice of reverence. I was afraid he would charge me a fortune to tell me what his nose found.

"I don't know what you charge to evaluate a person's odors." I offered him a hundred dollars if he would tell me, right on the spot if I had, in polite terms, a disagreeable odor about me.
"Keep your hundred," he said. "I have known women who burst out in ecstasy smelling the vile odors of laborers, farm hands, and the crudded sweat of a ditch-digger. Napoleon always wrote Josephine, days before he arrived, asking her, begging her, not to bathe. Look for the woman who enjoys your odors, or as you say, your stink."

He showed me his door. "Keep your money," he said and bid me "Au revoir."

I never felt as lonely and as devastated as I did that afternoon, standing in the doorway of Maestro Monsieur Ziphetirie's house. I felt I had been thrown out. As if my odors offended him and he was too polite to tell me.

The Doctors

The smells

The doctor

The Chinese doctor

Gaining back my confidence

There was no doubt in my mind that a standard of odors for modern humans had been established, but what was it? *Smell good* was important, but what was *smell bad*?

The smells

I heard a testimonial from a man who said that he changed his underwear and socks three times a day. He was so afraid of the smells that he didn't bother to wash the changes, he just threw them away in fear that the smells would linger, even after the clothes had been laundered.

There were so many questions in my mind. I was a prisoner of my own imagination and fears.
If I do stink, why wasn't that smell around when we first met each other?
Did I smell different to her then?
Did I eat something or did a change of nervous energy create a new odor that was unbearable, and now I not only smelt different, but I stank?
Did something happen to me during the period that I lived with her?

Did smoking good weed finally reach a certain level, where you start to smell like a wild animal from personal neglect?

I was convinced that somehow I had developed a public smell which I couldn't detect. It made no difference what I put on, what lotions, fragrances, soaps. The smell was always there, identifiable, with me. Even the advice of the Bulgarian Nose couldn't distract me from the thought.

I started changing my clothes twice a day. Just before she'd come home, I'd put on clean underwear, pants, socks, shirt. I'd powder myself, put deodorants on all the right places, throw a swig of mouthwash down my waiting mouth and hope for the best.

I had become so obsessed with odors that I made an appointment with a dermatologist. I deliberately didn't put on any deodorants, nor did I take a shower or a bath the day of my appointment.

The doctor

"Your problem?" he asked me.

I got to the basic issue quickly, and without any hesitation I told him, "I think I stink, and it's affected me to the point that I think I'm ready to get a divorce from my wife."

He had to give me an examination, and I could see from the look on his face that he had developed the necessary moves to smell me out. He had that look of professionalism that is required in order to charge for giving me the once-over with the nose.

He got close to me, asked me to lift my arms up. I looked at his face as he gently inhaled a few sniffs. He was letting me know that he was engaging his nose.

"Drop your pants please."

I did as I was told. I stood there feeling stupid, while he bent his head down, and got as close as he could to my balls without seeming impolite.

Sniff...sniff...sniff...his nose whiffed.

"Turn around," he said, "and bend over."

I did, and he took a few more whiffs.

Sniff...sniff...sniff...sniff, as close as he could get to my ass.

"Nothing a good bath won't cure," he said.

"You smell alright to me, but many diseases have a certain odor to them. I'll be honest with you, I'm not familiar with all the odors that a particular illness emits, nor am I really familiar with the psychological problems presented by the odor. Now," he said with a notepad in his hand, "how did all this come about? Did you just wake up one day and say 'I stink'? Or were you just finishing dinner and flatulated, and never got rid of that odor of methane from your nose? Did you begin somewhere at a certain time, and feel you didn't smell right?"

"It just came about slowly," I said, with a feeling of sadness in my voice. I told him of my wife's indifference towards me and how she avoided me. That the only conclusion I could come up with was that I might have a bad smell about me which I had developed since we got married.

"I haven't heard of such a case," he said. "There might be some truth to what you're saying, but I don't smell anything out-of-the-ordinary in your case."

He told me of healthy odors that the body emits, and that one shouldn't become annoyed by them. He told me of body odors coming from your feet, your crotch, your armpits, your mouth, your hair, your ears, your pores, your penis, and the one that every one knows of, the odors that pass through you daily. "Every part of the body is capable of emitting, and does emit odors," he told me in a soft voice. "They follow you like your shadow on earth. They come like an unwanted guest, but normally bathing will take care of that. Then each disease has its own odor, each depression, each sadness. The nose understands what is right and what is wrong, and blessed are those who can detect it and identify it. I really don't know what more I can tell you, other than to recommend an old Chinese doctor I know, who could probably help you."

I thanked him for telling me so much about odors. I asked him how much I owed for the visit. He said, "See the nurse at the front desk," shook my hand...and my pocket for $135.00. This included his conversation, smelling my balls and my ass. Seven heavy whiffs…I counted them…and a few quick whiffs covered the rest of me. I paid the smart-looking nurse at the desk. She smiled at me. I wondered if she had been peeking in some 2-way mirror. I wish she had sniffed my ass. At least I would have gotten the result straight from a woman's nose.

The Chinese doctor

Maybe I needed a psychiatrist who would tell me that the smell was merely a justification, a reason, an explanation to give meaning to rejection. A mental need to give an explanation for the other lover. But I must have had some odors because he gave me Doctor Chester Chan's phone and address. An office in Chinatown on Jackson Street, just around the corner from Grant. I made a call and got an appointment to see Doctor Chan the next day.

I walked into his office and immediately smelt the fragrance of Jasmine. There was a young Chinese nurse dressed in an old-fashioned, starched white uniform, with a tricorner white cap sitting on the center of her head. White shoes and lips painted cherry red. She was sitting behind an oak desk that was more like a table, where I could see her legs in those white silk stockings, the dress riding up past the knee. I sat in a chair in front of her so I could look at her without having to move my head around. It was a wonderful sight and she didn't seem to notice me looking at her.

There were 4 old Chinese men sitting silently on old wooden high-back chairs, staring out into space. There were no magazines to occupy you. No pictures on the wall. There was only silence, and the lovely nurse to tempt your imagination. It reminded me of the silence of an opium den in Cambodia where I used to go, lie on the bench and fire up an 18-inch-long pipe and dream.

After an hour of sitting there, staring with the rest of the patients, I was called into his examination room.

"Your problem, Sir?" he asked me.

I told him my story and what I feared…that my wife had become ill from having to endure me. He took me by the hand and asked me to lie down on his examination table.

"Chinese medicine," he said, "has allowed for all of this."
He ran his nose across me like one would run a wand or a divining rod to find water, or a vacuum cleaner over an old carpet. He'd stop at certain areas of my body and sniff, two or three extra times. He lifted my leg and took another whiff. I've seen dogs do this...now I know why. I looked at his face to see if there was a curl of the nose or a twitch of the face, but...nothing.

Doctor Chan had that inscrutable face of an old master who could probably detect and differentiate what you ate by the smell of your shit.
"You're healthy," he said, nodding his head, "but I will give you an order for some herbs. It will make the natural smells of the body work in your favor."
"Does that mean that I stink?" I asked him.
"It depends on who is doing the smelling," he told me in a serious tone. "The fly finds the scent of the dung heap with her nose, to have her family, and the bee the nectar of the flower. Who can say what the nose dictates to the brain?"
His explanation was so philosophical that it sounded more like poetry to my ears than medical advice.
"It will take some time," he said, "to be able to trust your presence around others. You have, through fear, lost your Moo-shin...come back in a month if you feel you have to."

Gaining back my confidence
I so believed in Doctor Chan, and the herbs he gave me, that I tested out my odors on strangers. I purposely rode the buses and streetcars for the next week. Leaving early in the morning, when the streetcars were loaded, really going nowhere. All I wanted to do was sit with strangers and see if their noses would be offended by my proximity to them.

As if I was invisible, no one showed any recognition of a bad smell. All my empirical tests seemed to confirm that I didn't have "the smells." One day in particular, when my stomach hurt a little, I found it a perfect day to test out odors. I took some Malux, which always caused me to fart a lot. I got on the K-line at the West Portal Station, and rode through the Twin Peaks Tunnel. I just farted away and watched the faces of the passengers. I could see that the odors were hitting them. They didn't dare look around to see who it was, in fear of provoking some screwball and getting shot on the streetcar for smelling some nut's cracker-pops. I felt protected from any embarrassment, but it was evident the passengers weren't numb in the nose. When the methane odors cleared, I entered the olfactory zone, that area where one can detect your presence by his nose. The Moo-shin as Doctor Chan described it to me. Nothing...no look...no twitch...no odor.

I called up Doctor Chan and talked to him personally on the phone. I thanked him a hundred times, and according to Chinese custom...having been cured...I paid my bill with such happiness and satisfaction that I would have gladly kissed his ass in front of his lovely nurse, or if he wanted, in front of all the people on Market and Powell who were waiting for the cable car to take them up the hill.

The Video Wife

Meeting a cuckold husband

The magic of Mario's coffeehouse

The betrayed lover

In a complete state of madness

Truth is a verb

The ON button

The naivete that creates an illusion of respectability

I was a novice in the big leagues

Meeting a cuckold husband

It seems that when you become aware of something, other things appear to confirm the awareness. It was as if the devil didn't have anything to do that day, so he set me up for a meeting with a poor cuckold husband, who told me his miserable tale which really undid me to the very core of my existence, and helped to open new passages of suspicion in my head.

It was on a Monday morning. I had spent the weekend in dull conversation and almost alone. Nomi said very few words and when she did, it was the same old shit about her job. I had to get the hell out of the house before I came unglued.

I jumped in my '64 Dodge Dart, and headed for North Beach. I needed to be around people for a while and not really have to talk to anyone.

I drove around for about 20 minutes, looking for a place to park. Finally I spotted an opening in front of the church of Saint Peter and Paul, and almost had a fight with a guy driving a Mercedes convert who was trying to get the same parking space. What a place to have it out. In front of the church that was named after the two toughest Saints of Christendom.

"We can't fight in front of the church," I told him. "It's bad luck. I was just going in for a prayer." I was a true Christian. "I'm passive. I believe in the thought of good works. I have faith in man, and respect and venerate the Virgin Mother."

I laid it on him as thick as I could, conversation being cheaper than a busted face. "Get your ass out of that parking spot," he yells at me as I walked across the park to go to Mario's coffeehouse for a good cup of cappuccino.

The magic of Mario's coffeehouse
I figured Mario's was safer than going into the church. There is something sacred about coffeehouses that Europeans know and Americans are just starting to find out. You don't fight in coffeehouses like you do in bars.

First of all you have a table, and anyone sitting with you is sharing the same magical surface of this earth with you. It's part of some magical element that is in us. Maybe it's something that comes from some prehistoric time when people who ate together had to be friends, or else you ate each other up.

No matter how pissed off you are, sitting at a coffeehouse table with someone takes it all away. It's a place where you can sit by yourself and enjoy good coffee with a book, with a notepad, or just staring outside at the people passing by.

All of a sudden, all the thoughts that I had about coffeehouses, about the magical effect of a table, the mild effect of caffeine on the nervous system, all of it was going to be tested in a moment...because coming through the door of Mario's coffeeshop was the loudmouth from the Mercedes. Jesus what a place to start a commotion and no back door to get out.

He saw me sitting toward the back, and Mario was just bringing my cappuccino to me. Keeping my eyes glued to the coffee cup, I pretended I never saw him. I stirred my coffee slowly so I wouldn't destroy the milky foam.

I heard the loudmouth above me.

I heard the chair being pulled back, and his ass finding the landing in the center.

"No hassle," he tells me, "I found a better spot right down the street. Saw you come in here, and figured this is where you get ready for that prayer you were telling me about."

He introduced himself. He said he was new to the area, that he had come up from L.A. He once lived up here when he was in law school at Hastings College of the Law, down on MacAlister Street.

"Jesus those were the days, when the dean of the school taught contracts. Loaded to the gills, he'd sit in his throne with a little green shade pulled over his eyes like a Faro dealer looking for a cheat."

He started pouring his past out in little bits and pieces. It was like listening to a guy who was on the front line who started telling you all about his life because he knew that he might die, and it felt good that someone would hear the story. That once he did have a life. A life that was dear to him, and people who knew him once, and he had a burning love for some woman or some pimply-faced girl. Would she remember him when he was dead? Did she care? Was it all worth it?

He talked about a lot of things. You could hear that he needed to talk to someone, anyone that would hear him. He was cleaning out the storeroom in his head and needed to put everything in its right place.

After bouncing around from subject to subject he started to zero in on the main theme of his story.

How he quickly came up the ladder of success, and how his suspicions and accusations sent him right back to where he started out years before, at the bottom of the ladder. He told me of getting a job at a bank when he got out of law school.

"After I got out of law school I went back home to L.A. Worst thing I ever did...that has to be the armpit of the world, but I got lucky. I knew a friend who knew the owner of the bank, at Beverly Hills National.

"I met the owner who said that I reminded him of himself, when he was young, and for whatever reason people like people, he took a liking to me and my style.

"He was an old bootlegger who had made a lot of money and eventually he opened up a bank. I got invited to his house, and pretty soon I was involved with his daughter, and a year later I got married to his beautiful daughter.

"That's not a bad score...from rags to riches...the great American dream come true, along with the great American woman making it all possible."

"Nothing like that has ever happened to me," I said, thinking of my sleeping, indifferent wife.

"You're lucky," he told me. "It wasn't all that dreamy. She was a woman who needed a lot of attention. I don't mean 'good morning sweetheart' or 'bless you' when she sneezes. This woman needed a love machine to keep her quiet. Even though she had a very quiet type of personality, a 24-hour-a-day job of handling her wouldn't have been enough. She suffered from having too much, and therefore nothing stood out."

I listened to the poor guy tell me about her...how beautiful she was...how she had all those nice qualities. But he had the misfortune to stumble onto her secret life.

His story started to fit the thoughts I had in my head. Maybe life is so similar that we mistake it for being complex. Maybe everything is the same, and we just can't believe it.

He skipped most of the bullshit someone tells you before they get to the zero point, and quickly got down to the part that makes it all hurt. His face now became more serious as he started to unfold his misery.

The betrayed lover

"I saw her one day as I was coming home from a bank meeting in Santa Barbara. She was in a pickup truck with a Mexican farmhand. The guy had on a straw hat with peacock feathers on the band. I couldn't believe it was her, maybe it wasn't. But it looked just like her, I mean identical. I almost drove into them. I got so close I could see the dirt in the guy's ears, and she's holding on to him like he was Adam and she was Eve."

Here was a person who was a star in the old man's bank… married to his daughter, and she's baiting farmhands who haven't taken a bath, probably, in a year...whose assholes are probably dangling with dingle berries, their armpits gassed with smells. And he was shadowing them in his Mercedes.

The thought of men who smelled, being with beautiful women was taking ahold of my thoughts. It was like Doctor Chan had told me. "What's stink to one is fragrance to another."

He was looking at me with the stupid look of a betrayed lover, who can't understand why his woman would want something less than him, someone so low on the ladder it would take a year of climbing down to reach him on the bottom rung.

"I can understand her running off with someone who's got deeper pockets but this guy had nothing. I kept telling myself it was just someone who looked like her, but really wasn't her.
I followed them, and sure as hell she drove up to our house at Kensington Circle. It was a beautiful house with pool, elevator and six huge bedrooms."

He told me how happy he had been in that house. He lived the life of a man of means, a man who had it, a man who had arrived, and was still climbing. There was no end in sight. His father-in-law was a multimillionaire. A multi-anything is better than a monodic nothing. Yet his pain was brought about by the presence of his wife in a pickup truck with a gardner who wore a straw hat, sandals and who hadn't washed in a year.

At least he had a face to work with. All I had was a suspicion of what my wife might be doing.

If only I had a face to work with, a person, a name, a place. But I had nothing, only the thoughts in my mind that it could be anyone anywhere. A faceless thought, an anonymous caller, a hat without a head, a shoe without a foot, a pair of pants without a body.

"What the fuck was she doing that far away from home?"
His voice brought me back to the table. I found myself staring at my coffee cup while he continued.

"What was she doing in the guy's old pickup truck...snuggled up to him...playing with his ear and him laughing? She was so wrapped up in this fucken wetback I could have taken her wedding rings off her hands and she wouldn't have known it. I came back that nite and said nothing. She started telling me that she had a busy day. She had the gardener, Margarito, over. 'What a beautiful guy,' she says, 'really is a hard worker. He worked all day...never stopped.'

"She couldn't stop talking about him, like it was necessary to share with me all this mojado's virtues. She was in love and you could hear it. I never said a word about seeing them, but whenever I came home I found him there...sitting, talking, elbow-to-elbow. If they got any closer they would have had to fuck. They were tied like Siamese twins to the same umbilical cord of life."

"That's very poetic," I told him.

In a state of complete madness
It seems that all men become poets when their woman take on other men. There must be something to that type of inner pain that causes a person to look inside himself for some explanation to his suffering. In a state of complete madness the male utters words that have the ring of desperation. The Universal 'Why' circles the whole male cosmos. The tears of betrayal, sleepless nites, a thudding in the ears telling you she found another who satisfies her more.

"Then, as if the wind blew him away, Margarito quit being there and I never saw him again. Then another guy comes who she introduces as Pablo, and he looked like the other guy, a guy who works in the dirt. Then there was Angel and Rudolfo and 4 or 5 others who all looked alike. My house became like a fortress, built to keep me out. I felt like a stranger in there. I could never get close enough to the house without being seen to find out what was going on. A house that big you could have someone living in there and you'd never know it.

"The Canadian Consulate owned the house before I did, and had it rigged for catching spies. It was equipped to detect a mouse moving in the kitchen. If a cat crossed the threshold the alarms would go off. If the garage door opened a bell would ring, a red lite would flash in every room. Once you were in it and the drawbridge pulled up, you were as safe as being in a bank vault. Not even a high-tech burglar could help you.

"Not only was she with them all the time, but she talked about them when they weren't there. Even when I was screwing the bitch, she would talk about Rudolfo or Pablo, Tereso, Gonzalo, Roberto, Victorio...and how exotic they looked. How mysterious the Indian face was with coal-black hair and black olive eyes. She had found her subject like a rock collector finds a vein of turquoise.

"They were all from the same pueblo, she said, in the state of Oaxaca. They all talked Mestixo, an Indian language that she found absolutely fabulous. She suggested that she'd like to go for a vacation and spend time at their pueblo. She was so into becoming one of them that she renamed the dog we had and gave her a Mestixo name, Ti-na-lo-lo, which meant dog in their language.
Maybe it was all just fun, and she was doing a hands-on anthropology course, but there was never any gardening done. I told her one day that I didn't really see what the hell her gardeners had been doing because the garden always looked the same.

'That's what takes so long,' she told me, 'just keeping it up so it looks the same.'

"She always had an answer, an answer that sounded so innocent that you had to believe it. She covered up the truth by not talking about what she did. She always said who had been over but she never said anything about her drives in the pickup truck, where she had been or where she was coming from.

Truth is a verb

"Being a lawyer had developed in me the natural distrust that a lawyer and a priest develop toward mankind. After hearing all the constructed confessions, one realizes that truth is a moving object...a verb, a variable. Truth was in that truck going from point A to point B. But I had to work, man. I just couldn't follow her around. I had to work. I knew I should keep my nose clean and not try to find out too much. Sometimes you shouldn't know too much about your wife. If you like what she tells you, then it's enough. If you push too far, you're going to find out some painful shit."

I had to agree with what he was saying. I was on my way down the same road of marital suspicion.

"Suspicion is a heavy-duty feeling," he said, as if he had just been introduced to something so foreign that it was as new as stepping on the moon for the first time.

"If I suspect someone at the bank, we cut the deal short, do a lot of checking and asking, but this was different. I never hung around a woman long enough to get suspicious about her. I split before I could find out anything to disturb me, but now I was stuck. I was married to her, like a pair of shorts on a bare ass. Suspicion was not enough. I had to have more before I could leave. I had to know the whole story."

All of a sudden the conversation took a break, a little lull before a storm.

"I never got your name?" he asked me, sticking out his hand to shake mine. He told me his name and out of habit gave me his card.

Larry Learner, Attorney-at-Law
Beverly Hills National Bank

I had no card therefore I really didn't have a name or occupation. Any name would do. I wasn't tied to a name or to a job, so instead, I bought him another cup of Mario's cappuccino and said my name was LeRoy Smith.

I must have been the one-hundredth person who he told this pathetic story to. The story had been rehearsed. It was stored in his memory, in precise little paragraphs. All the details, all the compressions, the editing. He would probably repeat this story a million times more, until he found some reason, some answer, as to why his wife took to liking unwashed wetbacks instead of this fine-looking man with a bankroll, ambition, an education, good manners, and her Daddy's trust.

"Can you believe this?" he asked me. "I hire a private eye to do the job for me, and he tells me that she checks into the same motel up the coast...2 to 3 times a week...with a different Mexican fieldhand. I couldn't believe this shit, but what could I do about it? Catch her in the act? What then? Tell her father that his daughter is a screwball? But I wasn't really sure what the hell she was doing. She always stopped at the same motel, always used the same room, 309. She went there an average of 3 times a week, all this was in the reports. That's where she was coming from, the day I saw her.

"I asked the investigator...what could we do? I wanted to catch her. It wasn't clear in my head why I wanted to catch her. It must have been a feeling of betrayal. A feeling of being a victim to her plans. It was my ego wanting retribution. I was on a dangerous road and I knew it. I had tapped into another person's energy, someone else's world that I had no business being in. She was a sick puppy, man. There is no other explanation for it.

"If I busted into the motel room, the lover might pull out a knife and put it in me, or I could get involved in an assault-and-battery trip with her. If I was a truck driver it would be different. I'd stomp her brains out and feel good about it. But this was a delicate matter. I had a lot of ties. A lot of things would come to an end. I had to figure it out, but definitely there was a change in the air. No matter what I did, it would mean that things were going to change.

"The investigator I hired had imagination, and his imagination was my downfall. He made a living out of following wives for the downtown crowd. He worked for doctors, lawyers, and big bucks. 'You can't leave them alone for too long of a time,' the investigator told me. 'They break the chains and go like a dog in heat. They more-or-less all have the same pattern. They meet somewhere, do a few hours together then go home. It's hard to catch them at it, it's too quick. But with your wife, she has time to select the one she wants, and can keep him around the house till she's ready then she takes him somewhere else to ball him. She's wise, she's done this a lot, she's a pro, Mr. Lerner,' he tells me, 'and she doesn't want to do it around the house. She keeps it clean with no monkey business. Keeps her lover under control that way.'

"'Her activities are so habitual that we could rent the room next to 309, and for a few bucks to the owner of the motel, make a peephole in the closet of room 308 and film them.'
'Go to it,' I told him. 'Get with it quick.'
A few weeks later he brought me the video tape of my loving wife and her gardeners. I put the cassette in the VCR, I sat down on the couch, picked up the control, and pressed the ON button.

"I couldn't believe what my eyes were looking at. There in front of me was my wife...with a wetback's prick in her mouth and another one aceing her from the rear.
It was the most frightening thing I had ever seen. I sat looking at it. It was a triple-X-rated movie and my wife was the main actress and the bean pickers were climbing over her like flies on a piece of flesh. My blood rushed to my head. I got dizzy. It felt like my heart was going to pop out of my chest. I had a feeling of wanting to throw up. I wasn't ready for this. You have to grow into these activities. You have to start out slow and easy. First you have to see your old lady...maybe kissing your friend or just hugging someone and you work with it for awhile till you get used to the action. Then it gets a little heavier, and you talk about it. Maybe you join a swingers club and go to one of their parties. You start to swap, and become a wifeswapper. But I wasn't a swapper, I was the guy paying the bills while the bitch was having her cunt hairs parted."

The On button

"I had something in my hand that no other period of history could have dreamt up...the ON button. I had found the modern man's way to torture myself...with a 4 x 10 cassette showing my wife giving it to her lovers. I press the button and this screwball appears on the screen in front of me. I played it again, again and again, hoping to flood myself with images, that blended together and became meaningless. I stopped it at certain places, and just stared at her with her eyes closed in deep, blissful satisfaction. Can you imagine Chaucer's Canterbury Tales and the Miller's Wife done on video?"

He laughed...the same laughter I heard once from a man who had lost all his money. He seemed to find great delight in letting me be part of his wife's orgy.
He wanted me to smell the lovers...the way he smelled them.
He wanted me to make it with his wife in our conversation.
He wanted the man at the next table to hump her.
He wanted the newsboy outside to watch as we all fucked her.
Mario was too old or he'd have asked him to join us.
He wanted the whole world to line up at his wife's bedroom and wait for their turn to screw her.
He was caught up in the frenzy of destruction.
It was cleansing. It brought everything in perspective. The eye was focused. The cleansing properties of destruction were just as profound as the burden of creation.
He overcame the embarrassment of what the Latins call curnudo...horns on the head of a betrayed husband.
Another man's child in her.
Another man's smell.
Another man's sweat between her legs.
Another man's passion...his sperm...saliva.
There was a whole world of problems with a clown for a wife, and the senses themselves had to be altered to accept it.

"Over and over I looked at that video," he tells me with a look of being lost in the universe.

"As the next scene kept coming up, I could feel my heart thudding in my chest, but I kept looking. I was possessed by my own wife's secrets and depravity, and the pain it caused me to look at it."

Then his pathetic story moved into the midpoint.

"One nite she walked in on me while I was looking at one of her films which I thought was the wildest. It was a new one that my investigator, Lester, had brought me the day before. I was dying to see it. It was like someone had placed my future...my pain...my life...my depression...in a little black cassette, waiting for me to put it in the VCR. I swear," he says with a look of absolute piety on his face, "I never was a porno watcher, and here I was going to the movies with my wife as the star. I made myself comfortable, poured myself a double scotch, took a good stiff drink, and pressed the ON button and there she was with 3 of them on the bed with her.

"She had on lace and garter belts, black panties and 6-inch heels, but the farmhands didn't seem interested in all that fancy turn-on gear. They wanted in, and all at the same time. One was pushing the other off her just as he was going to put it in her. While these two guys are wrestling with each other, the third guy sneaks up and puts it in her real quick, and they both laugh. He got it in and she helped him fool the other 2. I didn't recognize 2 of the lovers. The other one seemed to be her favorite because he was in every scene, in every film.

"It seemed that he would bring his friends over and provide her with more farmhands to garden her cunt. He would direct the other 2 as to what to do. He'd tell one to place his head between her legs and the other to place himself on top of her face. Then, not being satisfied, he would rearrange them and put himself in the composition. Then he would break out laughing, and start to pull his root, and spill it all on her face...while she tried to catch it like it was rain from the gods.

"It's undescribable as to what it feels like...to watch your wife being had. It's painful, and yet breathtaking. You look at her face for that feeling of satisfaction...her lips curling in a look of desire, of wanting more.

"I guess there is always the fear in a man that this could happen to him, but like a bad disease you never think it will hit you, and when it does, you feel a sense of relief. It's all over with, another button goes off in your head. You faced it. It was her world, her cunt, her ass, and yet it drove me nuts, her giving it to the hired help. If you asked her why...she couldn't say it was for love. How could you love that many people all at the same time?"

He paused for a few moments, took a swallow of his coffee, ran his fingers through his black hair. I could see that the story was just beginning. He was building up his energy to tell me the next chapter.

"I had become obsessed with the thought of trying to figure out what the hell to do. It was like living out a nitemare. She was wearing me out along with the Mexicans.

"Then one nite, as I sat alone in my study looking at the videotape of her last encounter, she walks into the room and asks me, 'what you looking at hon?' She asked me like she was exuding love and wanted to interrupt me...so I could put it in her like the guys on the film were doing. 'Can I sit by you, and look at what you're looking at?'

"I pressed the Off button and the tube went blank. Here it was, do I let her see what I got, or do I play dumb? If I let it all out, either I go along with it, or I have to divorce her, and then I might as well kiss my sweet job away. If I stay with her, I might own that fucken bank someday. I had a lot of time invested in it. So she screwed around...now I knew, but what do I do? It's not as easy as if you had nothing. My future was tied to her cunt, to her morality, to her madness....do you know what I mean?" he asked me, his eyes wide open, waiting for me to realize his pain in trying to decide the great question, On or Off Amigo?

"I have no way of knowing what you mean," I tell him, "it's beyond my understanding."

"She sat next to me, and I had the button in my hand. I had to make up my mind now, as to what I wanted to do. How long this bastard had done this wasn't important any more.

"I had moved into the world of acceptance, the way a cancer patient waits for death. I had put her ass on the scale of life's fortunes. I felt betrayed, done in. It could be all over in just a few more moments. All that fucken work gone down the shit tube. I had accumulated 5/3-hour videotapes. Fifteen hours of fucking filled with her and different guys.
I had a full collection of X-rated films, with the main actress being my wife, along with her Oaxacan buddies, whom she called exotic, at the cost of $15,000 dollars.

"Maybe I was lucky and didn't get a dose of clap, or syph or worse yet. There were no rubbers on these bastards' cocks, and she was putting them in her like they were notions at a New Years party. I asked Lester, my investigator, how he felt while doing this video. He acted dumb. 'It was all professional, Mr. Learner.'

"I begged him to tell me. It was important to me to find out if he had a hardon when he was doing this film. Maybe he got into her too. I don't know what sort of psychosis had developed in my head, but like a pain that you get used to, you learn to think around it. I felt like I wanted the whole world to know this bitch was fucking everyone around. I didn't want to keep it a secret. I wanted the world to know. I wanted the whole world to fuck her. I wanted the world to share not only in the delight of the celebration, but also in the big question...Why would a woman want to be screwed by these peasants dressed in semi-rags?"

"She wants to be like a barnyard hen," I told him, "and get screwed by some real honest-to-goodness farmhands.
She wants to get close to the earth, to the smell of humans, to the smell of sweat rather than deodorants. These guys have a strong odor to them. It might be her nose is driving her to do these things. Take her to a nose doctor."

I knew what he was talking about. I had just experienced that awful pain of the nose and odors, but this guy's wife was the opposite, she loved the smell of sweat.

"You might be right," he utters in a low tired voice. "She had them guys over on their stomach and her tongue was heading for places that the Arabs use their left hand to touch."

I was amazed that he would talk about his wife and her outings, without any hesitation, without any embarrassment or shame. Most men won't say anything concerning their private lives, only to boast about the women they've had. Here this guy was telling me all the men who had had his wife. He was telling me he was duped, that he had to pay to find out the virtues of his wife...he was talking to a stranger, to someone he had just met an hour before. And he was telling me the agony of freedom, the release from doubt and suspicion, the view of clarity, the pain of knowing.

He was free and it was killing him. Where was the happiness that comes when you don't have to think of it any more? He was drowning in sorrow.

"She asked me if she could look at the film that was so interesting to me. Can you believe that? A feeling of I-don't-give-a-shit hit me, the way one gambles his money away at one throw of the dice. I had nothing to gain and everything to lose. I had lost my cools.

'Do you really want to see it?' I asked her.

'Yes I would, you know I like to share things with you.'

She said the right words, the magic words. The timing was perfect. The time had come to let her know I had discovered the slut. All her politeness, all her make-believe, all her secret world was now on a magnetic tape waiting to unleash itself to public view. The whole fucken world would know of it. This was my day of judgment and retribution. Somehow the feeling of righteousness overcame my better judgment."

The naivete that creates an illusion of respectability

"The trial began with the pressing of the ON button. A sense of power came over me. I felt a surge of the divine come through me. What would she say?

What could she say?

I became impatient to find out.

Would she cry?
Would she tell me that she's nuts and needs help?
Would she beg me not to tell anyone, or would she attempt suicide? Or worse yet, confess to me that she was a raving sexaholic with stories that would make the films seem calm and sedate?
What would I do?
Would I forgive her and start over again?
Would I pity her...hate her...despise her?
I knew I could never look at her the same way again. I had lost something. I had lost my emotional virginity, the naivete that creates an illusion of respectability. She looked like a fucken buffoon bouncing on the bed with three other clowns...a real circus act."

"You need more than just Mario's cappuccino," I told him. "You need some good weed, the kind that makes all this shit seem like passing a day at the races."

He didn't hear me. He was in the middle of reliving a lucid dream. His mental image of seeing his wife on film, and her wanting to see it with him, had caught the moment. "I have to admit," I told him, "I've never heard a story like this in my entire life."

"It's tough man," he said, " it's really tough. You'd think that I could handle it. The stakes were great enough. I could afford to look the other way and let the nut do what she wanted to do, for a piece of her father's bank.

"It was the video that did it to me. It felt like I was there being the fourth man. I was still ahead of the game. She didn't know I knew. I could still turn back and just find some way of entertaining myself when she was out moteling with her pals. But it just wasn't meant to be.

"For the last time I asked myself...was it worth telling her that I knew about her private life? But it wasn't private anymore, it was on film. A half-a-dozen fieldhands had been with her. My investigator knew about it. I could make hundreds of copies and send them out to the world...it was on its way to becoming public. Would she care? It dawned on me that it might be a setup. She might have known all along that I had had her followed, and she was bringing me into her world. The stakes were big enough for me to consider it. I had to make up my mind in the next few seconds.

"Someone told me once, you can't wear that hole out. You can stretch it a mile, and it won't rip an inch. I could leave the pig do what she wanted and still come out ahead. Someday I would get her old man's bank, then I dump her. Maybe it was my ego, maybe I came from a different world and fucken money wasn't as important to me as I thought it was. Fuck the whore, it was too late now. I didn't really want to sink my prick into a cesspool. You never know what shit is floating in it.

"'The die has been cast,' Caesar said.
Agamemnon had sacrificed Iphigenia.
The wind had filled my sails.
The moment had arrived.
'Come on,' she begged me, 'Let me see what you're looking at.'

"She sat next to me and held my hand. 'Love you,' she whispered in my ear.
'Here goes sister,' I said, like a paratrooper leaving the safety of the jump bay...and into the enemy below.

"I pressed the key to my future, and in front of us appeared the darling little Margy.
There she was...crawling...climbing...doing...like a woman who had been given Spanish fly. This cold thing that had laid around like a dead mackerel. This cold whore that had a hole as dry as the Mojave desert. A woman who was such a bum lay, that when I first started making it with her, I thought I would give up sex. Now, on the film in front of me, she had become a woman gone mad with passion.
Her face had that look of total abandonment.
Groaning
Moaning
Screaming.

She was coming…she was yelling…'Mas fuerte.…mas...mas...mas.'
'Si...Si...Si'...the beanpickers yell back. The earth was exploding.

"She sat quietly next to me staring at the film with cold indifferent fish-eyes. Within a few seconds I was in the most agitated state of my life. I was so excited that I was hyperventilating. I waited to hear what she was going to say. I had plunged the knife. I had pulled the trigger that fired the final bullet. The truth was out, it was staring at both of us. This was her film debut. She was a star. Now she had to address her audience.

"She looked at the woman on the screen and didn't say a word. Then she got up from the couch. Her eyes showed no anger...no passion...no shame...no guilt.

"She looked at me with a coldness that I still remember. I knew then that I had made the wrong move. I wasn't a husband, I was a social front for this nut, and I was talking morality and condemnation to a woman who had probably done this all her life. Man...Oh man! Did I have things yet to learn. I had stepped into a nutgrinder.

I was a novice in the big leagues
Her mouth opened up and a sound, like the hissing of a snake, came out of that cesspool.

"'Is this what you do with your spare time? You sit and watch filth? No wonder you're so cold,' she tells me. 'You probably sit here and play with yourself on these kind of films.'

"I couldn't believe my ears. It felt like I was in a horror show. Then her face slowly turned into a look of disgust, like she had practiced it in front of a mirror for a close-up. The lips snarled, the eyes became inflamed, her face started to twist.
'You mean you don't recognize the person in the film?' I asked her.
'What do you think I do, look at porno? That's your game mister,' she hisses at me, 'don't include me in it.'

"I found myself trying to convince her that she was the one on the video, and the more I tried, the deeper in the shit pool I got. You would have had to be there to understand what I'm talking about. She threatened to have the cops drag me off.
She moved from threats to warnings, that if I didn't leave on my own she'd have me arrested.
'For what?' I asked her.
'For forcing me to look at that crap with you.'

"She went to her room and locked the door. I just couldn't go get someone who knew her, and ask that he identify her on the film. She would deny that it was her, and I couldn't prove that it was.

"The woman on the film had a different look on her face. She was laughing, giggling, groaning. The face looked different. It was alive with pleasure. It was in its own element, its own environment. I might as well have saved my money and just lived with my suspicions. It became the topic of my thoughts with her. Not what she was doing, but that it was her who was doing it.

"In the week that followed, my whole fucken life changed. It was obvious to me that she was crazy, not because she wanted another man, but that she needed many men in some strange authoritarian way.

"She had found a source of men. She hired them as gardeners, and part of their job was to garden her, and when she got tired of them, she sent them on their merry way. She laid them off...can you imagine that? She lays off her lovers.

"She also needed a husband. A social front, someone she could come home to after a day at the motels. A husband was necessary. It made the lover cautious. The husband was like a guard dog in the eyes of a burglar. The lover always had to figure on the husband being around somewhere. He had to go home because the husband might catch him.
One day I made the fatal mistake and let frustration get me. I knocked her on her ass. It was the first time I ever hit a woman. Her face snarled like a rat that's been cornered. I had a bad feeling in me. I knew the bitch had outwitted me.

"The cops came. She was right, if I didn't leave she would have me hauled off, and they did haul me off for knocking her on her ass. It was all over with. I paid for my own funeral and watched my own demise take place in front of me, and what I got left is 5/ 3-hour films...of my wife's hobbies...in the trunk of my car."

He told me of how the father threw him out of the bank, with a horror story of the first order, warning him if he ever showed his face in L.A. again he'd be buried in a pile of rubber tires. All because...the poor bastard moaned that his wife needed a "love machine" that produced lovers like they were gumballs.

"You can live with your wife's infidelities as long as they are given to you as words in the form of a confession, but once the eyes become a witness to it, and it could be repeated over and over, something new has been added to the concept of reality. An image that burns itself into your mind demanding that you look at it again and again. Maybe this is what madness is. Maybe the Video is the road to eternal remembrance...the soothing effect of forgetting gone...forever."

Suspicion and Accusation

Accusation and its nature

The job of the accuser

Six alternatives

As the days passed the story of that poor bastard banker kept going through my head. It made me sick to think of it. It was the study of a male gone berserk over his wife's moteling. It was a classic case of what books are written about, doctors investigate and money is made on.
But the truth of it was, he got caught up in it and something snapped, and like Humpty Dumpty, no one could put him back together again.

I knew from experience that love appears as some form of disorder disturbing your hormones, moving them around, creating a strange unexplainable emotion that engulfs you like a riptide.
There also seems to be some hormonal mixtures that trigger off in a man, turning him into a raving lunatic, when he finds out that his woman has been laying up with someone else.
Maybe this is what makes dogs howl at nite or birds sing in the daytime or lions roar in the jungles, a deep-rooted frustration.

Maybe the sounds that came out of Noah's Ark were the sounds of contentment when all of God's creatures were paired up and there was no third party trying to cut in. Who knows what the evolutionary intent was?

Dogs, cattle, birds, seem to have the instinct to get rid of other males, so they can breed. Humans created doors and they shut them, in order to keep other males out when getting ready to give it to their female.

The story I heard from that poor cornholed banker filled my head with another possibility…as to why my wife found sleeping more pleasurable than lovemaking with me. I felt I was looking in the wrong place for my answers, and now that the seed of suspicion had been planted, I could see the problem more clearly. I felt that there was someone around, someone with a hardon. Not only was he around but he was close by. But who? Who was he?

Suspicion comes when a pattern is broken or a new one is being created. Something catches your eye, your ear, a contradiction,
a mistake in time
a look
a matchbook
an unpaid bill
a quiet voice on the phone.
Something caught my attention.
My ears went straight up, like a dog who has heard the sound of a leaf falling to the ground.

The thought of someone else made more sense to me now. Her yawns, her indifference, her general lethargy, were caused by spending her time with someone else and she came home tired, her panties in her purse and his fluids trailing behind her, like the tracks of a snail.

Even though I felt that she could be going the way of the banker's wife, I had nothing to go on. There was no evidence of any activity. It was always the same. She came home on time, never late. Never a need for an excuse. I couldn't say a word. I could never ask the question "Where have you been?"

I could suspect her, but I still had to find something to accuse her with, something I could prove.
All I had to go on at the present was…she wasn't giving me what I wanted, which was her love. She resisted all my attempts to love her and she hid behind the words of tiredness. There had to be some reason why she fell asleep on our wedding nite. Was she being faithful to her lover, not letting another man get into her sacred altar?

Was it a temporary thing?
Was she making me wait until she broke up with her lover?
These were some of the questions growing and developing in my head. For my own peace of mind, I had to know the answer. No matter what my feelings were, I had to be very careful and not try to accuse her before I had some information to go on.

A feeling of gloom came over me, a feeling of sadness covered my whole existence. For days the suspicion grew in me. I could see the end of something was about to begin and my own curiosity was leading me by the nose.

If I entered into her world and discovered similarities to the banker's wife, what would I gain? I might not be able to handle what I found. The same thing might happen to me that happened to poor Larry. I might discover something I wished I had never known about and end up traveling the world...telling my story to anyone who'd listen...as to how I was duped by my wife.

Accusation and its nature
What would I do if I found out that she was pulling her dress up and letting her panties down…for one or more men during the day? Or that she was seeing another woman or molesting a young boy or having it with her boss, what then?
Accuse her?
Then what?
Leave her?
Beat her?
Shoot her? Or make the same mistake everyone makes and try to understand why?

A moment of tranquility and lucidity came over me. I should leave her now and forget all this crap, but curiosity and the high that suspicion brings with it were starting to invade and overcome my better judgement.

I was tempted one evening, as we sat and ate our dinner in silence, to let her in on my suspicions of what I felt and what I thought. I was tired of my existence with her. It didn't take a genius to see that what I thought was the look of tiredness on the face of my wife, was in reality, a coldness...an indifference...a feeling of uncaring…and now the suspicion that her love was for someone else.

With my new awareness, brought about by my suspicions, I could see her face at times changed its color, its shape, its purpose. I could see the eyes looking through me and never at me. The words, few as they were, fell like lead bars from her mouth. There was nothing I could put my finger on and point to. The minute you said something it would be gone. I couldn't take a picture of it and tell her, "This is the look that is creating all this suspicion."

I knew the look on her face before she got this way. She was warm and considerate. She never did, nor said anything that made me feel unwanted.
Now I had a suspicion and a story coming together of her indifference.

Only a fool would try and accuse her prematurely. If she realized that my accusations were pure fabrications, she could see that I was reaching for straws in the wind, that I was suffering from the terror and pains of suspicion. She would eventually get the upper hand. She would get disgusted with me, laugh at my childish attempts to find the truth and have her lover throw me out.

The job of the accuser
If I had something to work with it would be easy. A motel bill, an address, a note. I had nothing to go on. I realized I would have to play it out like an actor does and pretend I knew everything.
But I was too much of a gentleman or too sensitive to her needs

to make an issue of it and accuse her. To feel the suspicion is one thing but to prove it, I would have to follow her.

I would spend endless hours waiting, watching, looking at my watch. Disappointed if I found nothing because I wasted my time watching her drive off by herself. There were moments that I saw myself as a slimy, slithering little bastard, waiting in the dark. The thought itself disgusted me. What could I tell myself? My suspicions were feeding me like one would feed a furnace until it became a roaring blaze. It's a morbid fascination that man has with death, destruction, pain and his wife's infidelities.

It was a simple fact, I didn't have the money to indulge my curiosities like the banker did. He hired someone to spy on his wife, caught her at it and it cost him his job, his career and all he had. If he'd been broke, like me, he would have gone through it all with a wife who was, as far as he knew, straight up, solid, boring, and whatever it is that nice women are called.

I sat down one day and wrote down
Six Alternatives I could choose from.
1) I could spend all my time monitoring her and try to find out what the hell she was all about. I really didn't know her. Who really knows anyone? It would take so much energy that I would have to shift my emphasis of life from doing to watching, looking, asking about someone else's life, and leaving mine go to hell.

2) I could find another woman to make love with, and just live with this one, but that would necessitate that I create new habits with the new woman. Make up stories, keep secrets, false time-schedules and hidden conversations. It would raise hell with me. I'd be with one while thinking of the other. A world so distorted that one slip and I would lose myself in it.

3) I could give up the thought of loving. Resign myself to the sexless condition. But I would need help, like a celibate monk does, to overcome the need for touching, loving, smelling, tasting, and screwing a woman.

4) I could beg her to quit work and see if she lost that tired feeling. If she didn't, I'd know for sure she was getting herself hosed at the local motels.

5) I could find some other way to be able to enjoy her, maybe while she slept. To wake up in the morning, so satisfied, so invigorated with each other that we couldn't wait to go to bed at nite and fall asleep, and dream of each other in the most divine ways.

6) The sixth alternative was the quickest and cleanest. I could leave her and not bother with all the useless conversations that really don't go anywhere. Conversations create more problems as to who did what and when it was done and with whom.

I finally decided on the following two options. Either uncover her or don't bother with it anymore, but which one should I pick? If I stayed I'd have to develop a more devious attitude. One that disbelieved everything she said, until I could prove otherwise.

I had never been in a situation like this before. I didn't know how to get the information I wanted and what to do with it when I did get it. An interesting question kept coming up in my head...how would I react? What do you do with information that is painful and destructive?

I had to begin somewhere and by the most obvious methods available. I had to look around me and see what was going on. I had to take notice of things, little things, things that the normal eye would never see.

I would have to learn to read the signs. Since I never did this before I had to learn the alphabet of a suspicious observer. I had to learn how to collect information, interrogate at the proper time with the proper questions and properly accuse her, with a final solution to the problem all worked out.

I had to develop a systematic method that took all things into account. Like studying a piece of music where the smallest detail is examined over and over until it reveals its hidden secret.

I had to learn to pay attention to details that the eye would normally overlook. To check things out. To prowl around in the dark. To look in places that politeness or etiquette told you to stay away from. All the hip words pouring out of the word mills, supposedly to help you see your relationship to a screwball, aren't going to make the suspicion, depression, sleeplessness, loss of appetite, then violence, go away.

Something kept telling me, turn the other ball James, don't be greedy, share with your brother, live and let live. It will stretch a mile before it will rip an inch. Be generous, be understanding. But it was all bullshit to my ears.
I didn't want to share with my fellow man because I would get the leftovers, cold and dry like a dog's dinner.

It was her treatment of me that I found painful and disgusting. The more I thought about it the more I started to see similarities between the activities of my wife and the wife of that poor bastard Larry, the banker. I didn't want to go crazy like he did.

He was traveling around the country with 5 video films locked up in his suitcase, in the trunk of his car. Waiting to prove that his wife was screwing others. He wanted to prove to the world or anyone who would stop and listen that he was betrayed, that he was forced to eat social shit and had to swallow it. He got the leftovers, a love hole filled to the brim with that day's catch.

The filth of it all gave me a strange feeling of euphoria, like a terror that knocks on the doors of your mind and you want to run but there is nowhere to go.

Spying on a Woman

Man-wise

Monitoring a woman's activities is a necessary art in modern times

People stay in line because someone is looking

The mysterious woman

There is no greater emotional pain than to suspect a person you live with. When you suspect them everything they say sounds like a well planed-out lie. I remember the jive asses that used to hang around the street corners, playing their steel-stringed guitars, singing about a lying mama...

> ***If they say up, you know it's down.***
> ***You find yourself getting sick***
> ***just being around...***
> ***You hate to ask cause you know,***
> ***the story you get is smelly and old.***

My feelings were starting to get laid out on a tape measure of disbelief. A psychic measuring-rod that starts out in a feeling of self-pity and ends up in the depths of suspicion and fear.

Man-wise

There was no question in my mind that she was "man-wise". In the early days of our lovemaking she guided me through maneuvers that only a skilled pilot, flying through a mountain pass, could have done. She let out sounds and sighs, moves and squirms that drove me deeper into my passion. She went through physical positions that only a skilled yogi could pull off.

I remember one nite I went to see her at her small apartment. I knocked and no one answered the door. I thought I heard a noise inside. I knocked again, there was a strange silence like the world had stopped breathing. I left and never gave it a thought.
Another time I came over unexpected, there were cans of beer in the garbage can. I saw her look at me while I looked at the empty cans. I said nothing. She closed the garbage container and asked me if I wanted coffee.

There were other little incidents that I noticed but never put it together in my head because I really didn't care.
Somehow I knew that it would all end sometime and she'd go on her way down the same road that all past events go to...the junkyard of memories. But things worked out differently and I married her. Now all the little incidents that were almost forgotten reappeared in my head begging to be looked at again.

It was the first time in my life that I knew what the real power of a woman was all about. I knew a woman could free you of every fear you possess and a woman could give you fears you never knew existed.
I became the string on the kite that held her on this earth, and then it all ended. It stopped…like the breath of a dying carnation, and she started drifting away. She must have been drifting away from someone else when I first met her. Now I was stuck with her.

Monitoring a woman's activities is a necessary art in modern times
The period of indifference was starting to fall on me like a blanket of fog. It was impossible to see the road out of this problem. By the laws of necessity, I had to find out where I was and who I was with. I had to accept the fact that I had to, if not spy on her, at least monitor the activities of the woman I lived with.

The thought of spying on someone seems like a disgusting occupation as well as an occupation that requires a great deal of training in observations and correlations. It was either professional or it was amateur and sleazy. I was brought up thinking it was an embarrassment to get caught at it. An invasion of someone's privacy. Even the words spying or invasion of privacy had the connotation of the sinister. I decided to replace the word spying with a more sensitive word, a word that included me as a necessary participant. I had to monitor my very existence the same way that I monitored my diet, my health, my money, my time, my music. Everything needed looking at. Modern man has a need to know if there is crap in his life's matrix. I had to be able to get it out of my system. It was toxic waste, being dumped on me, and I had to monitor it in order to get rid of it. I had to find out what information I needed. What really concerned me and me only. It was a very basic social need to want to know. It's the nature of mankind, to look, to search, to talk about someone, to gossip, to praise and defame.

People stay in line because someone is looking
I could see that a well-run society depends on spies and informants to keep it clean, pristine and functioning. A woman should know that someone is looking. Her natural propensity and desires for lovemaking are brought under control by the hidden eye. God spies on you. He wants to know if you have been good. All the holy hierarchy spy on you and report their findings to Him. Your country spies on you. Your neighbors know what you're doing at all times. Communities are kept together by spying on each other. People stay in line because someone is looking and keeping tabs. People spy on each other as naturally as the rivers flow to the sea and instead of spying they call it monitoring the activities of another for the benefit of one and all.

I knew from the very beginning of my life that I wasn't made for pain nor for sainthood. My dedication to myself was to endure as little pain as possible and to fall asleep nitely in the arms of my woman. It wasn't an unreasonable demand of life, it merely advocated the philosophy of *It's just nice to be nice.* I wasn't interested if she was a person or an individual, an amazon with one tit or a modern draconian female. All I wanted was love, the kind of love that's soft, attentive and necessary.

It had become impossible to have a conversation with her. She was silent about everything, other than immediate events that weren't in any specific order. The words just fell out of her mouth like turds from a horse's ass. "I'm tired...food bores me....I seem never to get enough sleep."

On the surface she did nothing more than sleep and yawn and push my hand away or turn her head when my lips wanted to lock on to hers. But by doing nothing she activated my imagination to search, and the more my mind searched the more my suspicions grew and the greater my distrust of her grew with them. Every move she made was another piece of suspicious information that was placed in the big puzzle of her developing duplicity.

She was really a mystery to me, a person from another world, who spoke a language I thought I understood and yet I knew nothing about her. She never said anything. She was a blank piece of paper. All I knew about her was that she was born in Bismarck North Dakota, 32 years before. She had no past life. She was the person of the present. She was the immediate person, the person of the moment. She came from nowhere. She had no historical existence, no opinions, convictions, no prejudices, no names or places, merely the hum of an animal existence coming out of her in the tones of grunts, monosyllabic words, snores, farts and sighs.

It raised the fear in my mind that her history must have been so active with events, so filled with madness, that she kept it to herself, like one keeps a photograph of some frozen moment hidden in the bottom of a trunk, afraid that someone will see a photo of you on top of a windswept mountain staring at your own asshole with a look of amazement and fear on your face. A fear that others might see it or hear of it and think you would repeat it.

The mysterious woman

Whoever said that the mysterious makes for the alluring was mistaken. A lover finds a secretive woman mysterious and exciting. A lover goes home at nite and feeds his imagination a mental dinner...that he will overcome all obstacles in order to get into that woman's love triangle, and then her mystery will be no more. But the mysterious creates great gaps in the history of a person, gaps easily filled with doubts that give birth to painful suspicions.

I began thinking of her as a masterweaver placing the threads of duplicity, denials and silence into the tapestry of existence.

The ignorance I had of her, created a fear in me. It manipulated my thoughts. I had no doubts in my mind about her duplicity. I needed no further convincing. All that came into my mind existed, its only limits were the limits of my own imagination in proving it.
My existence with her had exhausted me. I was tired of the silence that secrets create.

The Woman's Purse

Looking for the lover's Identity

The lover paid for the room

Sharing the bill

She paid for the motel

The ethics of rifling her purse

I had to begin somewhere to materialize my suspicion, so I started out with the most obvious, I hit the purse, the bastion of a female's world. If there were any secrets they would be in the purse. This is where a woman's primary world exists. All her immediate possessions, her home away from home, her survival kit, her life raft on this earth are in her purse.

When I first saw her in the park, on that beautiful day, I realized that her purse was an essential part of her beauty. Hanging from her shoulder on a long leather strap was a big, brown, soft leather bag, that closed with a big shining brass clasp.

She made my eyes salivate as she played with her purse. She moulded her body around the god damn purse, like a vine around an oak tree. Her hand holding on to the strap…her hip at an angle, she created the look of independence, dominance, freedom, indifference, pensiveness, anger, happiness, using a purse for a prop. And now I was looking at the purse with the desire to enter into its mysteries.

I lifted the clasp, opened the big leather flap and looked in. At first glance it looked like a messed-up throw-in drawer. But that wasn't the case. The more I looked in it the more I realized I was looking at a developed sense of security packed into her purse. Everything necessary to survive in the megalopolis was placed in there. It was a survival kit put together by some inborn instinct and cultivated to each woman's taste and need. Maybe the purse to a woman is like a lifeboat to a sailor, that will be there waiting when the ship goes down.

The first thing I pulled out from her purse was a key chain with eleven keys. Car keys, house keys, locker keys, other unidentifiable keys. Followed by a pocketlite, tampax wads, tissue paper, lipstick, mirror, wallet, credit card, checkbook, changepurse, perfume, comb, hairpins, mouth freshener, toothbrush with holder, hairbrush, eye makeup, chewing gum, notepads, pen, a matchbook with no address on it. Scraps of paper with numbers on them, sunglasses, sunblock. A pack of silk stockings. A sewing needle with black thread. A pack of aspirin, eyewash.

I was looking for something, and hoping that I would find a motel receipt, a pack of Trojan rubbers, a phone number written on a piece of paper. A note from her lover. But all this would be too obvious, too easy to hope for. If this woman had a lover she was making it hard for me to find him. A mountain of questions was starting to be raised by the innocence of all that junk in her purse. The everything and nothingness of human existence was staring me in the face, waiting for my imagination to put it all together.

I started out with the credit-card company. I called them to find out of any unusual charges to the credit card. Nothing. I checked out her checking account. Checks for groceries, clothes, gas, electric, rent. Normal stuff, the kind everyone writes. I didn't know what I was looking for. I had never rifled a woman's purse before, but maybe she expected me to look and left nothing for the searcher to find.

Looking for the lover's Identity

I was looking for the identity of her lover and was hoping that she had left part of him, no matter how small, in her purse. I needed to find some evidence, a clue of his existence. Who was he?
Where did they go between the time she left the house and the time she got back? It's hard to go screw in the back seat of a car in daylite, so she would have to go to some motel and that could be expensive. Or there was the possibility that she went to his place. She always got home later on Wednesday and Friday. She said they had to work two hours later on those days. If it was anyone it most likely would be someone in the office with her, but then again that might not be the case.

Three primary questions came to my mind after studying her purse. If she went to the motels, who paid the bill and how was it paid?
Did he pay for the room?
Did she share the bill?
Did she pay for the room?

These were important questions at the beginning of my search and I felt that the purse would somehow reveal to me the truth.

The lover paid for the room

If the lover spent the money, there would be no evidence of cash flow. His name would be on the motel register. It also meant he cared enough about her lovemaking to spend money on it. It meant that he probably had a wife, because he didn't take Nomi to his place but to a motel. He might become more demanding as time went on. I would have to pay attention, not only to her, but also to him. He would become part of the household. He would affect my life. Eventually he would make his appearance. But how would he appear? As an address? A name?

How are the mysteries revealed to us? Where is the lover hidden and when does the lover appear?

If he was a lover with money, a man of means, he would give her gifts, personal gifts...a perfume that he likes…a dress that he feels makes her more beautiful, a pair of shoes that shape the foot...maybe a gift even more personal, like lace underwear. But why would a man with money pick a married woman to load up with?

It didn't take much of an imagination to figure it out. A married woman, for a busy man, is a premium. She has no venereal diseases. She has to go home at nite to tend to her other obligations. She doesn't ask too many questions.
It's quick and therefore it's intense. She goes back to the office with wads of tissue paper stuffed in her drawers to catch the fluids of her lover's passion. He would share what was mine and I would be left to guess who he was.

In her own way she would share him with me. She would leave his imprint on me. As a lover in her dreams. A lover she could caress and dream about while I floundered in the dark stumbling over shoes and nitestands looking for the elusive bastard in her purse, while she snored just a few feet away, in the arms of her lover. I had to remind myself that the axiom, a lover is never left outside on the doorstep for long, was going to work in my favor.

Sharing the bill
If she shared the motel bills with her lover, I was dealing with a lover who was moderate in his lovemaking. Probably a married man bored with his wife. An honest man, an unpretentious man. A deliberate man. A man with a limited income. A man who would tell her, "I can only afford half of the motel bill. If you want me, you'll have to pay half of the bill." The chances were that she bought him gifts. I would be looking for purchases of little things, the kind of things that thoughtful lovers buy each other. They would be things she charged on her Emporium or Macy's card. A little wallet, a little trinket, something to show her love. This might be an habitual thing.

She paid for the motel
If she paid for the bed I was looking at a deeper problem. I would be looking at a woman who buys a man. A woman like the banker's wife. Not any man in particular, but men that have a price tag on them. Men who can be bought and sold. Men looking for a bed and a woman thrown in. She must have realized that it

costs money to get laid as often as you need. I might be looking for a secret bankbook, a deposit slip. I had no way of knowing what her accounts looked like. This might be the reason that she went back to work. She had to find a way to afford her habit.

Her purse revealed nothing to the prying, untrained eye. I knew I was reaching into the jagged areas of suspicion. If I went any further I might suspect that I married a hollow baby, a woman who couldn't remember how many men had screwed her. Someone who had a need to be loved by people on their way to somewhere, looking to fill her life up with disposable people. She probably had spent as much time developing a hidden world as I had in the study of my guitar. I felt as if I was standing in quicksand and sinking by the minute, and I was too preoccupied, stupid or thrill-seeking to appreciate the danger to my very existence.

The thought that this woman didn't seem that crazy quieted me down, but then again, what did I really know about her? She never talked about anyone, ex-lover, brother, sister, mother, father, friends, not a word did she ever mention as to who she was.

A blank book had entered my life and I was compelled to write the story in it. If she had any friends she kept them a secret. No one ever called for her and she called no one. She had no phone numbers in her purse. Why didn't she have any friends?
It seemed strange that a woman so beautiful knew no one. Were all her friends, ex-lovers better left as secrets? And if this were true, how and when did she make contact with them?
If I could interpret the secrets in her purse, all of it would clear up. I had to learn how to correlate the various objects in her purse. Objects that looked innocent at first glance, but correlated with other innocent objects, told a story.

The ethics of rifling her purse

Her bizarre behavior brought about my suspicions, and I merely did what I thought was natural. I started looking at the world around me more carefully. I was now monitoring my own life, keeping a secret watch, as the saying goes, on the affairs of another.

I felt I had the right, after I became suspicious of her, to invade her privacy. This I felt was a moral right that was due me. Life was complicated enough without having to live with a woman who created further complications for me that were as serious as a debilitating illness.

Then there was always the problem of getting caught rifling her purse. Her private property...but this was a legal thought of property and trespass...and it might have some legal significance to a judge or a lawyer, but to me, it had as much meaning as a pile of dogshit to a passing truck.

I started a systematic categorization of the contents of her purse. I noticed one day that she had changed the flavors of her chewing gum. There was an absence of aspirin, of tissue paper. At one time her toothbrush was missing for three days, then she bought a new one with a new holder. Where was the old one? I searched the garbage cans in the house. If she didn't throw it away, where did she leave it? The purse was starting to reveal to me its hidden secrets. I knew with constant effort and daily diligence I would be able to piece together the missing parts so necessary to my agonizing suspicions.

Unknown to me I had crossed that line which divides the world of lite and belief from shadows and suspicions. Not because I wanted to, but she took me by the hand and walked me there, inch by inch, step by step, until I realized that my thinking had taken on another dimension, painful to the touch, agonizing to the thought. I had become a slave to suspicion…a black hood had been placed over my head and I could see nothing around me other than the darkness of doubt.

The Interrogation of a Wife

The denials of a promiscuous wife

Developing a method to accuse

The logic of interrogation

The beginning of my interrogation

Developing the interrogation

Daydreams vacillated between guilt and innocence

Becoming an Interrogator

The methodology of interrogation

Empathy

Sympathy

Trust

The denials of a promiscuous wife

Every day I felt I was coming one step closer to the core of her treachery and every day I felt one step closer to losing my mind. The time to accuse her had arrived but the techniques of accusation were still a mystery to me.

If I accused her now, I knew instinctively, it would be a disaster. All I had to work with were suspicions and suspicions are useless without facts. I would end up in reverse accusations. She would accuse me of being an idiot with pangs of jealousy and complaints of neglect, accuse me of insensitivity, shallowness. I could become, in her eyes, a basketcase of bad habits and attitudes.

She had a perfect defense to any accusation. She was tired from working and according to her, working people have a different attitude toward love and lovemaking. We had divided our worlds between my need and her rejection.

Developing a method to accuse

I had to develop some way to accuse her. I knew that the best reply to an accusation was either a strong defense to counteract the accusation or an avoidance of the defense, by being silent or denying it. This would allow the accuser to rant and rave to a hollow baby who's not listening. A tactic that would make the accusation become meaningless and the accuser become exhausted from the silence or frustrated from the denials.

To be accused and to say nothing requires that you appreciate the silence of the sages. The book of Tao, the works of Lao Tze, advocating the effort of doing nothing. Doing nothing is the means of attainment. If she had the wisdom of the sages she would say nothing and leave me to hang myself in front of her.

To be accused and to deny the accusation means you have a way out, either you're innocent or you have an alibi. Her purse told me nothing conclusive. I had nothing to go on other than my feelings. Even if she was guilty she wouldn't admit it. It's natural for a person to deny an accusation, and the denials of a guilty person can be works of art.

The banker went wrong when he accused his wife without first developing the grounds for his accusation. He threw the films in her face, and she denied that the person in the film was her. The person might have resembled her but it wasn't her. He accused her but he never developed the logic for accusation and interrogation.

The denials of a promiscuous wife are as detailed and as carefully laid out as a battle plan in the hands of a general. "Not me," would be the first reply no matter what the evidence.

"But I have your fingerprints and your photographs and ten honest witnesses that say they saw you there."
And she will say, "Not me...you're wrong...how can you think of me that way?"

The logic of interrogation
I knew very little concerning the art of interrogation and how to pull it off. Somehow I would have to develop some form of systematic interrogation. I had to see if I could gather enough information from bits and pieces of our conversations and try to correlate it with what I felt. I knew it would take weeks to gather any information from her. We had few conversations and when we did they were about nothing. In the meantime I would have to be very careful and make sure she didn't catch on to what I was doing.

The beginning of my interrogation
At the beginning of my interrogation I would have the upper hand. She didn't know what I knew. She didn't know if I had been following her, or had paid someone to follow her like the banker did with his wife, or had found a new piece of evidence, something she forgot to dispose of…something left in her purse.

Developing the interrogation
How much more developed the banker's story would have been if he had casually asked his wife how her trip to Santa Barbara was, or he could have dropped a hint that a friend of his had stayed at the same motel...without a word about seeing her. The seed of suspicion would have been planted in her head, left there to grow as more sightings were told to her.

I knew it would take someone with far more experience than I had, to work his way through the accusatory process, but I had to try. My first attempt was to isolate my problem. My problem was different than the banker's. I had suspicions but no proof. I didn't have any information and I would have to bullshit my way into planting suspicion in her head and have her believe that I knew something. What that something was, was still a mystery to me. Somehow I would have to get her to believe that I did follow her.

That I did have a noose hanging over her head ready to pull at the right moment. I had the element of surprise on my side.

What I needed now was a carefully laid-out plan. If she did have a lover they both shared the feeling that I wasn't aware of their existence. There was no doubt in my mind that she was telling her lover that I would never find out. She must have referred to me as indolent. I sat and played the guitar all day. I had no awareness of the world nor the people in it.
All this was in my favor. They would never suspect that I was on to them, but I'd have to be very careful how I presented my accusations. If my suspicions didn't translate into the right questions, properly placed in the right order, she would immediately know I was playing a game. She would accuse me of instigations, of a paranoid mind, of a devious and suspicious nature. She would call me sick. She'd get up and walk away, ending the conversation, and further deepen my frustrations. One mistake and it would be curtains for me. I had to make sure that I didn't give her a fact that she knew to be wrong. She would know immediately that I had nothing but a suspicious mind. Then again, my suspicions hadn't become absolute. There was still a possibility that she was telling me the truth.

Daydreams vacillated between guilt and innocence
In my daydreams she would kiss me when she left for work in the morning and when she came back at nite. In my most loaded moments she would ask me how I was and how I felt. If I sneezed she would bless me, if I coughed she would say "Take care of yourself." Little things that meant so much to me. It was in those precious moments of my own hallucinations that I felt guilty of accusing an innocent person.

But the reality of it was, she always had the look of indifference engulfing her face like a blanket of cold snow. When she left in the morning for work, she would look at me with cold indifferent eyes. Her lips were sealed shut like an envelope filled with empty sheets of paper. She had a mouth that opened only to be fed and to yawn. It was in moments such as those that intuitions flared to a heated blaze. I couldn't ask her a direct question, since I had no direct knowledge of anything she was doing. What she was doing was going to work and avoiding my existence at least 90 percent of our time together. If I made the mistake, like I did one day, of asking her why she was so indifferent and cold to me, her reply would be, "I'm not." As far as she was concerned, she was the same as she always had been, loving, kind and filled with consideration.

It was my feelings, my fears, my lowgrade appraisal of myself that she would accuse me of projecting on to her. She could deny anything and everything, which made it important that I document her attitudes and her activities with me.

Becoming an Interrogator

The thought of becoming an interrogator fascinated me. If I was to take on the role of Torquemada, The Grand Inquisitor, I would have to know how to interrogate. This wasn't an easy role to fit into. My only hope, which kept me going and which propelled me into this world of deviousness, was to uncover her and her lover, who by now had become, in my mind, the destroyer of my existence.

I had to begin somewhere and I had to begin with simple questions. They would have to be simple questions, the type that wouldn't raise any suspicions. It had become not only a matter of principle, but a great concern about my safety. If she was screwing around, how would I know what this idiot was doing with her lover? What was she telling him or promising him and how ambitious was he?

The question kept appearing, how intelligent was my dear Nomi, and the same answer kept coming up, that only a stupid woman would let a situation get to the point of suspicion. But this might be her intent, to make it look as if she was stupid...too stupid to try and be a devious woman.

I had convinced myself that there was another person involved in our world. I didn't know him, but I was sure he knew me. I had to figure out how I could unearth all this intrigue and how I could become an interrogator and still remain a devoted husband.

The methodology of interrogation

When one doesn't know what he's doing an air of confidence is what he needs to fool someone. Confidence is the look of assurance. It's authority presenting itself, dressed in a dark somber suit of clothes with a finely shaped Fedora. A card with a title. The confident smile of one who knows what's going on.

Confidence is a theatrical and practical posture, a posing for a photograph as a character wearing a uniform with gold braids. That complete look of knowing to the very last detail.
I had already established an air of confidence in her guilt as if I knew exactly what she had done from the time she left the house till the time she came back. Now I needed a look of knowing on my face rather than a look of wanting to know.

To uncover her duplicity, I would have to somehow convince her that I had everything ready and all that was left was the necessary act of presentation. Like a grand dinner that was served bit by bit, plate by plate, till she choked.

Good interrogation depends a lot on the depth of understanding the subject. The subject in this case was Nomi and the subject matter was one of duplicity. It frightened me to think of it.

I had such a small knowledge of this vast subject that somehow I had developed, maybe because of my ignorance, a thought that duplicity could be uncovered. That duplicity could never be perfected to the point of never being able to be detected. Something was bound to show through. If you're looking you might see
a glimpse of the stage
a look in the eye
a word
a gesture
a contradiction.
She didn't just find a lover to love, she had to develop a system of avoiding detection, and duplicity is the essential ingredient in the system. I knew, more-or-less, all of god's creatures possess this remarkable talent for duplicity. Animals which change their color

and shape, flowers which fool the birds. Plants fool the flies in order to eat them...even god wore two faces, one of forgiveness and the other of vengeance, so that you never knew which one you were dealing with at the moment.

My real problem was...I didn't know the essential makeup of duplicity, its mechanism, its history, its philosophy, its psychology. I would have to learn, step by step, what a duplicitous person thinks like, feels like, acts like.

Before I could ask the right questions I would have to learn enough to develop confidence in what I was asking. That in itself is the interrogator's greatest asset. He can raise a question that he already has the answer to, but unless I had a way of making her talk I would become the accuser, victim, judge and jury.

The predicament was obvious. To develop a procedure for questioning a person is one thing, but to get them to talk to you about it, is something else.

Everytime I tried talking to her about my problem she'd tell me I was a chronic complainer. All my attempts to talk with her were always just attempts, like trying to make a hole in an ocean wave with a broom handle. So reluctant was she to talk to me about anything that in the middle of a conversation she'd yawn, roll her eyes, shrug her shoulders and just wander off to bed. Maybe she felt the conversation itself would lead me to the mysterious secret that she had buried in her. Talking would, by its very existence, expose the name of her lover.

Empathy

I wasn't ready to begin my interrogation, but I had to, for the sake of my own sanity. I had to start as quick as possible. I decided that I would first approach her with Empathy.

Empathy is such a wonderful way to enter into another's feelings, and she wouldn't have to talk, I would do all the talking for her. I would take full responsibility for all her actions. Blaming myself for the insensitivities I heaped on her. Accusing her would be like trying to turn back the tides. I had to go with it and let the current take me to the point where she realized that I was strong enough to provide a shoulder for her to cry on. I had to get her to trust me to the point of talking to me about her lover. I had to pretend that I understood her tender feelings, that love is such a powerful force, no one can resist it. I felt I could convince her that I understood the poetic flavor of love.

Empathetically I understood that this was no back-alley affair she was having. Her love had in it the substance and all the elements of true love.

Sympathy
I would somehow try to show her that I understood, that maybe in her situation I might have done the same thing. I would have to reduce her moral guilt by minimizing the moral seriousness of the act and suggest a less revolting and more morally acceptable reason, or motivation, for the betrayal of her marriage vows.

I must sympathize with her, and not condemn her and her lover for their indifference to my position in life. I must condemn myself, even cry if I had to. I'd have to show her that I had been the insensitive one, if possible even the immoral one, to give her a way out.

Trust
I must get her to trust me.
I must learn to display an understanding motivated by sympathy for her and convey to her that this wasn't all that bad and that we could iron out our differences. Maybe we could invite the lover over for dinner. There was no guilt, no shame. I had to make sure that no antagonism was in my voice. I had to have a clear-sounding voice...a voice one could trust. The voice of a priest, a doctor, a lawyer, a man in love.

I had to appeal to her pride, to her honor, to flatter her, to tell her a beautiful person like her needed the attention of another man. If I had consideration for her feelings, I would have introduced her to her lover. It was my fault and my neglect that had created this problem.

It's a known fact, amongst women, that most of a woman's problems have been created by some man.
A frigid woman is merely the creation of an impotent man.
A fornicating female is the doing of some devious lecher.
Whoredom was created to fill the needs of men.
Boredom was created by an inattentive male. She might be sleeping because she was bored with me and if she showed reluctance to being with me, it was my fault.
I was now taking the easy road, and blaming her for all my troubles.

But if history was a cyclical affair and human creatures merely the compositions of bad cyclical habits, the way she solved her problems of life, before she met me, was the way she would continue solving them now that she was with me.

But I didn't know her history. She was a blank page, a forever-present problem. My thoughts about interrogation now fed my imagination from the deeper waters of doubt. Interrogation would work if she cooperated, but what would I do with her after she confessed to her duplicity?

What road would I follow after she told me that she was in love with another man? Would I continue being the empathic, sympathetic, trusting, forgiving husband? I was in deep waters. I was trying to uncover her and yet I didn't know what to do once I did uncover her. In some strange way, I might find a way to enjoy this pain that was enclosing my total existence. I was entering the mysterious world of a woman, when she has decided to take on another lover and juggle two men in her bed.

There was no doubt in my mind, the power and force that was simmering in the emotional cauldron would erupt. Something would ignite it when all of it met, somehow, somewhere, in the coming weeks ahead.

The Sex Counselor

Competing with a lover
Seeking a counselor
I called Dr. Boyle's office
Sympathy begins with concern
Time to let the counselor hear my song of love
Aural state of sexual expression
The sounds of love in the dark
Sexual patience

It's amazing that dealing with a woman can make you walk the waters, or it can make you scared of stepping on a concrete floor.

The whole matter was too complicated for me to handle on my own. I needed help and it had to be professional help.
Now that my suspicions were more than just aroused, advice from a friend was not enough. I had embarked on the road to prove my suspicions correct. It was too late to do anything else, even leaving her now was too late. Once the doors of hell are opened you might as well enter.
It was time to see someone who was versed in the subjects of marriage, suspicions, infidelity, maybe mental illness. It might be that the woman I was with had gone nuts. Unknown chemicals

working in her system that could be triggered by a bird flying, a bee buzzing, the wind blowing through the doorway of a building, a shadow throwing its darkness over a table, a word, a look that caused the chemicals to form into some strange molecular structure that created some other identity, a person I knew nothing of.

Competing with a lover
No matter what I did, I thought, or tried to do, she had needs which were unsatisfied and only another person could satisfy them. For some reason she needed someone else. I had to accept the fact, that for some reason, I wasn't getting her hot enough to keep her awake, or to satisfy her.
Also my techniques weren't good enough to screw her when she was sleeping. If these were things I could learn then I had to find someone to teach them to me, the way one is taught to ride a horse or to hunt for the doe.

How to tap into that mysterious connection between body and soul, spirit and mind, desire and sleep? I had a need to seek advice the way one seeks the advice of
a banker
a doctor
a lawyer
a priest. These people have been trained to advise you, and the advice I needed was the advice from a person who knows sex. The thought of a prostitute came to my mind, but a whore provides ready-made stories, she comes with the words and stories all put together. More money...better stories. The whore tells you what you want to hear, she doesn't tell you what a woman wants. I knew what I needed, now I had to find out what a woman needs.

Seeking a counselor
I started looking for a marriage counselor. Since I didn't know anyone who had been to one, I had to follow the same road that all newcomers follow.
I picked up the phonebook, the holy bible of names, and started thumbing my way through 485 marriage counselors. I didn't know what I was looking for in particular, but I imagined it

would be the same as looking for a dentist, a plumber, a builder, someone to do a job that needed doing. I had a definite idea of what I wanted. The question was, how could I find the right person to help me do it?

I had developed certain questions by the order of their importance. The first question was, what do I do with this suspicion that is growing in my head by the day? It's a strange feeling when you start losing trust in someone. Everything they say or do you see as being against you, even the things they don't do.

Second question was, should I stay around long enough to find out if my suspicions are correct? Why should I bother?
The world is filled with women of every size and description, each one different from the other. Millions of female possibilities, each one probably just a little bit better than the one you just left. Maybe it was my curiosity that kept this ever-growing suspicion alive, maybe an inborn desire to inflict punishment on myself out of the sheer boredom of my existence, or maybe some long-ago forgotten guilt that needed daily punishment to remind me of my worthlessness. I never seem to know why I do what I do, and now for the first time in my life, I did know.

I wanted to know what my wife was up to. I knew that I wanted to discover her most secret activities, her vilest acts. I felt jealous of the banker and how he found out his wife. He faced what was, and his disgusting wife became a film celebrity that he packed around on videotapes in the trunk of his car.

Another set of questions was created as the thought of finding a professional to help me came into my mind. How would I know if I found the right critic of my life? I'm sure that 485 counselors don't say the same thing, follow the same rule book, drink out of the same cup, piss in the same bowl. Some might feel that my toilet training was influential in developing suspicions toward my trainer's real intentions, which in turn created, in my adult life, suspicions toward all those around me. There were so many reasons why I was the way I was, that it would be like trying to undo the Gordian knot.

The question was...which one did I need? Was one better than the other? Would I eventually go to all of them, once I started going? Did I need to go to some precounselor to tell me which counselor I needed? Some of them had to be outright frauds, shoe salesmen, carpet layers, posing as the Oracles of Delphi, ready to help and give advice for a few bucks. Just by the sheer force of numbers, the odds were great that the area was filled with three-card Monty busters. Frauds looking to make a buck. I had to make a choice, and everything had more than one possibility to choose from.

I spent days thinking about the counselors, looking up the various schools they claimed they belonged to. It was like a stewpot of psychological mumbo jumbo that consisted of the following:
Analytical Schools...with dream analysis thrown in
Gestalt Schools
Behavioristic
Functional
Structural
Dynamic
Reflexological
Psychonormic
Morphogenic
Topocentric
Schematalogical
Value orientation
Twelve point electro-stimulator activities that can bring you back to your youthful, bouncy self.

Each one of them had its own peculiar explanation of why things are the way they are and why you aren't happy. Each one had its own way to identify, to correct, and conquer your fears, hit your mark, make your life obedient to your will. That was the secret, how to make your life obedient to your will.

Finally one day when I was at the laundromat waiting for my clothes to get out of the dryer, I saw an ad in one of those papers that float around free of charge. I rested my eyes on one ad, like a fly picks a crumb on the table to land on.

Dr. E. Boyle, Ph.D.
Sex Counseling with Human Compassion
Individual and Group Counseling
Relationship and sexuality issues a speciality
Gestalt
Hypnosis
Psychosynthesis

I knew I had found the one I would feel comfortable with. I needed someone with human compassion. The word human turned me on. The word compassion made me feel like spring was just cresting the horizon. It had to be the right one. If nothing more, at least I could find sympathy in a world that lacked it, or was afraid of it.
A world that found the thought of sympathy to be as close as you could get to being antimodern, anticapitalist, anti-American, antiprogressive. A flake of dandruff on your shoulder.

I knew I had found the counselor I was looking for, a counselor with human compassion. I spent my day in preparation for my final attempt to save my love for Nomi from the junk heap of oblivion. If Nomi only knew the effort she had put me to, would she have sympathy for me?

I called Dr. Boyle's office
An answering service told me that Dr. Boyle had an opening in two weeks. Evidently other people felt the same way I did. The thought of human compassion had turned them all on. People who are hard to get a hold of, like Dr. Boyle, must be doing someone some good. The word must be out on him. There might be a waiting line going around the block a few times, or it might be just a ploy to keep people waiting, to let people know he is important, then when it comes to giving you the bill…you'll agree to whatever he wants. How could so many people trust him, if he wasn't as compassionate as Christ?

I was feeling optimistic. Here was a person who took into account the human side of the problem. I wasn't going to be fitted into a theory like it was a ready-made boot, waiting for my foot to be squeezed in it. Here was a counselor that was going to fit me up with what I needed. Tailored just for my needs and no one else's. I finally made up my mind, made an appointment and showed up two weeks later. Parked my car in the Westlake Mall, took a few hits on my nerve regulator and found my way to Dr. E. Boyle's office.

I was ready for anything, ready to confess my troubles. Human compassion was the key to it all. I had no doubt in my mind that he'd understand my predicament. I was ready to tell all in a last-ditch attempt to save my soul from eternal damnation. "Stay silent," I told myself, "and lose your kingdom. Speak up in defense of what is yours, and heaven shall reward you."

I entered the waiting room, and a bell connected to the door sounded my arrival. No one was there to greet me, to take my name and number, to fill out the endless questions, followed by social security number, insurance number, bank references, friends who will vouch for you, mother's maiden name, and whatever they can think of to find out if you really exist and are not a money freak trying to run out on the bill.

A beautiful dark-haired woman, dressed as if she was invited to a business meeting as the guest speaker, opened up the door and stood there. I looked at her from the shoes up, the way she must have intended me to look at her. It was difficult to take my eyes off of her, and she knew it. She looked like she was modeling the new women's fashion for the finally arrived...professional woman.

On her feet she had a pair of Italian-made, black-brushed shoes with 4-inch heels. She wore a dark, pin-striped, one-button roll suit-jacket, with high shoulder pads and a flared collar. A gray woolen skirt, a vest, a button-down Brooks Brothers shirt with a gray broadleafed tie.

She emanated the look of authority as she stood in the doorway. It was a special type of look which has the ability to create in you the calmness of belief.

"I'm Dr. Boyle," she said, "and you must be James?"

For a moment I felt like running. I wanted to run out of there and forget about Nomi and marriage and paid counselors. All this shit was taking me away from a life devoted to music and pleasure.

I nodded my head like a mendicant who has taken vows of silence. She stuck out her beautiful hand with long slender fingers and long unpainted fingernails. I felt her hand in mine and it felt cool and soft.

"Come," she said, "come with me." It was a voice beckoning me to come into her bedroom and my body obeyed without any hesitation. I couldn't get my eyes off her fragile beauty.

She led me into her office, like I was tied to a leash, and asked me to sit in a chair in front of her. Behind her hung all those silent introductions that are very important to a person who is going to charge you for their advice. Those silent introductions that are hung on the walls of a church, a lawyer's office, a doctor's room, any place where it's necessary to turn belief into faith.

There was a big overblown diploma from Sonoma State University, and a Doctorate Degree in psychology from the University of Chicago. A few other important-looking documents on the wall. A certificate of completion from the Institute of Advanced Hypnotic Studies. She belonged to the National League of Women Counselors. There were numerous other framed certificates which were hard to read without my glasses. She had a trophy for tennis, a trophy for golf and was a Black Belt in Aikido. She had a picture of a sailboat.

A picture of a teenage girl, sitting on a horse, wearing an English riding habit and a bowler hat. There was enough to tell you she had a family, a daughter on a horse, a picture of a man, maybe her husband with a tennis racquet in his hand. It was all laid out. She wanted the one who sat in my chair to feel like here was a woman who had a family, and it was all put together because she knew the answer to the problem.

Maybe I was in the wrong place? How could I talk to this woman about another woman? She would take sides, she would say I goofed and got what I deserved.

I put it all in my head, bit by bit, without saying a word while she shuffled some important-looking papers on her desk, straightened things out, and prepared herself and me for what was to come.

My eyes came off the wall and she was satisfied that I had filled the empty spots in my head with who she was. A soft voice filled with compassion asked me,
"Well James what seems to be the matter?"
The weed had just set in, and I felt friendly, talkative and like a benign tumor…nothing to worry about. She had the look of concern on her face.

Sympathy begins with concern
I started to tell her of my problem, but like all problems, if you want the problem to be understood, you have to do a lot of editing before it's ready to be told to someone.
I had rehearsed my woes, like one does the rosary or an actor does his lines. Over and over in my head, I emphasized the pain and the depressions I had suffered at the hands of an indifferent woman.

Feeling something, and having to tell someone what it is that you're feeling, somehow doesn't sound the same. It was so perfect in my head, and now what kept coming out of my mouth was a lot of whining and poor-me things, of how I felt I was being betrayed.

I didn't know how to pinpoint the real issue so I wouldn't sound like a little boy who had his valuable marbles taken from him by a bigger, stronger, more dedicated boy. Maybe I didn't understand what it was that was really bothering me. On the surface it looked like neglect, but there might be something else hidden in the story that I was ready to tell her and didn't know how.

"My wife is a beautiful woman," I told Dr. Boyle, "Full lips, good breasts, slender hips which move in such a way that they promise me great pleasure if I lie in between them."
"It's important," she said, "that sexual attraction exists towards your sexual partner. Now, what's the problem James?" she asked me in that beautiful, soft voice that one learns how to use in a

broadcasting school, a bedroom, on a stage, or a counselor's couch. After a long hesitation I finally summarized it for public announcement.

"She won't let me have her anymore," I said. There was a long silence, then a soft sound of sympathy, compassion, and unmitigated concern.

"Ohhhhhhh...My...my...my...myyyyyyyy. How long has it been, James?" The concern oozed out between her lips like honey from a jar.

"Three or 4 months," I said, with my voice holding the sound of self-pity like an altar boy holds the holy crucifixion, afraid that he might drop it. "I've lost count of the months...I don't know."

Another sound of sympathy. "Ohhhhhhh my...my...my...my, James. Did she tell you why she didn't want you to have it?"

"She keeps telling me that she's tired, and all she does is lie there and sleep."

"Do you sleep?" she asks me.

"We sleep together. I wake up, look at her, maybe touch her, run my hand up and down her legs. She groans and pulls away."

"Do you feel like, or do you masturbate when you're looking at her?" She caught me by surprise asking me that.

"As matter of fact I do, if I didn't I would really go nuts."

"Do you masturbate in the same bed?"

Evidently the counselor wanted me to be precise. She was a scientist and she wanted to know exactly what went on in the bed.

"Yes," I said, "I do it right there next to her."

There was a long pause and the counselor waited for me to continue my story.

"My mind is engulfed, like a roaring blaze, in fear that she's got someone else in some other bed somewhere." I didn't even bother to try to disguise my fear that she was spreading her legs somewhere else. "I keep trying to hop her, but she's shut down. It's been so long now that it has become a way of life. I get dreamy just looking at her." I stopped.

"Don't stop James," she tells me, "Keep going, tell me about it."

A strange urge came over me, I felt a twinge in my saddle. I felt the desire to tell this woman, who I had just met, what a wonderful fucking felt like. I wanted to tell her every little detail of the pleasure I had with my wife before I married her, and how depressing and painful the whole affair had become. It was important that I describe how I felt then and how I feel now. How deep I went into my details would depend on how accurately I described my pleasure.

The weed was really kicking in. I had never talked to a woman about another woman. Talking to a woman about another woman is difficult, but talking to a woman about you screwing another woman creates a different feeling. It was a feeling I had never felt before, nor could I describe it.

Time to let the counselor hear my song of love

"All her movements were part of the desire that made me want to slip her clothes off, climb in between those soft legs, and let those hips rock me like a child in a cradle. Thinking of those long legs, curved around me like an octopus its prey, drawing me into her for one last emptying of the vessel of love, sent shivers of passion up my scrotum and into my stomach."

The counselor liked what I said. I could see it in her eyes. I doubt if anyone had ever described a fuck scene with such beauty. This was possible because I was in love. I wasn't just putting my meat in a hole. I was connecting the passions of strength, like two beasts who have met each other for the first time in the confines of a zoo.

"Why don't you tell her all this James?" I was asked in a professional tone.

"I don't want to tell her that, I want to do it to her. I want to know how to stop my wife from sleeping everytime I try making love to her."

This was the perfect opportunity to tell Dr. Boyle, in minute detail, all about my marriage nite, and see how she'd react to it. I told her the story of how my new wife yawned in my face while I stood there in front of her, ready to put the sword in its scabbard.

"She yawned with such a look of indifference that I felt like shoving my club down that gaping mouth. The only reason I didn't put it in her mouth, was, I was afraid she'd bite it off when the yawn was finished."

I became braver with each sentence as I described my marriage nite to Dr. Boyle. I felt like a soldier at war after the first shot has been fired. An overpowering urge to explode into a million little fragments, all going into a million directions at the same time. "The son-of-bitch fell asleep on me. On our marriage nite."

I didn't know if I sounded amazed...rejected...or pitiful. "It's the same as if a priest fell asleep on you while giving you holy communion or the sacraments or your last rites, or a surgeon fell asleep holding your heart in his hand. I don't give a shit what you say," I told the counselor, "there are certain things one does where falling asleep is forbidden. A soldier falls asleep while on guard duty. The court martial finds him guilty of falling asleep on duty. He will be shot by a firing squad of ten erect men. Cold rifles will be pointed at his hardened prick. A sycophant would never sleep while scandalizing you, nor a thief fall asleep while stealing. A lover would never fall asleep on top of his woman while entering her mysteries. Some things are just too important to fall asleep while doing them."

"I think you're over-reacting James," she told me in a very sympathetic voice. "You felt rejected, pushed away, you felt unimportant at the moment. Overexpectancy. You placed too much emphasis on your wife's lovemaking with you. A very common thing amongst men. You're not allowing the whole thing to take place more naturally."

My story was going the wrong way. I was a man with too much expectancy about lovemaking. I wanted to fuck my wife when my wife wanted to sleep. Now I had to explain to the counselor my suspicions of why my wife didn't want to fuck me, and hope that I didn't sound like I was losing my mind.

The story was all jumbled up and not in any order. I hadn't repeated the story enough to have it all laid out. It would take a year of saying it, to different people, to sort it all out before it made any sense to anyone trying to understand it.

I told the beautiful lady my problem the best way I could, but what I couldn't tell her was the confusion that it had put me in. The state of agitation. The looking through her purse for some clue as to her whereabouts. The systematic methods I had developed to find out if she had another man in her portfolio. The money I had spent trying to figure out if I stunk. Actually, I did tell her what I had gone through with my fear of odors, that I had gone to a Medical Doctor, to a Chinese herbalist, to an Aromatologist.

I had considered going to an astrologer. I had talked to an ex-priest. I had read Dr. Barbara C's book on *Love in The Modern Times.* A soul-searching book by a woman who said she had personally fucked 850 men, and was still searching for the proper man to really turn her on.

I told the counselor of the time I spent looking for the famous work that was written by Gardner Millstone, *The Sex Habits of a Modern Woman.* I feared that the Feminist movement in the late 70's had burned the book in mass retaliation for his portrayal of the modern woman as more of a high-tech machine with buttons hidden on her, that once touched, the lovemaking process would be engaged and her legs would snap open, like a Jack-in-the-Box. A happy healthy voice would say "You did it lover, it's yours." As simple as that.

I continued reciting my woes to Dr. Boyle because this is what I was paying her for. To listen and to make an announcement that she would give me the right words to open the Cave of Ali Baba.

I realized like a drowning man does when he grabs on to his hair to save himself from a watery doom, that I had reached the first law of separation. That the unity of two separate bodies is equal to the square area of the attraction.

Aural state of sexual expression

In the weeks that followed Dr. Boyle introduced me to a book she and her husband had written concerning the relation of sound to the sexual process. She gave me the book and charged me $145.00. She told me to read it, because we would be referring to it as we progressed.

She began by introducing me to her method of seeking pleasure through the words that we use on each other while making love.

"The sounds we utter are so very important to lovemaking, the ears transmit the sexual energy to the neurological system of the human. Silence, like babbling, can destroy the magic of the moment. Sexual pleasure should be transmitted, not only physically, but also aurally, and the right sounds are very important to the climaxing of the sexual potential. There are certain questions I want to ask you," she tells me, "just to see if you're up on it, and to see where you need some help."

1) What are the sounds that are most pleasing to the ear when lying in bed with a woman?

"Do you know?" she asked me. I answered…no.

2) What are the divine sounds of lovemaking?

I thought for a moment.
"They change from time to time," I told her as if I had paid great attention to them. "Sometimes I like to hear heavy breathing, sometimes a heavy fart as I plunder the cave of the Minotaur. Sometimes a command to give it to her hard and fast, sometimes a groan, a moan, the sound of wetness and slurping."

3) What are the sounds that bring about a provocation of sexual desire?

Again I had to think for a moment. I really never gave it much of a thought before.
"The sound of a woman walking, that click, click of her heel hitting the floor...the tone of her voice."

4) Have you ever engaged in an erotic conversation with a woman that stimulated you and brought about an orgasm without touching the woman?

"Yes, it was a dream I was having, I'll never forget it. It was a woman I knew who was married, and we met in front of the altar in church. She had taken her wedding rings off and

asked me if I approved."
"Did you?" Dr. Boyle asked me.
"I remember my body trying to explode through my cock...the feeling lasted in me for days."

5) Were there sounds from a woman that turned you off?

"Yes."
I told Dr. Boyle that a woman snoring made my bubble blow, and my cartilage crawl back up my gut. Lying in bed with a snoring woman was like a trip through the horse barns.

The sounds of love in the dark
The Good Dr. Boyle told me that the most important part of a marriage was how things sound in the bedroom. Most sex encounters are at nite when the eyes are of little help in creating sexual excitement.
"We have to learn how to develop our images with words to really get our partners all worked up and ready to go. In a dark room the ears are the primary source of sexual pleasure."
With a feeling of bravado that comes an hour after you have smoked a good joint, I offered Dr. Boyle my mental and spiritual resolution of toleration. I was ready to listen in order to learn whatever it was that I was missing. Since I was a musician, and the ear was the seat of my art, I couldn't deny the power of the voice and sound in the pursuit of pleasure.

The voice commanded, led and deceived, opened and closed the doors of heaven and hell. I knew that God spoke to Moses and Noah and to Mrs. Noah as she cleaned up the mountains of animal turds on the deck of the Ark. In the darkness of my bedroom it was the disgusting sound of snoring that my ears had to listen to. My wife's yawning and snoring drove me crazy.
Dr. Boyle didn't feel that there was anything wrong with my wife. It was a perfectly natural response to a hard-working day. But for the moment we would concentrate on me, and my problem of keeping the woman awake by the words I use to guide her to the love-world of a man.

The counselor advised me that I was probably out of sync. My biological timing was off. I might feel like I was being patient and sensitive, but I touched and wanted at the wrong time of the day or nite. I was warned that I was probably saying the wrong things at the wrong time.

"If you're off a picosecond, you might as well be off at least an hour. You have to be right on. You have to really concentrate on it. You have to wait for the right moment. You must create an atmosphere." I was, she said, like all men...in a rush. I should start examining myself, and get ready technically to be able to handle it properly when the right moment came.

"Your vocabulary has to be adorned, James," she whispered, "along with your awareness of what to say and when to say it."

I was told sex with a modern woman was not a necessary daily diet. The modern woman was busy, had learned to take care of things on her own, and at times she would rather have a private masturbation dealing with her daydreams, than have her lover crawl on top of her, violating her body. It was more important to be loving and sensitive than to be climaxing all the time.

Sexual patience

Dr. Boyle told me parables of patience, of a Zen archer who waits in front of a tree for a leaf to fall before firing his arrow. She told me of a Hindu mystic who kept his arm stretched out till a bird built a nest in the palm of his hand, or for that matter waited for a bird, any bird, to take a shit on that open palm. Then Dr. Boyle started purring as she told me,

"We have brought our love life into the speed of the moment. We have become so influenced by speed that it has curdled our love life. Do you understand James?"

It all sounded so right, coming out of Dr. Boyle's mouth. She had said it so many times she probably had memorized it without a flaw or a hesitation. Something so perfect coming out of one's mouth has to be the truth. Authority comes dressed in a suit and a tie carrying the gospel in a shirt pocket. But would it work?

"You're going to need a helper," she told me, "to practice on. I'd like you to be able to come here ready and practiced, so we don't spend a lot of time just talking about it. I'm here to see that you're doing it right."

She smiled at me as she wrote down an address on her notepad. "Try to get it before next week. I've written down three models for you. I suggest that you pick up a P.P.D. 38-363. It's a little more expensive, but believe me, it's worth every penny."

The Robotic Lover

The dialogue with Judy

The note directed me to Grenshaw's, a discreet little shop off Tenth and Clement. The door was locked. I rang the bell. A tall thin man with a very serious, somber, clerical face opened up the door and asked me if I had a prescription. I showed him the note Dr. Boyle had given me. He opened the door wider and let me in.

I asked him, Why all the mystery? He said there was no mystery, that they served only patients from Doctors and Registered Sexologists and were not open to the general public.

He introduced himself as Rodney and told me Mr. Grenshaw was out, and assured me he could take care of my prescription.
"Hi!" I told him, "I'm James," and stuck my hand out for the immortal gesture of friendship.

I really wasn't sure why I was there. I looked around. I had never been in a place like this before. It was a plastic-part shop of human plumbing, placed in glass cases, recommended by smiling women, endorsed as
"The best-feeling dildo made."
I really didn't know what I was supposed to buy.

"I was sent here for something," I told Rodney.
He looked at the note that I handed him, while I looked with amazement at those huge dildos in the case.
"Do women actually use those things?" I asked him.

"Certainly," he said. "I have them in African black, Mexican brown, Irish red, Jewish cut, name it, we have it."
"I don't want something in her, other than me..."

"Yes of course," he sympathized with me, "that's everyone's dream. What you need, according to Dr. Boyle, is a P.P.D. 38-363."
"A what?" I asked him.
"A P.P.D." he says again, looking at me as if I was stupid in not knowing those call letters. From the look on his face they had to be international code letters for Male Distress.
"A Play Partner Doll. Dr. Boyle thinks you should have Ms. Judy."
"Another woman?"
"We have Ms. Judy May," he tells me. "She's the hottest number out. Feels and acts and talks like the real thing. She's like a grown Barby Doll that's programmed to give you the latest in high tech."

The dialogue with Judy
"You have to give Judy the right answers or she won't let you have it. You have to touch her the right way or you're in the doghouse for the nite. If you learn to handle Judy, you can probably find your way through any bedroom without too much trouble." He talked about her as if she was a real person, whose purposeful creation was mainly for the acts of pleasure. If your imagination fancied something else, you merely changed the program.
"She's programmed to cross-reference ten cultures, and to cross over gender lines. In other words," he tells me in an authoritative voice, like a man who knows his product, "she's capable of being an Oriental woman from three different Asian countries. She can also be a Mediterranean, Italian, French, Spanish, Greek. She can be a Jew or a Moslem, Swede, or English, and the latest program can have her an African black, or American black, or if you like

she can be a bisexual woman relating to you all her needs, or an Sado-Masochistic Amazonian. You know," he tells me, changing the tempo of his monologue, "that each culture has its own sexual hangups. Africans don't kiss while making love. Cocksucking isn't the thing with the Greek women. Assbanging is favored in Spain where virginity in a woman is a prime thing, and is a no-no with the English women. If you travel a lot, Ms. Judy is like a Berlitz course in sex, and all of it can be understood because she does all her culture-things in English translation, with the proper accents to give it an authenticity that brings you as close as you can get to the real thing."

"Going to the moon is nothing compared to this," I told him in utter amazement.

"Here," he said, "I'll give you a chance to hear her."
He dialed Southern American on the cultural selector, and pressed the start button. The doll started talking in a beautiful-sounding Savannah Georgian voice. "Hi, I'm Judy May...do yu'all think I'm beau-ti-ful?"
I stood in front of her petrified, as Judy May looked at me with eyes that looked human. They had a gleam in them and a built-in promise, her eyelids fluttering like a fan on a hot Savannah afternoon.

"Say something," Rodney told me.

"Yes I do," I replied, feeling strange that I was talking to a doll. "I do think you're beau-ti-ful."
"Do yu'all think my tits are big and pret-ty?"
"Yes I do."
"It's soooo...warmmm...would you like to take my blouse off and look at me, sweetie pie?"
"Yes I would."
"Now...cuz you been a right nice type of good fella...yu'all can lift my dress up...and while yu'all at it honey...if yu'all want...yu'all can take my panties off too."

I lifted her dress up, and she purred like a high-tech engine being started. She enjoyed the fact that I was getting started on her. She

wore a pair of velcro-strapped panties. I had never seen them on a woman before. None of this pulling them off the leg routine, you just pulled on the lace strap and the panties popped off.
"Do yu'all like what yu'all looking at darlin'?"
"Yes I do..."
"Then you can touch it and if I like...and remember...I said...if I like how yu'all do it...I'll let yu'all work it over with that lovely...lovely looking...long tongue...yu'all have."

I hesitated, and Rodney felt my reluctance.
"Feel the hair on her cunt," Rodney tells me. "The hair on her cunt is like the real thing."
"Amazing what those Japanese can do," I said.
"That's blond #8 fine. We have 6 different colors and textures, all interchangeable."

I touched it and it felt like silk. My mind was at the crucial point when reality is questioned only for a moment, until the deception itself becomes the real thing.
"Stick your finger in it," Rodney says, "and play with it."
"It feels wet and a little sticky," I told him.
"The fluid is adjustable," he told me, "but you should have it a little tacky to get that real feel that she's horny."
"Lay me on the floor honeypot," Judy May tells me, "and get on top of me quick. OUuuuu.... AHhhhhhh...Oh honey...Oh honeylove...put it allllll...the wayyyyyy in."

I couldn't believe my eyes or ears.
I felt my prick get hard in my pants. I felt embarrassed to have Rodney see it getting hard on a modern programmed Barby doll, but it was so goddamn real.
Rodney immediately saw that I had a problem showing up on the horizon. He reached over and pushed the stop button on her wristwatch.
"Jesus in heaven," I said with the bewildered sound of a child.
I asked how sophisticated the doll was.

"It's not just a doll by any stretch of the imagination, it's a robot that is highly sophisticated, and the nice part about Ms. Judy May is, she can be converted to other situations with the change of programs."

Rodney's voice became softer as he told me, "You can get the program which makes Judy into a nun who needs convincing that it's God's way. She has an automatic digital selector that can scan postures of your mind. If your conversation isn't persuasive, Sister-whomever will engage you in some corrective discourse. If you give her an argument that has some merit, she'll let you do it to her. It's like having honest criticism without any gender bias. That program is an extra $520.00, including the nun's habit in white and black.

"We also have a schoolteacher program where you're kept after school, and she keeps you under the desk for punishment, letting you stare at her crotch. If you confess to your naughtiness, she will let you have her. It's $150.00 for the Styrofoam desk, and $485.00 for the program. There's also an intellectual program. A real popular party program. Ms. Judy becomes a librarian who helps you select subjects suppressed by the police, church and the Rotary Club. The depth of your curiosity determines if you can have her. The program goes for $230.00 including 2 volumes of essays on sexual subjects."

He told me of programs he had of "a nurse who discovers you have been faking it while she's washing your balls and starts to masturbate you. We also have a really interesting number for the real go-getters. A business woman who outwits you and you have to eat her shit. We also have a model who is in love with her face, and like a painter who has just finished a canvas, keeps asking you if you see the real meaning in her work. All 3 for $685.00."

Rodney continued with his sales. "There's a lot of happy people out there with a play doll next to them. You can turn her on at nite with an electro-timer and get the following." He touched a button on her watch.

"Hi darling, sweetie pie lover-man. I just can't sleep. I need it bad...how about giving it to me? You want to fuck?"

"You can turn on her confession button, if you like that kind of thing, and she'll fill your inquisitive nature with all her naughtiness, asking you to understand and forgive her, but she just couldn't help herself."

Then Rodney gave me all the technical data which I had a hard time remembering.

"They're all advanced Japanese robotic models," he tells me, "with digital neuromemory enhancers, equipped with a digital sound-system, multiple interchangeable programs, a built-in 8-track audial-response system that gives you whatever conversation you would find necessary for your enjoyment. If you like, we can let you have a demonstration, but you have to use condoms...health regulations you know."

This was what my wife's indifference had driven me to, buying a rubber-plated fuck machine, like the kind cows are milked with.

Surrogate Wife

The next best thing to a robot
The little death
The human approach
Igniting the great sexual engine
The great secret
Touching is expensive

In my next meeting with Dr. Boyle, I found her wearing a blue denim skirt made of tightly woven cotton, with a fluid drape that made her shape the dominant part of our meeting.

The next best thing to a robot

I took notes, like she asked me, concerning the progress I had made, how I created a lovemaking atmosphere, how did I get Nomi and myself ready for our lovemaking, and if I was comfortable with my newly acquired P.P.D. I told Dr. Boyle, with a tone of failure in my voice, that there was no way I could take home a P.P.D. 38-363. Sit and talk to it, touch it, fondle it...then take my hose and hose it, bang it, love and caress it, like it was real female flesh.

"You'd be surprised," she says, "how many of my patients use the surrogate-lover doll. There are those who are very inhibited in their gender relationships, both men and women. This helps them overcome certain obstacles."

I told her the thought of it made me sick. I needed the feel of real flesh for my fingers to touch.

"You'd be surprised at the advance of science in the sex field," she tells me. Then the counselor, with a very clinically objective set of words, offered to be my surrogate. In other words she offered to be the next best thing to a robot...all this in order to develop my sexual-technical abilities...which I was, according to her, in need of improving.

The little death

"It would be expensive," she told me, "but it could be very beneficial in solving the problem of sex and sleep appearing together on the same stage, but in the wrong sequence. Ideally," Dr. Boyle said with a look of serious sensitivity on her concerned face, "the sequence should be the following. Coupling, climaxing, then a moment of the little death when you just lie there between her legs for what feels like an eternity. The little death that comes at the hands of a woman, La petite morte, that wonderful feeling of total indifference that comes after a good unloading, then sleep."

Dr. Boyle offered to be my surrogate and to pose as my wife. She would guide me through the whole procedure of touching, and letting the feelings go through the fingers.

"It's important," she said, "to touch the right place with the right sense of feeling."

I told the counselor of an incident that took place with my wife just two days before. "I waited for all the conditions to be correct in order to make it with her. I was ready to put it in her after a lovely candlelit dinner, a few glasses of wine, soft music, and then the sonofabitch yawned in my face just as she always does. I tried to revive her with a few soft kisses. I laid her on the couch, lifted her dress and let my tongue slide up her leg. It was no use. She went to sleep, with a look of indifference on her face that I could have mistaken for the look of death."

The counselor crossed her legs and looked at me with those eyes of a wanting woman, half-dreamy, half-open, half-staring.

"Shall I continue?" I asked her.

"Oh yes, by all means."

"I really should have been leaving her instead of marrying her. We had reached the uppermost areas of pleasure before we got married, and we were on our way down to the 'blahs' of just being together. Something else had to take place because all the newness was over with, and I had to come up with something better. I knew I had blundered by staying. I knew I had made a grave error in marrying, and my mistake has brought me this far...to a counselor's couch. The passion was gone, the habit remained, and I felt somehow that the way things were could never be again."

The human approach

I asked the counselor if there was some simple way I could nail my wife, just like we used to do before this sickness of her spirt took over. I needed a more simple, more human approach, rather than a state of mind that one prepares for a lifetime.

"I don't want to devote my entire life to preparing for the big screw, waiting to be screwed, hoping to be screwed in some future moment, when all the moments and all the signs of the zodiac line up, when all the secret incantations of Nostradamus, Alistair Crowley and Boulon reveal themselves. When all of it falls together under the great book of the I Ching. Life has only so many moments, and for sure, it has more pleasures in it than just a woman's ass."

Igniting the great sexual engine

Dr. Boyle convinced me that the real secret of womanhood was...that no two women are identical but they both can have enough similarities to make generalities possible. She carefully told me that there were areas on the female body, if touched in the right way at the right time, that would ignite the great female sexual engine. This, I was told, was a difficult task and required great study to accomplish.

The greatest problem being, the woman has to let you touch her before anything can happen. You have to somehow convince her that she should let you touch her. The next problem is, you have to know what it is you're supposed to touch.

The great secret

What were the erogenous zones of the female body? Dr. Boyle would instruct me where hers could be found, how they could be touched, and what to do when they were stimulated.

"You have to understand," she tells me, "that once the areas can be identified, one has to learn the right pressure to exert, the right stroking, the right friction, the length of time required for each area."

According to Dr. Boyle it wasn't just a hit-and-miss proposition. "It requires a talented and trained hand and a patient attitude in order to 'fuck' the highly complex and sensitive modern woman."

Touching is expensive

It would be an expensive undertaking, but if a marriage was worth saving, then this might be the right moment to try to understand the whole area of stimulating the woman the right way. Dr. Boyle was a professional woman who could teach me the way. Her counseling would amount to a hundred dollars a visit, and any surrogating which opened up the gate to her sexual affections would be extra, figured by the area touched or the services rendered.

"It could be very expensive," Dr. Boyle said. "That's why I sent you to Grenshaw's."

I asked her to explain to me how the surrogating was figured so there would be no confusion later. She was very frank and open about it, and all the parts had a price tag on them.

"If I let you touch my nipples," she said, "it's one price. If I let you touch my cunt, it's another price. If I let you lick me, it's another."

It was cafeteria style, you paid by the item.

"And the pay scale?" I asked.

"That depends on the session, sometimes touching is part of the counseling and the demonstration, but If I'm teaching you arousal, and I know you'll get aroused, then it's different."

I was ready to follow Dr. Boyle and the sessions she had worked out for me, like a lamb following Little Bo-peep.

The Language of Love

Touching with fingers and tongue

The tongue

The breathing of a woman in heat and
the properly placed mirror

Looking in the mirror

The difference between licking and tickling

Third session: The language of love

In our third session, Dr. Boyle raised the issue as to what language we were going to use between us while we conducted our exploration. She said she liked using colloquial terms rather than clinical terms...because of the casualness, the nuances, metaphors and innuendos that daily usage gave the words. "You're not embarrassed, are you," she asked me, "if we use words that we are all familiar with?" I asked her to explain, knowing what she meant but wanting to hear it come from her beautiful mouth.

"I like words to flow out of me naturally. I don't like using words out of context. If you get me aroused, I might ask you to put your cock in me for a while, and cool me off, or I might ask you to lay your tongue on my cunt. Do you hear where I'm coming from?" She paused for a moment, then told me, "Any other word just won't do."

By the end of her conversation I was as hot as a hummingbird seeking out the red bottlebrush to feast on.

Dr. Boyle spent the fourth session introducing me to touching with fingers and tongue

She was wearing a parchment-color straight skirt with a white-piped jewel-neck blouse, black high-heeled shoes, a golden bracelet on one wrist and a golden Omega watch with a black band on the other wrist. Her visual simplicity made it all look so erotic. She told me to sit on her leather couch. She came over and sat next to me, then she took my hand and held it. I sat there waiting for the next order. Her soft voice asked me to put my arm around her and rub her neck gently. I did and felt her cool skin on my fingertips.

"Are you comfortable?" she asked me.

"Yes."

"Good, now take your tongue and pass it over my ear."

The tongue

I pulled her closer to me. My arm felt her body give way and she started breathing heavier. I let my tongue leave its cave...where it had been quietly lying in wait. An organ so sensitive that it could be used to talk to god or lick her earlobe. I pushed her earring around with my tongue, like a dolphin pushes a hoop in his tank at Marine World U.S.A.

"Let me take them off," she said. The words "Let me take them off," ignited me like a match to a Roman candle. It could mean so much. It could mean…let me take my clothes off. Let me take my panties off. Let me take my wedding rings off. Something was coming off...so I could get to it easier. I felt a throb in my cock, like a fire bell had been turned on at the station. She was lighting me up by the second. A hundred dollars for 45 minutes...to hear words come out of her mouth, instructing me what to do with her body. "Touch here, kiss there, lick that." While my tongue was working away, like an anteater on a hilltop, she looked at her watch. My prostate was aching. My head was buzzing. I felt awful. It was time to pull my tongue in, zipper-up my fly, get up from the couch, thank her, write out the check, put my jacket on, and leave out the side door while the next guy was getting ready to come in through the front door.

The following week she gave me a new area to lick, to touch and to squeeze. I asked her what she intended to do with the pains in my groin, as my balls swelled up for the big blow that never came. "We are going to empty them out at the right time," winking at me as she said it.

"How am I doing?" I asked her on my way out.

"Let's get into it more deeply," she said, "before I tell you."

I felt there was hope. The word "deeply" sounded to me like she was intending to let me put it in her at the next session.

My fifth meeting: the breathing of a woman in heat and the properly placed mirror

At this session she started out really quick, like she was in a hurry. "We're going to talk about breathing and the woman," she tells me. "The woman will let you know she's getting ready. Her breathing becomes heavier. You must pay attention to the breathing. It is the female prana. The woman's breast will start to heave, her skin flush, and the breathing become deeper. This is her highest moment of sexual prana. Her eyes close, and she lapses into a world of semiconsciousness. Her legs start to open like a clam shell, ready to take a drink. Her cunt will be well-lubricated to the touch. You must be sure you're near a couch or a bed, and if not, the floor will do fine, but you must get it in her quickly and gently...like one would pump a fragile well."

I thought of my tool being ready, cleaned and oiled like a hunting rifle, ready to ram her deeply, splendidly...and to fire a hot load of lead deep into her belly.

"Using condoms is like taking a bath with a raincoat on," she tells me. "The woman doesn't like it. If you're afraid of getting a dose then you shouldn't be fucking the woman. Any fear whatsoever will turn her sex mechanism off."

While she was talking to me, Dr. Boyle started to undress herself. It was to encourage me that all wasn't lost. How beautiful her soft movements looked, as she took her dress off, then her blouse. She left on her brassiere, her lace panties, stockings, her garter belt, and her high-heeled shoes. It was a pleasure to watch her undress. It was so dainty, so delicate. One wonders if a woman's delicate movements have been rehearsed, or is it just natural to a woman to look so dainty as she takes her clothes off?

There is something about a partially dressed women which is so much more inviting than a nude one. The parts that are covered are the parts that you want to see. Gawking is so much a man's way of looking at a woman...that I'm sure Dr. Boyle had it all worked out. She made sure she could see the bulge in my pants as she got ready to show me the rest of it.

Looking in the mirror

She went to the couch and sat on it, then told me to come sit there with her. She looked so wonderful, sitting in the soft leather couch, waiting for me to come pet her like I would a puppy. I sat next to her and she took my hand and placed it on her leg, just above the knee. There was a mirror on the wall in a perfect position for me to watch myself touching her.

"It's like a dancer," she told me, "who looks in a mirror to obtain gracefulness and poise." I stroked her leg up to where the silk turned to flesh. I placed my hand between her thighs and her legs opened slightly. I could see my hand in the mirror heading for Hector's horn. It was as if I was looking through an opened window at someone else. Then I smiled, stuck my tongue out and watched it wiggle as if I was licking an imaginary piece of flesh. I saw her hand move towards mine and felt its strength as it stopped me from going any further.

"Not yet," she whispered in my ear as she looked at my frantic tongue in the mirror. "I want you to take your tongue and lay it on the inner part of my thigh. Just lay it there and don't use it. Let me get used to it. Let me dream of it going in me. Let me be just a fraction of a second ahead of you."

I adjusted myself so I could see my tongue obeying orders, doing what she told me to do. Her legs parted, and I could see the inner part of her thigh. That part of the female anatomy, that when it's exposed, the drawbridge to the citadel is getting ready to be let down. She told me afterwards, as we summarized our session, that the whole procedure was to stimulate her imagination so that I could supply her with the rod at the right moment. The timing was of the upmost importance.

I left that day with a pain in my groin. I had blown the fuse. I had come in my pants like a teenager at a drive-in movie.

The sixth session was devoted to the tongue and the difference between licking and tickling

She began with her discussion of the human tongue, how profound the human tongue is, how it could magnify a small hole in the tooth and transform it into a crater. That of all the organs in the human body, the tongue alone was involved in six distinct functions, not four as has always been assumed:

speech...............articulation
chewing ....mastication
tasting.............gustation
swallowing.......deglutition
licking.............glyfication
tickling............gargarlismatation.

Then she told me that the tongue made the ear listen to the words that it articulated. The tongue could raise sexual images in the mind, with words created by the human species to evoke great sexual anticipation. The tongue was capable of gossip, of destruction, of resurrection, of love. One could, by the use of his tongue, charm a bird out of a tree, the pants off a woman, the money out of your purse. It could sell, it could buy. The list of what the tongue could do in articulation could go on forever. The tongue was so important in sex that it was without any doubt the second penis. The tongue could lick and with the proper strokes could bring about an orgasm in a woman with the intensity of an earthquake.

In this session she wanted me to take her clothes off, and begin kissing designated parts of her body. While I was undressing her, she told me to tell her what my eyes saw and what I felt. To use the mirror and to learn how not to get distracted watching myself. What she was doing, she said, was evoking a sexual synesthesis whereby all the senses work with each other, getting the mind into a high state of sexual excitement.

She had a beautiful body. I said I was amazed that the hair covering her altar was as dark as coal, and hidden in the dark forest was a pink opening, waiting for the right moment to be worshiped. She corrected me, and told me not to use poetical words to describe her parts.
She directed me on how to take her clothes off.
She told me when and where to stop.
When and where to kiss.
When and where to use my tongue in licking her.
Licking, she said, was a very advanced technique. A man could turn a woman off if his tongue tickled the woman instead of licking her. She lay her head back and brushed her dark hair away from her face.
"There's a big difference between thrusting the tongue or licking with the tongue. Tickling is to be avoided at all costs since it causes the female to become distracted. Most of the time the tickling is brought about by the tongue being stiff. This stiffness is caused," Dr. Boyle said, "by the nervousness of the male in not being relaxed, and his prana not being used properly."

There seemed to be so much to learn. One wonders how mankind ever survived before the good Doctors took over.

The Art of Tasting a Woman

Learning to taste a woman

I felt like a little boy being told how to pee, and how to lick his lollypop. I wondered why my father hadn't taken me to a Dr. Boyle when I was young to show me how I should touch a woman. And now she was going to teach me how to taste her. This should have been part of all little boys' training along with baseball, basketball, gym classes, music lessons, and all activities that prepare you for manhood and good civic character.

She ordered me to breathe properly and let my tongue relax. Then she told me to slowly, very slowly, run my tongue up her leg as close as I could get it to her altar, without causing any tickling.

Up to now I had spent a thousand dollars and I hadn't put my throbbing engine in her. Nor for that matter in my wife, who was increasing her constant complaint that she was tired, and told me not to bother her while she tried to get some sleep.

"You have to learn how to taste the woman," Dr. Boyle tells me. "Taste the saltiness on her skin that's produced by her excitement. When she's turned on, her saliva has an aroma that can raise a sexual activity to new highs. Her secretions have a sweetness to them that allows a subconscious flow of energy to enter your lower house, disintegrating your little ego…the little self. Rather than looking for a mutually explosive climax, you should learn how to enjoy the taste of a woman, letting your tongue seek out its own pleasure without being guided by your intellect."

I ran my tongue up and down Dr. Boyle's shapely legs. She opened them up, just a little, for me to look at her. "I'm not going to let you taste me down there," she said, "not today. I want you to understand first the pleasure of tasting the woman's perspiration, then her secretions. I want you to develop the awareness of sex as an energy-giver, a concept of pleasure that we miss in our modern rush to have an experience."

I didn't fully understand what Dr. Boyle was talking about, but it sounded good. I knew it was just a collection of words and thoughts jumbled up, but the application was what interested me. While I was with Dr. Boyle my suspicions about my wife with another man quieted down. I was being occupied by another woman.

Sex Education

Dr. Boyle was such a mysterious person. I couldn't help thinking, what type of a person would want to make sex her livelihood, or for that matter, what was the difference between what she was doing and what a whore would do? I wanted to ask her how she learned so much. But the diplomas on the wall were there to tell me that she learned all this at the university taking the following classes:

The tongue and its artful usage	201	M.W.F.	10:00
Cunnilingus and the modern man	202	T.Th.	1:00
Fellatio and urban living	190	M.W.F.	11:00

Deep-Finger Manipulation for the Modern Woman, given with special permission from the department.

The Philosophy of Sex from Pre-Socratic to the Patristic Period. With emphasis on Plotonius, Peripius, Demetrios and Augustine. This is to be given with the prerequisites of comparative Sex 300.

Sex must have fascinated her in order to become a sex surrogate. She must have taken her Doctorate in sex management. With a diploma on the wall, and a few terms, she was running a modern whorehouse right in the middle of a shopping mall and getting away with it. How many guys a day did she have tasting her ear, her leg, getting close to her cunt, and how much did you have to pay to put it in her? It was amazing what a woman could do with a diploma on the wall and her ass on a couch. It changed the whole atmosphere of sex.

The study of familiarity

After the 8th session I started calling her Ele, and she called me Jim. It seemed stupid to sit on the couch and finger her and call her Doctor Boyle. We had become clinical lovers. She cautioned me, and said that we weren't lovers. "We are humans trying to understand the mystery of sex, and the thought of a lover brings with it rejection, confusion and gender prejudices."

I asked her what her married life was like, and what her husband thought of her being a sex counselor. Without a moment's hesitation she told me of her husband, and how they had a wonderful relationship with each other. That he was an alternate-gender person. That he had a practice right down the hall, and he dealt with alternate-gender women who have problems in their relationships with alternate-gender males.

The thought was too confusing for me to understand. "In a way my husband and I are very lucky being able to compare notes with each other and find where our faults are at. After one of our note-comparing sessions, we really get turned on and create in us a great desire…to fuck each other."

At first, the way she described things and her choice of words confused me. She had a way of mixing clinically antiseptic words which made my feelings cold, with street words, which had a way of making my feelings hot.

She would sit on the couch with her legs wide open so I could see the inner part of her thighs, then ask me "Is your libido active?" Then ask me if I liked looking at her cunt. Which part did I like looking at the most, "the minor or major labia?" Or if I could describe to her the various female genitals I had seen in my life, and compare them as to shape, contour and esthetic beauty. Did I ever see an "ugly cunt"…one that made me cringe? Was there one that had a peculiar odor to it that repelled me? Then she would talk to me of marriage and her husband and my wife, and love, and people, while she took her clothes off, touched her "carpet" and asked me if I was ready to do some serious pleasure-seeking.

Aphrodisiacs

During the 9th session I asked Dr. Boyle "Do you have any pills for getting a woman turned on? It certainly would save us a lot of time if we could just take a pill when we are tired, and recreate the passion which has been taken out of us."

"What good would the pill do, if you don't know how to use your hands and tongue to bring pleasure to that excitement? There is no royal road to pleasure...pleasure must be taught."

My problem was, my woman couldn't stay awake long enough to go through the basics that dogs, cats, and all the creatures on Noah's Ark knew about, let alone all this touching and erogenous hunting.

What Dr. Boyle recommended would take up half of the nite. Pleasure requires time. The rich know about pleasure because they have the time to explore it. The poor are condemned for indulging in it.

The female breast

Maybe this erogenous-zone thought was merely crap. A fable that men developed to describe the mysterious woman. If parts of the woman were touched in the right sequence, in the right way, a combination of feelings will happen and turn the woman into a great fornicating monster, capable of devouring you. Somehow I felt that the fountain of youth had more chance of being found than a woman's trigger points.

I was told by Ele that "Man has always had a fascination with the woman's tits and the nipples that adorn them. He's given them poetic names to immortalize them. He's described their color, ranging from the subtle pastels of early spring to the deep reds and oranges of autumn."

I knew the breast as the place a man lays his head when tired, weary, sad and troubled. The first warmth outside of the womb was given to me by the beautiful tit of my mother. It's where I got my first taste of food and its life-giving nourishment, my first comfort, my first feeling of softness, my first fear that it would be taken away.

I told Ele that I cried my eyes out when the tit was taken from me and my mother made me drink from a cold tasteless cup. The tit has become a shrine to my life, not because it's a trigger, but because it's the first source of life. But what can a man tell a woman when he's lying on the bed with her, "Give me milk, nourish my soul..."?

It's a memory of pure pleasure making me cry out for the tit of my mother, and in my head I think that, because I want it so bad, I hope the woman needs to be sucked and her nipples tickled by my thirsting tongue.

Ele moved her bare legs a little to make me comfortable. "Here, lie on me," she said. "I'll let you suck my tit, but first you have to become a little baby lying in my arms with your little head in between them warm tits."

Touching a woman

The thought of laying my head in between the mounds of Venus made my insides bubble with pleasure and my heart palpitate, missing a few beats in the process. I laid my head down on her, while she whispered in my ear, "Take your hand, and with your tender fingers reach down and gently, very gently touch my…" and with a faint voice she whispers in my ear, "my……cunt."

I was startled. I felt the surge of excitement blow itself through me like a killer wind. I had become aware of not touching correctly. I was told that I was doing something wrong.

My mind drifted as I started to think of a woman's genital sensitivity. Would I touch it correctly?

I remember the first time I touched a girl...Eleanor…I touched her hand, then I held it. What a wonder touching was. I could spend a whole afternoon just lying under the sun holding her hand. I remember touching her lips with my fingers, letting my fingers enjoy the pleasure of touching and feeling the different textures of each part of my lover's body. But according to Dr. Boyle my senses, like my sense of tasting a woman, had been seriously deprived.

The price of touching

So far I had learned from the good therapist the following...that a tired bear won't dance, and for a hundred dollars, every week, I could talk to a live human for 45 minutes. If I touched, or fondled her, it would be an extra charge according to what I touched and played with. Or I could go down to Mr. Grenshaw's and pick up a doll for a few hundred, and amuse myself by changing programs to suit my fancy.

Money creates thoughts

It seems that when you pay for something, you start thinking more about it. I found that for every dollar spent, 30 minutes-worth of thinking goes with it. I was spending a hundred an hour, therefore I spent 3000 minutes of thought.

The Lexitorium

Words were invented in Dr. Boyle's lexitorium. Words that could make your ears perk up, or lie down, or just hang on the side of your head like a mop on a handle. I was paying to listen to words, like one throws money in a tray to hear the preacher tell him of heaven and hell, of the land of milk and honey awaiting him. It was a church I was in, a new type of church. It was a temple disguised as an office, where the temple whore, knowing the secrets of man, was willing to teach you the secrets of womanhood and the words that go with it.

I had entered a high-tech American-style psychological whorehouse, where words, promises and temptation were converted into money. Where promises were dangled in front of your eyes like pieces of candy behind a glass case. A place where things began with a diploma on the wall, a leather couch, a good-looking woman dressed like a window mannequin, and words that promised you a walk through the rings of heaven. It was a place where you go to tease yourself, to look, touch and listen, then go home, and carry the promise with you stuffed in your pants.

The examination of truth

It had become difficult to look at Dr. Boyle once a week, touching those well-shaped tits, touching her clinical sex organ, rubbing my finger up her butt, putting my tongue on the lips of her lubricated pisshole, and not being allowed to put it in her. "Look!" I told her, "You've been bullshitting me for the last three months. True, I've been able to keep my mind off my wife, but that's because I've had it on your ass instead of hers. If I haven't got you hot enough to let me fuck you, that means I've failed the course, and I have learned nothing other than how you get the money out of my pocket and into yours. Where once that hundred dollar bill was, now there's a hardon in its place waiting to be yanked on like I was trying to pull a root out of the ground. I got screwed," I told Dr. Boyle, "through my ears with a little left for the eyes and a little for the touch."

I was in a strange situation. I was now playing with two women. One was asleep and I would occasionally get my finger into her dried-up well. I would pull the covers back and shine my flashlite on her, flashing up her nude body with my Nifty Lite. Then I would begin with my tongue to gently taste her like Dr. Boyle instructed me. It was a wonderful eyeful but she was asleep like the Briar Rose, activated only by my imagination and nothing else. The other woman was awake, but was merely a paid surrogate who promised me I could have it if I touched the right places at the right time. It was the re-creation of Tantalus' punishment, a constant awareness of the ever-continuing pain. The torture of not having, when the object was right there in front of me.

My mind was teased beyond what it had ever known before. I had dreams of having both women in the same bed. I would lie there with Nomi snoring next to me, and dream up this scenario of lying in between both of them, of being smothered by the soft flesh of a woman's body, each hand touching another woman at the same moment, my tongue rushing from tit to tit, flooding my mouth with different tastes. Exhausting my tongue, I fall asleep. Knowing that both women had been bought, one with a 10-dollar marriage license, and the other with a weekly 100-dollar bill, plus handling expenses, which were totaling an average of $175.00 a week and going up.

There were certain things I had learned about touching, licking and other uses of my tongue, but it wasn't worth the money to go any further, and I think she felt that I was on to her scam. The closer I got to that golden pot she called her cunt, the greater the cost. I was touching her, then I was tasting her, and that cost more. Touching was the first step to reality, the first step to sexual bliss. Tasting was the second step. It was a trade-related problem, the customer was waking up.

But when you buy in, you always go back for just one more time, filled with hopes that you didn't make a mistake. I was condemned like Tantalus, Sisyphus, and Prometheus, to be nourished only on the dreams of having.

The last taste

I could tell she wanted to squeeze the last buck out of my pocket, when she told me at the end of our 19th meeting, "Look I'll be truthful with you, and I feel it's very important. If you're going to learn anything from this," she paused for a moment, her eyes wide open as if she just saw the resurrection, and with a great relief in her voice she tells me, "You're almost there. Every time you lay your tongue on me, I feel that moment getting closer. You've almost got me ready." She paused a minute, closed her eyes, slowly waiting for the thought to clear the air.

I finally understood the following...Dr. Boyle was not a woman...she looked like a woman, smelt like a woman, felt like a woman, and tasted like a woman...but really wasn't a woman. She was a dart board, a pinball machine, a wheel at a carnival that would lite up if you hit a bull's eye. She was like Ms. Judy who had a "wired-up rubber-plated pussy and a big asshole, programmed to squeak, to sigh, to moan and to fart all in different tones, pitches, and dialects."

The Last Session

The mirror of the imagination

How do you know when it's ready?

Paying to get rejected

What's real?

The good counselor was working on me again, using her voice like a can opener to pry open my wallet and get the last few bucks that were lying in it. She was pretending to succumb to my newly acquired abilities that she'd taught me. The test was, if I got to screw her...a woman who knew all the problems and answers about sex...I could theoretically work any woman into the bedroom. But if I didn't stay and graduate, I would never know if I had overcome all those mistakes I had been making about women.

Then there was another thought in my head, that I'd been had. By an educated slicker who took my money like a carni barker with a promise of the golden ring.
A freak show with mirrors and diplomas on the wall.
I was part of the show and for all I knew, I was being filmed, or worse yet, being looked at from some peephole in the wall by a paying student sexologist.

I had spent nine months in the womb of my creator. Was it so strange of a thought that I would want to re-enter the place where my life was created, to worship the citadel of my existence with the same words and awe I use to refer to the holiness of life?

I came to Dr. Boyle's office seeking help, and ended up wanting Dr. Boyle. I forgot about my troubles, I forgot my wife. It was true, one woman will help you forget another...but Dr. Boyle wanted me to talk about my wife. She would ask me to describe her and to pay attention to the smallest detail. She wanted to know how I made love to my wife. "I want you to do to me...step by step...just what you do to your wife."

I put my tongue on her belly button. "Oh that tickles," she said. The lites came on in my head. I must have looked startled because she said immediately, "I told you not to tickle a woman."
"I'm sorry, I'll try again."
"Forget the tongue, and take your finger and gently rub my cunt. Is this the way you touch your wife? Be careful, you're hurting me." I started to feel like a spastic stumbling between the legs of a wanting woman. Dr. Boyle was holding my hand as it rested on her sacred thigh. "I don't want to criticize you. I want you to feel like I'm giving you a move-by-move response to the mistakes you're making, which might be why your wife is withdrawing from you.
I want you to tell me just how you put it in her.
Do you put it in hard and fast, or do you put it in just a little at a time, letting her touch it as you put it in slowly?
Do you tell your wife how wonderful her cunt feels? That you really enjoy the wetness and the slipperiness?"

We had covered a lot of ground in the world of male-female excitement, and Dr. Boyle was, as she admitted, an expert at it. I never realized how instantly street words deface the world of make-believe and the citadel of love. She would touch her cunt in front of me and ask me to describe to her what I felt, in simple words.
Words blew into my head in gale-force winds, carrying my feelings to places I had never been before.

The mirror of the imagination

"First we have to understand that I'm playing the role of your wife, and in your mind your wife has become the other woman that you want to have. I, as your wife, am trying to guide you through certain movements that will assure you of getting her. I am your confidante, your advisor, your helper in getting and having that other woman."

In her enthusiasm to get my money, Dr. Boyle kept forgetting that my problem was a sleeping wife, who snored, farted, mumbled, ground her teeth, and at times barked like a dog. Touching her was like touching a Kamodo lizard, snoring in a state of pure lethargy...afraid that the bastard would wake up and tear my hand off my forearm, break a finger, tear off a thumb. There was a certain danger in what I was doing.

"Only an insane man would continue trying to make love to two women at the same time, and not really getting one or the other."
"That's good," she replied, "having the desire to make love to two women at the same time helps you overcome the fear of losing one or the other or both. Maybe we should start out today by you telling me how you've been doing with Nomi?"

Dr. Boyle was not only playing the role of my wife, she had now become my wife who was going to help me have the woman who was sleeping in my bed.

I needed words that lite up the nite. Words that turn a lily pond into a pulsating ocean.
Something must be broken for a sound to be created.
Something must be destroyed for a feeling to be born.

She looked at me with eyes that had been created for the occasion. They were colored and painted to represent desire beyond even the limits of a bedroom.
"I feel this is the day," the beautiful Dr. Boyle said.
"I want you to take your tongue and bathe me with it."
She slowly sat on the couch, then without disturbing the air around her she laid her head back and partially opened her legs.

I stood there looking at her. I didn't know if I should get on my knees and open the legs wider or put my head under her dress...was I supposed to take her clothes off...was it a pay game or was this the real moment...the moment in time that she wants me and I want her...the perfect moment when desire must be satisfied.

I must have been gawking at her because I heard her say, "Aren't you going to do something?" It was the wrong question, the wrong set of words.

Certain words had the ability to bring desire down to its most basic understanding. I found myself paying to hear words that most women used in bars and in the streets.

It was the wrong morning. I don't know why, but the words felt like a bucket of cold water had been thrown over me. The words, the commands for my tongue to come forward like a wash rag and bathe her ass, all came together in my head at the same moment, like matchsticks being shook in a cardboard matchbox. The images were as cold as glass. My tongue was tired. My prick was fresh. For me to use my tongue as a wash rag, I would have to be in love with her this very moment and I wasn't.

I saw a blemish on her thigh. It was a vein with a red splotch around it and blue in the center. I had never seen this before. It stood out like a glaring headlite on a dark nite.
She sensed that something was wrong. The bird was ready to flee the trap. The words were flat. She depended on my stupidity for another round of 100-dollar bills to feed her and her pimp husband down the hall.

"Are you getting shy on me?" she asked me with a voice as soft as a mother cooing to her baby. She had tired me out, like a cat tires a mouse, and what was once temptation was now pain. Her beauty was turning into ugliness. I could hear the money tinkling in her words. Strange, I had really never gave this thought an airing before. What got me started on this thinking was a gap

between the promise and the performance. The stopping of something, not the starting of it. It started out OK. It just stopped short. I had no complaints at the beginning, it's when you look back, like Orpheus did, that you lose Euridice.
"My wife went to sleep for some reason or other and I can't get her up, and I pay you to tell me the secret to wake her up."

The daughter of a siren started out again with the same line and the same drumbeat. I had to learn about the moon and the moon sister, of hormones, eggs and cycles. There was a right day and a wrong day. A sensitive moment and a nonmoment. There was a right week and the wrong week. There were books to read and breathing exercises to follow. Everything from vitamins to vegetarianism, to pamphlets and testimonials. The whole world was waking up to a good healthy screw, followed by a good healthy shit and all I wanted out of life was to do the same, make love to my wife. It seemed that I had reached the final and most logical question after paying $3,000, and facing the possibility of paying out another $1,000. I wanted to know a principle, some guiding thought I could carry with me out of this little shop.

"How do you know when it's ready?"
I asked her. "Is it like a good roast that you can smell when it's ready to eat, or does it have an aroma like bread in the oven? Will there be a sign that tells me it's ready to have now?"
"You're getting it," she said, "but the signs are a little different, and the smells more delicate."
It would require another $1,000 for the next ten sessions. This of course meant that I was right there, as close as I could get to the good Dr. Boyle's lovenest.

I had passed the point of no return. Once you pay and are almost there you'll pay that little bit more to get there. One more dollar in the shithouse and I would stay for another 1,000 dollars. I told her out front. "Either I graduate now and do a postgraduate course later or you don't get another dime out of me."
She looked at me with a look of total understanding, it's that look of sympathy just short of a big laugh.

"I can't tell you you've passed your course if you haven't. I think you've learned a lot, but you haven't really aroused me to the point where I would let you have it. You must realize a woman is delicate in matters concerning who she gives it to and for what."

Paying to get rejected

I was paying this semiwhore to tell me I couldn't get it because I couldn't turn her on. Maybe this was the lesson…through rejection I would understand *Hope*.

I don't know what or how she did it but I bought in for another $1,000 worth of lessons. I finally figured it out weeks later. She had hit on my hope button. It was hope. I had been bit by hope. The whore of all whores is hope. It was the last thing that was left in her arsenal of gifts...hope. I was still standing in the doorway hoping and waiting to get in.

She said that the real lesson I was learning was to be able to be with a woman, and not feel the need to put it in her. She told me that women know that when men get it off, they lose interest in the woman and go back to their bad habits of looking for other women. "You have to learn to be with a woman, and not want to..." and she winked at me, "do it to her." She smiled when she said it.

I consoled myself over the loss of $4,000 with the thought that I got to see what a wonderfully educated woman's bottom looked like. A beautiful mind housed in a beautiful body. A beautiful body which required money to be touched.

What's…real?

The thought came to me again. Was this really a counselor or was she a smart whore with a new way of making a buck? But then again, what difference did it make? If the diploma was real or not, her ass was real, her tits were real, that bush in the tundra was real, the office was real, and the paper on the wall was just paper, like all paper. Its only value was if you believed in it.

Thoughts of Suspicion

A word and its power

Intuition

The creation and the manipulation of a story

A married woman's need for a lover

A ***word and its power***

A word has the power to bring things together, to break things apart, to make one remember.

A look on the face gives it all the look of authenticity.

What I needed was a word that goes along with the look. A word that had the power to electrify all my fears into a swirling nitelite, searching out the devious, the silent shadows of suspicion.

I didn't want to rush the word, it had to be a word that would convey the right information, a word that must put one on the alert that all things are possible...when the human imagination is at play.

I was entering a world that, once entered, you never leave the same. I had spent months developing my suspicions and now I realized that my suspicions were centered on the suspicion of duplicity, the age-old malady of mankind, duplicity, and no one knew any more about it now than they did during the Great Flood. As a matter of fact, we probably know less about it now than we did in Year One. It can't be measured, it can't be drawn, photographed, explained, tested, experimented with, it's a word so powerful, a thought so frightening, that it turns your stomach. It begins somehow in some mysterious cauldron of feelings stirred up by rejection. Finally it becomes an attachment, walking with you like your shadow, sitting down to eat with you, lying in the bed with you, talking to you, but to prove its existence you have to be destroyed by it. Otherwise, it is just a feeling of doubt.

I was suspicious that my wife had entered into the world of duplicity. This was the word that I was looking for. Its definitions suited my fears…for now. This was to become the basis of my accusations. This was the cornerstone of my thoughts toward my wife, her duplicity. Her face, the blankness of it, was perfectly suited to what I suspected was going on. The face showed no guilt, remorse, pity...love or concern. It was a face delegated to no commitment.

I realized more than ever that duplicity was my main concern and objective....this is what I wanted to search out, but how? As I came to find, those that knew the essence of duplicity denied that there was such a method of thought. Its method was a secret, its inner mechanisms a mystery. If I could read her face, what looked like the arctic tundra would now become the maps of contrivance, with every little movement of the face a story of its own.

There were feelings I looked for on her face. There were feelings I wanted to find on that face of hers and couldn't. The face had a look of blankness on it, broken now and then with a smile of no concern. There was no way I could describe that look of nothingness on her face, to myself or to anyone else, and that's what scared me.

Intuition

At first I told myself that intuition is the necessary tool to discover the schemer and her scheme.
My intuitions told me that there was another man in the picture, and my intuition told me they had fabricated plans with each other, plans that did or didn't include me.
I had to believe my feelings, even though at the moment I couldn't prove otherwise. I had to trust my intuition.

I had developed a great sense of intuition. An intuition that I had to trust. I could never give it reasonable explanations. It was something I merely felt. I had learned to trust what I felt.

My musical career depended on it. I had to feel the crowd when I played. I had to allow myself the freedom of feeling things, while my emotions dictated the texture of my music.
My feelings told me what interpretations I gave the musical phrases.
My feelings told me what the crowd wanted.
My feelings were never wrong.
My feelings and my emotions were the tools of my trade.
The way I feel about anything is all I have to really depend on, whether it's music, people, places, or a woman. But was intuition enough to allow me to follow the scent of duplicity?

The creation and the manipulation of a story

I knew that everything could be manipulated by the storyteller...by the way the story was told, by the tones in the voice, by the expression in the eyes, and the mask the storyteller wore on his face. Suspicion could be a good thing if used properly. Suspicion is a good preventative, an assurance against duplicity and betrayal. But suspicion must have confirmation the way holy communion must. It must be able to bring you to a position of acceptance, and end before it becomes a disease of the soul. You cannot live with someone you suspect.

As the days passed I kept developing the stories that a suspicious husband would create when he suspects his wife of taking another male to some bed with her or to some dark parking area in the back seat of the car.

It wasn't just another male in a bed, it was that she loved someone else, which was even worse. Now she would cater to her new lover, to every whim and wish, while she left me to fend for myself. But why wouldn't she just get up and leave, if she had another lover?

A married woman's need for a lover

The only reason I could give myself was that there must be some general law that I was missing. Was a woman's need for a lover greater when she has a husband? The lover is less threatening and the husband more bearable, and somehow she can balance both of them into a harmonious life.

The husband's main purpose is to serve his function as the high mark of security, a social front, and the psychological excuse for female misery. Tomes have been written by women...denouncing the destructive boredom and familiarity that men have placed women in. "Kitchen whores" they call themselves, bedroom slaves, misused, overused, overexploited...and yet she seeks a lover...who needs her.

It's the lover's insecurity that makes him so appealing. He is the man of the moment. He is immediate like a drop of rain on a thirsty tongue, tomorrow he'll be gone. While the fancy of the woman's imagination keeps murmuring that the lover needs her, she hears the lover sobbing in the middle of the nite.

"I need you," cries the insecure lover.

"He needs me," cries the tormented wife. The nite is filled with the horror of not being able to go to him. Chained in her bed next to her husband, like a prisoner in a paddock. The only escape from her husband is to fall asleep and let her dreams bring her to her lover. His newness...invented and discovered, he's waiting to be explored. He is always attentive. He can afford to be, he's only around for an hour or so. Everything about him is new, his breath, his lips, his body, his curiosity. Even when he's downgrading her, the lover is exploring all those new things that the woman has.

A modern woman needs a husband...it is the only sane way to handle a lover. What an interesting thought. It sounds so appealing to find reasons still left for a husband and wife to live together.

I knew I was on to something that the fine-honed counselors and psychologist couldn't help me with, since they were involved in a scam of their own and as a husband, I was the main ingredient to that scam. I, with my problem, was the source of revenue for my dear Dr. Boyle, and it was in her office that I first came upon the secret language of duplicity.

In Search of Duplicity

The beauty of duplicity
The mask of the actor
The mask of holiness
The mask of duplicity
Studying duplicity
Modern virtues
Searching the universities for a teacher
Critical thinking
Waiting is an artform in itself
Religion is a good avenue to the study of duplicity
Duplicity has scary connotations
The two-faced god

I was so fascinated by the thought of duplicity that I started to see it in my mind as a subject fit for an artist, for only an artist could depict its complicated beauty.

The beauty of duplicity

It lies in the virgin domain of the imagination. It is the area of thought where one enters and finds that his imagination needs, not only the clarity of good logic, but also the divine assistance of fate. You need, like an actor, a face that can portray believability. A face that can convey honesty, sincerity, love and devotion, while all along the intent is to deceive.

Like a cryptologist, I would have to learn how to read the secret language of silence and deceit. I had to learn how to look at the face, and understand what it was hiding. Somehow I had to find the Rosetta Stone that translated duplicity into truth. I had to learn to read the subtle expressions on the face, the subtlety that appears when you ask a question and the answer is a stereotyped blank face, with a vintage story of labor and devotion, waiting to be told. At the moment all I had to base my feelings on was my wife's reluctance, her indifference and my suspicions.

Her face had a look of nothingness on it. A blankness of no concern. Again the same fears came in me, that I couldn't describe that look on her face...to myself or to anyone else and that's what scared me.

The mask of the actor

An actor, like a pilot in a rarefied atmosphere, needs a mask to survive. I knew even if my suspicions were on the alert, my eyes and ears could be fooled, the way an actor fools you into believing his role is true. But what is the mask I'm looking for which hides the true expression of duplicity? Is there another universal law that governs the expressions on the face? Do all humans show the same expression on the face? Does happiness always wear a smile? Do the eyes always lite up in amazement? Does sorrow express the exact opposite? Was there an expression of deceit and duplicity the same as there is one for happiness and sorrow? These questions kept appearing in my imagination, creating new areas of suspicion.

The mask of holiness

The icons in the church had the mask of something holy, something ethereal, not of this world. The look of Christ on the cross is an expression of earthly rejection. Moses must have worn a mask of amazement when he came down the mountain, carrying the tablets with the 10 Commandments.

I remember my grandfather who sculpted in plaster the faces of saints in the church. He was always afraid that he would create the wrong look on the face of a saint, and instead of making him look holy and reverent, he could, with the wrong move of his trowel, create the look of irreverence. "I can't be angry or drunk," he told me once, "when I'm ready to carve the face of a saint. The look on the saint's face must be of devotion, the eyes must show his inspiration by the divine word. The viewer must never suspect that my feelings of holiness were fermented by the good wine of the church. My hand must be guided by a higher order...my mind must be clear of all earthly objects and wants or I could, by the slightest movement, create a greedy-looking saint or an unrepenting Christ. I could, by one little error of judgment, create a mask of duplicity and create suspicion amongst the devout."

The mask of duplicity

If I was to learn what the mask of duplicity was, I had to find someway, somehow, to study it...but where? I couldn't just study my wife unless I had some knowledge of her activities other than what she told me. I would have to compare what she told me with what I knew, and the look on her face when she told it to me...but that wasn't enough.

To the trained observer the ability to maintain two postures, one deceitful and the other the perfect example of honesty, has been the hallmark of great rulers, politicians, men of the cloth, great actors, and political philosophers whose advice was "If you want to get ahead, develop duplicity to a fine art and make it part of your education."

Studying duplicity

How could I study duplicity? No one was called duplicitous anymore, the word had moved out of our usage. Duplicity had become, as far as I could detect, so much a part of the modern man's attire that without it he would dissolve into oblivion, unable to earn a living, find a woman, have a home, pay his bills, raise his kids, keep his wife.

Modern virtues

Duplicity had reached into every corner of life. Two-facedness had changed into the modern virtues of ambition, salesmanship, leadership and tolerance, and yet there was no place I could go study it as a pure artform. There was no academic course, as I found out, in Duplicity. It was called by other names and categorized under other subjects. Duplicity had taken on, in my mind, the position of the mother subject of all of man's endeavors, the grammar of human expression, the matrix of all human creativity, the core of human art, the power of all observations, the theme of tragedy...and yet there was no school offering a course to study it at its basic level. The modern mind had failed to create a methodology in order to study duplicity systematically. We learn duplicity the hard way, "by being took."

Searching the universities for a teacher

Like the Platonic man possessed by the thirst for knowledge, I looked everywhere for a teacher to teach me duplicity. I began my search by contacting the universities around my area to see if they were offering courses in the divine subject that had reached humungus proportions in my head. The Department of Philosophy seemed to me to be the first place to begin. It seemed logical to me that philosophy would have asked the questions...
What is the nature of duplicity?
What is the relationship between duplicity and success?
Can one study duplicity without becoming duplicitous?
It was a worthy subject capable of arousing great expectations. I was sure that Philosophy had covered duplicity and its possibilities.

Critical thinking

I called the Department of Philosophy and asked if there were any qualified teachers teaching the art of duplicity. I was asked what I meant by duplicity, and they assumed I meant someone who merely lied to you for a philosophical purpose. They offered a course of mental purification called Critical Thinking. A subject which was almost guaranteed to ferret out the most devious minds by merely studying the structure of their language, the failure of their logic, and the grammar of deceit. I felt I had found it, the stone of recognition, the equipment necessary to survive, not only my wife's infidelities, but the attempts of modern times to destroy the human will. I made an appointment with the head of the philosophy department. I wanted to know what I was getting into, and if the subject was suited to my needs.

I met the professor in his office. A little man with piercing eyes...the eyes of a rug merchant describing his most prized rug. He looked busy, so I got down to the point of the matter as quick as I could. "I'm interested in studying human duplicity." Before I could finish he threw up his hands as if he had seen the Almighty. "Wonderful!" he yelled, "Absolutely wonderful. People are catching on." Then he got a serious look on his face. He told me that his subject seemed to fit my needs. "I named it," he said. "I have developed it. I have geared it to prepare the modern busy man to filter the news media for falsehood, deception and organized lies. I can show you how to spot false advertisement, phony phone solicitations, credit-card scammers. I can show you how euphemisms are used to deceive, how deception is fostered on the hapless, as Orwell had said so pointedly, 'by letting the meaning choose the word, and not the word choose the meaning.' Philosophy has finally found its way into modern life."

The good Herr Professor said that he was proud that he was part of the defensive team seeking out the pedlars of deceit. He continued to expand on his belief in his subject. "We are going to seek it out and destroy it. We are going to make Critical Thinking as common to education as butter and toast is to breakfast. Let's get down to business," he told me with his face glowing like a

lantern in the dark. "I have laid out an outline that critical thinking will cover in a semester." He picked up a piece of paper off his desk and handed it to me. "Here," he said, "I have the class outline, give it a glance." I ran my eyes down the list.
People management
Salesmanship
Marketing
Self-development
Leadership and the corporate executive
Race relationships
Mediation techniques
The deception of tolerance
Reading the newspaper

I handed the paper back to him and he looked at me, his jaw jutting out, convinced that he had discovered the operational law of bullshit. "Sin labore nihil," he tells me, his chest popping out of his tailored shirt. "Without labor there is nothing. This class requires a lot of work. Ten books, 3 term papers, 4 book reports, 4 class presentations, weekly quizzes and 3 exams."

He gave me the feeling that if it's spoken, written or read, you could catch the devil lying. But what if you were dealing with a woman who didn't speak to you, and only answered a direct question that had to do with basic things around the house? I felt, to be fair to the good Herr Professor, I should tell him what my real needs were. As quick as I could. I laid it all out for him.

"I'm trying to find out," my voice had the hesitation of a novice confessing to his first crime, "if my wife has a lover, and I need to study her duplicity in order to catch her." I told him I wanted to learn how to look at a face and know that it was lying to me. "I know what an honest man's face looks like. His eyes look straight into yours. His face has the wrinkles of honest toil, an honest smile, an honest hand, firm to the grip, calloused from work. But women don't have honest faces, they have beautiful faces, and anything can hide behind beauty. I want to know what a female's face looks like when she's practicing duplicity on me."

"I don't understand you," he said. "I'm really having a hard time following what you're saying."

I tried to explain to the professor what I needed to learn. "Rafael painted beautiful Florentine whores as the Madonna and Child, and gave them the look of purity, of virginity, of un-touchedness, un-slickness, un-deceivingness. That's why men wanted virgins, they felt purity was honesty in a woman."

He looked at me with those piercing eyes filled with apathy and disgust. He must have felt that I was going to use his subject to penetrate the foulest of subjects, marital distrust, wayward women, and a lover in the woodpile.

"I don't want to study the duplicity of newspapers, selling and management," I told him. "I want to study the duplicity of human emotion." I knew I was walking on shaky ground. I told him I never read the newspapers or looked at TV. There were too many books in the world, and most information was the creation of someone's imagination.

With a look of deep agitation on his face he asked me, "What is it you want?" By now I was starting to feel depressed listening to him.

"I know people lie," I told him. "Most of the time people don't even know they're lying, but it hurts no one. Some lie by not saying anything, letting you assume whatever it is you want. Others get a great pleasure out of it, their lives are built around it. You become important to their lie. This isn't a con job, it's an art, it's a performance, it releases magnetic fluids in the erotic channels. That's what I want to study. Can you teach it to me? If you know how, tell me, or tell me where I can go and find someone to help me."

I'm sure he felt my honesty because he told me that he didn't think his course would help me. He assured me there might be a course given, maybe in the political science department, and with a look on his face of one who had just smelt the foul odor of decaying fish, he showed me the door and closed it behind me.

The next day I called the political science department, and a beautiful female voice answered. Realizing that people take offence even at the mention of duplicity, I was more discrete this time. I didn't mention my needs, I merely said that I heard there was a class given on paranoia and duplicity in world politics.

Her voice was manicured to perfection. "The political science department," she said, "has given a class in Machiavellian Ethics, which included what might be considered the affirmation of duplicity." She didn't know when the class would be given again. I might try the Psychology Department.

The Psychology Department was giving courses in the following:
Stress management
The deviant personality in literature
Group counseling and the modern woman
Negative thoughts and gestalt therapy
But there was nothing on duplicity. They referred me to the Sociology Department who in turn referred me to the Lloyd Whittaker's Bible College. By now I was feeling discouraged. So far, it was a dead-end road. I gave the old Bible college a try, but I really didn't expect much.

I made an appointment with the Dean of Admissions, Dr. Horonemus Bolley, for 3:00 P.M. on a Friday afternoon.

Waiting is an artform in itself
I waited outside his office till 3:30 and he hadn't arrived yet. Waiting is always a way of purification. One waits for everything to happen.
One waits for success
for happiness
for vacation
for acceptance
for promotion
for love
for marriage
wealth
health
fame and death.
In the long span of waiting you either develop patience, or you get up and leave, and just as I was getting ready to get up and go, Dr. Bolley made his entrance.

Out of the blue smoke of mystery he appeared, his zipper still open, and a flash of dribbled piss still on the left side of his pants. Prostate trouble I thought, age has its own form of possibilities to wait for, diapers and rubber panties. Maybe Bolley was testing me out. If I waited I had something important to say, to ask and finally, to pay. "Sorry I'm late," he said. He stuck his hand out to greet me. I didn't want to shake his hand. His prick was on the left side of his pants, that meant he was right-handed, and Westerners aren't as clean as the Arabs or the Indians when it comes to touching body parts. It was no longer a secret that certain cultures always use their left hands for touching parts of the body that are by their nature foul. Leaving the right hand for greetings, eating and handling the sexual organs of a female.

He saw my reluctance to shake his hand, and probably felt it was due to some strange eccentricity. He more than likely had some of his own. He smelt of urine and his office was messy. I felt I had entered the wrong place, but since I was here I might as well tell him what my desires were all about. I asked him right out front if they offered courses on the study of duplicity.
"This is a Bible College," he said, "and we educate future ministers who go out into the world that's filled with duplicity. Though I must admit, Christianity did start out with duplicity and betrayal."

Religion is a good avenue to the study of duplicity

He was frank and honest with me. He really turned me on to thoughts I had never heard before. For a moment I felt I had found my man. He told me that the history of mankind was filled with the stories of duplicity, that if I wanted to study the darker side of human nature, it would take a lifetime of work. "And," he went on, "to what avail?" Duplicity by itself was meaningless. If I wanted to study human duplicity, then religion was a good avenue to the subject.

Duplicity has scary connotations

"The word duplicity," he said in a matter-of-fact tone, "has scary connotations. It implies moral corruption, deep-rooted psychological problems, even evil. *Diaboliko* was the term used

by the Classical Greek to describe duplicity. Diabolical to the Classical Greek meant coming at you from two different directions at the same time. It had been, in the recorded past, a term that was connected with betrayal, the foulest of human conduct.
It was considered by the classical Greeks that duplicity was the mechanism of betrayal. Without duplicity you can't have betrayal. Duplicity is the basis of sycophancy, of hypocrisy, deceit and cunning."
He stopped and looked at his watch. He either had more to say and checked to see if he had the time, or was baiting me to go for the whole course. I asked if they offered a degree in the art of duplicity. I knew Machiavelli had written a book on the education of the Prince where he mentioned that duplicity was essential to the ruler. "The Bible spoke of it," Dr. Bolley tells me, "both the Old and the New Testament."

The two-faced god
He told me that in his opinion, through years of experience, there were certain people better suited to duplicity than others. They had a face for it, a blank look that was like an impenetrable veil. It was the ability of an inborn genetic talent to be two-faced like the god Janus. "Without this ability it is virtually impossible to be duplicitous and not be caught at it."

He was describing that blank look on Nomi's face. This guy was really cooking. He had what I needed. With the proper study and the proper teacher I felt I could become versed in human duplicity without becoming duplicitous myself, and be able to appreciate the moves and machinations of my wife, and even learn to appreciate her treachery without condemning her. But I would have to study religion for the next four years, and by then my wife would have gone through another dozen lovers.

Sensing that I didn't look the type who would want to spend four years in a theological seminary, he ended our meeting by telling me, "You might find what you're looking for in a drama school where they teach the face of sadness, the faces of love, grief, despair, happiness, and thereby teach you the face of duplicity.

You might want to study Judas Iscariot's face as he kissed his friend before betraying him, but it would seem to me," and Dr. Bolley stopped and looked at his watch, then at me, "a person who is duplicitous has found a way to banish it from his face and eyes. The eyes are the mirror of your soul. It would be better if one could see the eyes of Judas on his way to the tree where he hung himself. Did his eyes have the look of shame in them?".

There was a long silence and he looked at me. I had a feeling that he was saying something to me that I couldn't understand.

He thanked me for considering his school, but was sorry he couldn't help me any further. He looked at his watch again. This time he didn't bother to stick his hand out to shake mine. He didn't bother to get up from the chair he was sitting in. I had disappeared with the last word of his sentence.

Having Someone Else's Wife

The woman is the celestial navigator

You have to be good friends with the husband

The requirements

The beginning of my search

Peter and Sissy

Sissy

Peter

Obedience to a woman

A man creates a beautiful woman

It takes many men to make a beautiful woman

In order to get rid of my suspicions I had to begin with some plan, some stratagem to unearth the duplicity of my wife. My methods to discover my wife's lover were not developed enough to catch a fish in a pond, let alone a woman who had developed her skills in bedrooms with other men. A woman who has learned how, does not get rattled easily. You just don't accuse her and hope that she'll break down and confess to you. She keeps her life clear, distinct, and secretive.

If I was going to catch my wife doing whatever it was she was doing, I would have to do something different in order to catch her. There was no use in wasting my time with academic nonsense. If I wanted to study a duplicitous woman, I had to find one.

I needed a woman that I knew and whose husband was my friend. I had to find a woman who would be willing to betray her husband and make love to his friend. I needed a husband that I knew well enough so I could be there and look at her face as she lied to him. I wanted to be so close to her when she filled his ears with stories and denials, that I could watch the corner of her lips twist and the smile of duplicity paint her face. This, I thought, was the most necessary element in my understanding of this complex world of duplicity.

I had to know the husband in order to be there to study her, her methods, the looks on her face as she moved facts and verbs, nouns and adjectives, threading them all together to achieve her divine objective...the betrayal of her husband. I could also, by being present, watch the husband in his gullibility, performing as her audience, and I, also her audience, amazed at her duplicitous performance and her talents to pull it off.
The same story would have two appreciations at the same moment...her husband appreciating what he thought was her honesty and concern for him, and I, her lover, appreciating the artistry of her dishonesty and her concern for me.

The woman is the celestial navigator
If I had told anyone what was on my mind, I would have sounded like a dangerous man to have around. A person who's not bound by all the cultural taboos, ethics, mores, and just plain good fellowship. I consoled myself and dissuaded my guilt with the thought that no woman will let you have her unless she wants you. She is the celestial navigator to the bedroom. She guides you with eyes and smiles, sighs and promises. You can dream all you want about which woman you want, but if she doesn't give you the green lite, your dreams are merely so much material for a round or two of masturbation.

You have to be good friends with the husband

I knew the husband would have to be a friend of mine so I could be trusted in the house. I couldn't show up and get that close to his wife unless I had the husband's confidence. I had to be his friend. My curiosity would be fed, not only by my study of his wife, but also by the confidential information the husband would tell me concerning his wife, as I posed in front of him as his friend. I would be the first to find out if he suspected his wife. I would hear how his wife loved him and took care of every need and want he had.

I would be connected to his emotional world as well as his wife's. There was also the emotional problem of having had her...to share her with her husband and the thoughts of her in bed with him.

Since I was doing the taking this probably would not depress me as much as the thought of Nomi being in some motel room with her lover.

The requirements

I needed a good duplicitous situation for my documentation. I needed a couple who had apparent love between them, while the wife was capable of being promiscuous. Not a sexaholic nor a nympho who would take anyone on for the nite. I didn't want a sick woman. I wanted an ordinary woman, a common woman, a housewife of ordinary intelligence, a woman who enjoyed having a lover every now and then to feel the strength and the exhilaration of love. A woman who didn't want to destroy her marriage or her way of life. I needed someone who had found a way to do this. A woman who in essence loved her husband on condition that she had others who fondled her in strange beds or the back seats of cars, on a sandy beach, in the grove of the park. All she needed were a few moments of darkness to keep the public eyes off the naked flesh.

I was looking for a couple whose husband was the most trusting and whose wife the most likely to betray him. It was a matter of proper selection. I didn't want to make an error, so I had to make sure that I was accurate in my assessments.

I had never done this before. The real problem was...I had no way worked out to select the right woman. It was in the hands of fate, and my expectations would have to be handled by luck.

I had to allow myself also a breath of honesty, and not try to make myself out as an idealistic victim, driven by my loveless wife to the bedroom of a friend's home. My needs were different. My intent wasn't to have a woman for a lover in order to satisfy some inner need for love. My interest was far more simple. I wanted to see with my own eyes and hear with my own ears…the presentation of love and devotion by a promiscuous wife to her husband, while I, the hidden lover, was standing there next to her as if I was invisible.

There were a few more requirements. The woman must not know why I'm doing this. In her mind it would be seen as a love affair, and I as a lover she had a need of. Her reasons for doing it weren't my concern. Her methods of execution were what my interest was all about, not her reason for doing it.

The beginning of my search

I had to begin my search for this woman somewhere, so I began by the selection of four couples I knew, knowing them well enough to be able to summarize their home activities, their occupations and depth of sensitivity.

Peter and Sissy

I finally narrowed it down to Peter and his wife Sissy. They kept entering my plans, but I kept putting them to the side because of my close connections with both of them and our long friendship with each other.

Not only had I known them for what seemed like an eternity, but I also liked both of them. Whenever they invited you to their home it was with open arms. You never felt like a guest, who is always a stranger. It felt as if you were in your own comfortable world and you always hated to leave. I felt a twinge of remorse as I thought of them for my needs, but they filled the bill so wonderfully that it was impossible to get them out of my mind.

There was also a footnote to the story. I had heard from a friend of mine, Richard, a painter of great talent, that Sissy had once posed for him at his studio and that she had "an easy way about her." He never said that he had gotten "into her," but knowing Richard as well as I did, all that was left out of the conversation was the exact word that pinpointed the act. But then again, men love telling others about women who have loved them, and attribute to women their own fantasies of conquest and love. Men have a strange form of deceit. It must originate in the mechanisms of masturbation where innocent women are used as the icons for the daily offering to Priapus and his hard tumescent prick.

Sissy

The only way I can describe Sissy is...a dreamy look in the eye and a soft voice. An attraction that certain women possess. She had a look on her face that promised the beholder a special kind of love. Before this thought came to my mind, I saw Sissy's beauty as a form of a woman's honesty. Goodness was beautiful. Innocence was beautiful. Moral and proper attitudes were possessed by those women who had beauty. An ugly woman was more than likely a bitch, a witch, a hag. Or for that matter, no one really gave a shit as to what an ugly woman's morals were.

Peter

Peter was an easier person to describe. He had good things to say about everyone. He trusted everyone. He projected his own world onto everyone around him. He was born, it seemed, without the ability to have suspicions. Why would any one want to harm him? If you came to his house, he made you feel at home. His sense of hospitality was profound. You never felt as if you were an intruder, you never got the sense that you shouldn't have called. His generosity was heavenly, his conversations were enjoyable. As a person I couldn't have found a better friend. It was all so easy.

We had known each other since we were students. We drank together, and as the Greeks would say, we broke bread together. I had been his confidant, his soul brother. We had spent much time together. When he became aware of Sissy's existence, I became his confessor. He told me how his heart palpitated when she came near him, that his hands became sweaty and his tongue dry and fat, lying in his mouth like a beached whale.

Obedience to a woman

He told me how weak he felt in front of her. If she had asked him to show his love by jumping off the bridge, he thought he would have done it. He wanted to obey her, totally, as if obedience is how one shows his love for another.

He was afraid to get too close to her. She dominated his existence and she didn't even know it.

A man creates a beautiful woman

I knew from experience that women can't see their own beauty, no more than a guitar can hear its own notes or a holy man understand his own holiness. Women forever look in mirrors, searching for their beauty, asking the mirror to tell them "who's the fairest of them all."

Sissy liked being looked at. Every time I looked at her the parts and pieces of her beauty assembled in my head and a smile came across her face as she looked at me enjoying her.

It takes many men to make a beautiful woman

One man tells the woman that her ass is beautiful, another man tells her...her eyes are so dreamy. Someone else says her tits are two of the seven wonders of the world. After a kiss someone says her lips are soft and moist, her kiss is passionate, her breath a fragrance from a petal, her hair so beautiful. Another says the leg is so shapely and firm, the nose sculptured by nature to utter perfection, the cheek bones deliciously high, the chin perfectly proportioned.

One word at a time...a word from tall guys, short guys and in between, by Joe Blow and Bobby Magee, by Sammy Spoon, Steve, Al, Larry, Art, Bob and Gonzo. Some smart, some stupid, some drunk, and the image of the beautiful woman has been created...and the woman becomes complete. Then the man seeks out his reward for making her beautiful. He shows her evidence of her beauty, a throbbing engine hidden in the pants, just a few inches away, waiting, like a missile to be launched.

How Peter overcame all the obstacles of Sissy's world I don't know, but one day he asked me if I would be his best man at his wedding. I still have the picture of his wedding with his beautiful wife Sissy. A big broad smile on her face. They seemed like a perfect match. They never seemed to argue with each other. Why did I even think that Sissy would become part of my scheme?

Sissy

Thinking of my friend's wife

Fate definitely must have been guiding the next move, because one day, while I was deep into thinking about

Sissy and what would be the perfect time to start on my plan to have a friend's wife, Peter called me up and left a message for me to call him.

It had been a long time since we had seen each other and it was natural that I repay his call with a call of my own. I called Peter and Sissy answered the phone.

I apologized for not calling sooner, but I had been, since my marriage, caught up in the problems of married life. She offered me advice and I thanked her for it. Then she asked me if I'd like to come over...there was a pause in the voice like a rest in a musical phrase.
Here was my opening and before I could make up my mind what to say I heard her softly ask "Soon maybe...even today?"

Fate was good to me this time. She said Peter was out doing something and by the time I got to their house he'd be back. Perfect timing, it was destined to be.

It took me about an hour to get there. I took my time. I wanted to be careful that I didn't look too anxious and yet I didn't want to waste any precious time. All the way to Peter's house I kept thinking how fortunate I was that I had both Peter and Sissy as friends.

It wasn't an easy task I had set myself. To want another man's wife is one thing, but to actually pull it off is a problem in itself. How do I convince her that she should have me along with her husband? How do I convince her that she should create a problem in her life? What words do I use to lure her? I was going to a performance and I didn't know what pieces I would play or what the audience wanted to hear.

I could play the flatterer, the man who pays attention to her, makes her feel important. I had to create in her a need for me. But to do this requires time, a great amount of time. There is no magic word. There are a lot of words, and when they are all put together they tell the woman that I want her, need her, desire her. Passion is the key to it.

Peter's not home

I wasn't interested in seeing Peter. I really had nothing to talk to Peter about. It was his wife, whatever that meant, that I was interested in, and the sooner I could get her alone the sooner I could pursue my ends.

I didn't see Peter's car outside the house. I thought he must be parked in his garage. I knocked and Sissy opened the door. She stood in the doorway dressed in a rose-colored housecoat and just looked at me, never saying a word. When I think of it now I feel like it was a dream created to satisfy my loneliness...but nevertheless its creation brought about a moment when something was going to take place.

You can feel the electricity in the air before a storm breaks loose.
You can feel the stillness before a hurricane.
The silence before an earthquake.
The magnetism of human chemistry.
The fragrance of musk, the stillness of passion.
I looked into her eyes and they were glittering with the fluids of wanting. She had read my cards, my intents, my wants, my needs. She was a woman, and like all women, she was a visionary, a prophetess, a conjuror of magic. In the aura of the mysterious the woman is supreme.

I was standing at the top of a 100-story building looking down. A feeling of dizziness overwhelmed me, a sense of panic.
My hands began to sweat
my tongue became heavy
my heart began to palpitate
my legs felt weak. I was afraid to move, as if doom awaited my next step. But once you miss the moment it's gone for eternity. It was now or never...no second chance. I didn't care if I got entwined in the awesomeness of the divine and fascinating female sex organ. There was no more time to think about it. Sissy was doing the arranging, the moving. I was the bull and she was the matador. Maybe she smelt my odor, my spunk, the magnetic fluid oozing out of my fingertips. I was a dog pissing on the doorstoop.

"Hi!" she said with a smile on her face. She had it all under control. I felt I could trust her to guide me through all the complications of the introduction.

When the feelings are waiting to be fed, nothing need be said. It happens without too many words or schemes. Her words broke the spell of the moment. I found myself in the house, the door closing behind me and on my way to the couch. There was no resistance, no lost moments, no inane babbling and dull conversation of who…you…him…her.

A feeling of gratitude overcame me. I felt like saying thank you. She saved me the effort of having to plan, scheme, create stories, give excuses, develop my contrived discussion. Spending hundreds of hours in high states of exaggerations...so I could screw her.

Where is the husband?
The most obvious phrase came out of my mouth. The words that would set the tempo of this play and the intent of my motives.
"Where is Peter?" I asked her slowly and with desperation in my voice. I had mentioned Peter's name. I was in Peter's temple and to mention his name, in such an informal way, was blasphemy. My prick became immediately hard. The exhilaration of something so profane made it all the more critical. It was something we had to do together, dupe the same person and both enjoy the duping. We could now plan our activities always with Peter in mind.
"He's not here," she said in a soft, faraway voice.

In its own strange way the play had beauty. We were becoming the loving parents of our deceit.
"When will he come back?" I was afraid too many questions would destroy the moment.
"In a few days." She uttered the magic words again, this time more distinct and slower. "He...is...not...here."

How strange the mechanics of fate are! If someone else had called ahead of me, this moment would never have happened…someone else would be getting ready to have her. I would have been placed on hold, lost in the confines of Muzak, and told "Please call back again...some other time...when Sissy is available."

It takes a great imagination to explain events, and trying to piece all the parts together can drive you out of your mind. The schemes and the plans in my head were meaningless. I came to visit and life changed. For three days, almost to the moment that Peter came home through the door, I was on top of his wife. She let me have her around the clock and in every imaginable way. What made it possible for me to continue was my intent. I didn't intend to break up someone's home nor did I intend to run off with his wife. My intent was to merely study deceit, duplicity and the effects on the wife when she has a lover. If we were careful we could do what we wanted and no one need be the wiser.

I wanted to study her, like one would study a fish in its own habitat, in its own world while foraging for food. I wanted to watch as it ate. I wanted to study its sexual habits. I wanted to study a woman in her own world. A woman who would, by her own desire, betray her husband. I knew what I was to do, there was no guessing, no hesitation. The moment was caught in the storm. The only thing that could destroy it now would be a change of heart, a moral twinge, a fear of being caught, getting up and leaving or Peter coming home unexpectedly, and having to show great hypocritical happiness at seeing him.

The power of the female sexual organ

I had to marvel at the awful power that the cunt has to the human male. Kings have fallen prey to it. Religious men have suffered trying to stay away from it. Sons have killed their fathers, the famous and the infamous determine their success by the beauty and quantity of females they have around them. Something so powerful to the mind of man that he has created hundreds of symbols of grandness and eloquence to describe it. It's been called a rose, an altar, black suns in the shining lite, a star.

Not only was this organ beautiful, but it was dangerous. Not only was it necessary but it was perfect and it was guarded. An imploding pit of the perfect (O). Not only did man guard it, he worshiped it, knelt in lingual prayer in front of it. He kissed it and brought gifts to it. Robbed and pillaged for it. Drew and carved it on the walls of caves and churches, resurrected it in every form possible. Made statues of it, created art for it, adorned every great city with it. Created laws to protect it and punished the transgressors with long imprisonment, floggings, burnings, hangings, quarterings. And now it was my turn to take the chance of being caught inside another man's house with his wife.

I couldn't use the phrase I-had-her, that would have been a simpler process. I was like an army of men all standing in line to have her. How and where I found the energy and the stamina to continue, I can only attribute to the magic a woman can have for a man. We couldn't stop long enough to piss. I was in his house, in his bed. I didn't care if hell opened its doors and drug me in. The deceit, the thought of something forbidden was driving me to a frenzy, a passion akin to madness, a profound feeling of doing wrong that took my breath away.

I wanted to ask her if Peter made her feel this good, but I didn't want to enter in competition with Peter. It would have changed the complexion of my plans. Instead of looking for the mask of duplicity, I would be concerned with the obligation of giving pleasure. I told her I never had a woman that made me feel so good. She smiled...a big smile of satisfaction for a job well done. Like a priestess that sets out the mantle on the holy altar in order to lay our naked bodies on it, she changed the bedsheets so we could have our own clean love-cloth for the evening. I helped her make the bed and fold the corners. She complimented me on how well I did it.

I thought of going home for a few hours, just to be seen, to eat with my wife, tuck her in the bed, watch her yawn, and leave as soon as she fell asleep. But while I was on Sissy I forgot I had a wife. I was tied to Sissy with my umbilical cord. My divine root was in her, swollen like a dog's swage. I had never been treated so well. She never let my passion cool. It was lit by her femaleness to a blazing fire. This was truly a woman's triumph, and Sissy gloried in it like a saint in her perfection, knowing that the secret was in the ceremony and the ceremony was in her bed.

I had a need to say something to her. I wanted to thank her for making it all so easy for me. In my wildest daydreams I never expected such a treat. "I can't imagine Peter leaving you for a moment," I told her. It was the second time Peter's name came up and a twinge of excitement came over me again.

The husband becomes my enemy

For a brief moment Peter became my enemy. This was my conquering vengeance. I was hiding from him and the thought bothered me. One doesn't hide from his friend. I had to make him my enemy, my adversary. I had to create reasons, objects, sounds, conditions that I didn't like about him. I never had any reasons before, nor was I aware of any, but now they were essential to the plan. He was my problem, my obvious regulator as to when and where I was to have his wife. He would, by his very existence, curtail my movements, keep me on my toes, and help develop in me the distrust so necessary to carrying out this plan.

Berating the husband

I felt the need to berate him, in the cruelest way possible, by soft, not-so-evident flattery. Even in this Sissy was willing to help me overcome the fear and other problems that a wife's lover faces, by telling me Peter had lost interest in her.

"Peter is too self-centered," she said,
"at times indifferent,
sometimes boring,
usually demanding,
extremely unreasonable,
carefully insensitive."

She said she just didn't connect with him the way she did with me. She felt comfortable with me as if I was some soul brother. Everything was right. Our chemistry was right, the nose hung right on the face. She knew the right stories to tell me at the right

time. She seemed ready to provide me with what was necessary to despise him at the right time. She felt justified in what she was doing, and I became Sir Perceval, the Virgin Knight come to her assistance on my way to find the Holy Grail.
According to her I was here to save her from her ultimate destruction, from a life of dismalness and utter gloom. But for the time being, it really made no difference. He was away, far up in the mountains and he wouldn't be back for three days.

The most exciting sexual activity
Though words have been created to make the intolerable bearable and the awful seem good, something lurks down deep inside the human creature that makes the fucking of another man's wife the most exciting and dangerous social activity. It has all the necessary forbidden ingredients for both man and woman. Secrecy, duplicity, and made up imaginative pleasure stories.
"There is so much I don't know about you," she said as we lay on the bed naked. How much of this conversation was memorized from constant repetition and usage in motel rooms, was hard to say, but I knew these were the opening salvos to being rediscovered by a woman. A beautiful woman.

She would fill in the me that was missing and in return I would love her for bringing me my hidden Identity.
Sissy was so exciting that I forgot at times why I was here. It was the same when I was with the counselor. I had forgotten why I went there, and I got involved with her instead. I found myself wanting Sissy to discover more things about me. To tell me what she thought of me. I wanted to hear it.

Fascination for the perfect (O)
I was hungry for the mental dinner a woman can give you. A dinner of what her husband didn't have and I did. Evidently Peter was not enough for her, she needed me also. I was attracted to her, a magnetic attraction a man has for a female, that defies explanations. The shape of her hips, the way she walked around the bed, the way her foot rested on the red bedsheet, the way words caressed her lips, her long slender arm brushing her

golden hair. A little pearl in the lobe of her ear. The attraction was so powerful that I was sure I had entered into the inner sanctum of the laws of attraction. The way shit attracts flies or sweetness the ant. The way a magnet attracts metal and the sun attracts the planets. A form of attraction that's frightening in its all-consuming power. A form of attraction that's fused with the fascination and reverence that my relatives, millenniums ago, had for that hole that has been referred to as the perfect (O).

Any thinking would destroy the animal pleasures I was having. Holding her bare flesh in my hands. My body lying on her bare tits. Jesus Christ in heaven, the thought was terrifying! He was fishing with his brother and I was plundering his wife.

The perfect arrangements

It truly felt like the greatest thing I had ever done. In essence all women are alike in a bed. Some are more aroused, others more passionate, but they still open their legs the same way…but this was different, she belonged to someone else. It was like conquering a mountain. It was like crossing the wildest oceans. I had done the thing I thought I could never do, I had fucked my friend's wife and I loved it so much that I continued seeing her after he got back.

I would call her and I could hear her tell Peter it was me. I could hear him yell out that he wanted to talk to me when she finished talking. She'd whisper to me on the phone that she'd meet me at the Castle Lanes Bowling Alley, in an hour. I'd finish talking to her and Peter would grab the phone. "How you doing ol' pal...when we going to see ya?"

"Soon Pal." As I said it...I felt a twinge...a semi-erection was coming on. This was the appetizer, the talking to the husband a half hour before having his wife, "as soon as I can get there, ol'pal."

"Maybe you could come over now and keep me company, play a game of chess. Sissy is going bowling with her girlfriends. She's always going somewhere nowadays."

He sounded happy that she was doing something that pleased her and sad that he couldn't do it with her.

"I'll be over one of these nites with the wife."
"See you later pal," he'd tell me, "Sissy is just leaving now. I want to tell her goodbye."
"Bye bye Pal," I'd say, "See you soon."
I wondered how she felt, as she stood in the doorway and kissed him goodbye. Did she tell him she'd be home as soon as they finished? What control her face must have had, to conceal the excitement of the moment. I wished I was there to see it. I was missing what I had intended to be able to see, the face of the duplicitous woman at work. But I had time. I would first enjoy Sissy to the point where I got tired of the repetition, then I would become objective with her and hope that I didn't become possessive from overscrewing her.

Pleasure and jealousy
Where the line is at that divides pleasure from jealousy was a secret. Becoming jealous is such an easy thing to do, it creeps up on you so quietly that you go to bed one nite feeling good and wake up the next morning with doubt oozing out of your pores.

I told Sissy one day that I felt very uncomfortable being in the house, especially when Peter wasn't there. I told her I felt very uncomfortable being in the same bed that Peter slept in with her.
I could smell Peter in the bedroom.
I could smell him on the pillows.
I was sure there were marks on the bedsheets, and the mingling of hairs made me nervous and when I'm nervous, I don't want to make it. I felt an anger come and go. I had to stay cool.

My total interest, I told myself again, in this whole affair was to study, as accurately as I could, the facial mask that Sissy would construct for her husband. I was sure there would be moments when I would feel the remorse of treachery and the foulness of my activities and the jealousy of sharing her with Peter. It could make me ill at first, but I would for the sake of what I was to learn, bear it like a true believer.

She agreed that we should do it somewhere else, but didn't want to do it all the time in the back seat of the car. She said that maybe it would be better if we went to a motel were we could shower together and really feel good.

I became the man who couldn't afford the motel. I told her I didn't have the money to go moteling and she said that she had a credit card. It would be no problem. She paid the bills and Peter never looked at what things he was paying for.

Her eyes told me that she had found the perfect solution. How often she did this I didn't dare ask. Since Peter was paying the bill, I had no right to ask how many times she did this. I was the bought man. I was getting her for nothing. It wasn't costing me a dime, but I wasn't getting what I came to get either. If I couldn't see her working on her husband, it was a useless exercise in orgasms.

Renting a room for a bedroom drama

She picked the motel. She drove up to it like she knew the way blindfolded. I waited in the car while she registered. She had the card to pay for the room and all I had to do was provide the hardon.

She told me it was the first time she had ever rented a room with a man other than her husband. I didn't believe her and she didn't expect me to. The story must be the same for all married women with a lover in a rented room.

There is a desire for some form of virginity and purity between lovers. There has to be something that's sacrificed for the first time in the name of love. She was going to share this moment of sacrifice with me. She was ready to lose the innocence of a devoted wife at the hands of the all-powerful lover. She surrendered and entered into the land of the adulterous wife, even renting the bed to flop on.

She knew how to use a rented room. She moved with the accuracy of a professional. She took her clothes off and placed them on the chair. She sat on the edge of the bed and took her silk stockings off. She laid her back on the bed, opened her legs and waited for me.

I didn't bother to take my clothes off. I just let my pants drop. Her legs became limp and I plunged it in her like the sacrificial knife of the high priest. The sacrifice was completed, the gods were happy, the motel manager was happy. She cried and I cried with her. I stroked her hair as she laid her head on my bare thighs. I felt erotic compassion. The more she cried the more I stroked her and the hotter I got.

She loved her husband because he was her husband. She loved me because I was her lover and understood her need. I was a witness to her betrayal. She was showing me that she betrayed her husband for me. She would let me study the strength in her face, the conviction in her voice as she fabricated her explanations for our evening's betrayal of the poor ignorant dupe.

I knew eventually I would become the devoted fan of a great actress as she pumped her lines. I could watch her timing, the rhythms, the very essential heartbeat of her movements. She was masterful, enthralled with her ability to convince me that she could move undetected through the mazes and obstacles that her husband could and would eventually place in her way.

She would protect me with her silence. She would make my existence and my lovemaking to her as safe as a baby in his mother's arms. She would rather be burned at the stake than betray me to her husband as the treacherous friend who came, sat, ate and took the wife as well. I wondered if Nomi and her lover went through this routine together. How many times did my name come up as the dolt who just played his guitar, and never looked to see what her sensitivities were all about.

Bedroom wisdom

"What love has ever existed?" I asked Sissy, quoting from some forgotten piece, "that hasn't been born in some pain?" She lay there quietly. I didn't know the answer nor where I found that piece of bedroom wisdom. It rolled out of my mouth in a moment of sexual compassion, a compelling need to say something. It had no greater meaning to me than if I were saying it to a hollow baby, to a cardboard figure, to a mannequin in a storefront window. As the Bible says, I rammed her in the loins again and she grunted and squinted her eyes and cried the delightful tears of pleasure. To me that was bedroom wisdom, making sure we got our money's worth.

She'd stop, look at her watch, "One more time, if you want. I have to get home and entertain Peter. I don't want him getting suspicious. You want to put it in a little bit more before we go?" She'd whisper to me as if she was hoping I wouldn't say no. Those were the words that made the missile erect and hard as steel. I lunged with it, two hundred pounds of flesh driving an iron rod. The pounding made her fart and grunt. "You're crazy," she'd say, "you're trying to put it through me."

Sissy was five feet tall and weighed 110 pounds. She'd get lost beneath me as I gave it to her on that squeaky motel bed. It was at moments like these that I disliked him so much. His very existence was interfering with my pleasure and ending my nite before I was ready. I wondered if I really had any justification to be angry at him. He was, after all, an important partner in this sharing of one woman between us. Without him there would be no duplicity and no reason for me to be with his wife.

There is a point where you can't turn back. The engine has been launched, its destination secure. The possibility that it might not happen drives you mad with fear. You move along quickly but with caution. How it happened was pure and simple, why it happened that way, was part of the fluid motion of water chaotically running through the pipes. I didn't dare open my mouth because I was afraid that the dream would burst out of the pipe, flood the theater and drown the actors. I would be thrown out, not fit for the role of lover, betrayer of friendship and the director of a little afternoon episode.

Dinner with the Husband

The dinner as a test
The look on the face
The husband catering to the lover
Concern is part of duplicity
Friendship
The ingredients of friendship
The forces that created friendship in man
The frightened dinner guest
Playing the word of friendship down
Everyone is a Friend
The day I almost got caught
Friends sharing wives
Trying to keep a secret
Attraction toward a female
The pleasure of deceit
Uniting friendship

The time had come when the lover meets the husband. Usually, the lover and the husband pass each other like ships bearing no lites, in the darkness of the nite, never seeing each other, never knowing each other, and yet they both ascribe their passions to a small hole, like the little hole at Delphi that the ancient world knew was the center of the universe. The only one who knows their identities is the devoted wife, devoted to both, the lover and the husband. Her devotion depends on who she is with at the moment. But in my case, Peter and I knew each other and like love, friendship blossoms under the test of time and we called each other friend.

I was nervous, as if I was going to meet the husband for the first time. I had been there before...many times...with or without his knowing. I wasn't a stranger, but now there were two of me and one was a stranger. One of me, Peter knew and loved, the other, Peter didn't know. It was this stranger that Peter didn't know that developed my nervousness to a high pitch, since I really didn't know him either. Strange passions ran through this stranger's blood which introduced new combinations of thoughts. It was like playing in front of an unknown crowd when I didn't know my material well enough. My hands started to sweat, wondering if I could handle the language of the betrayer. The language of small talk that makes no commitment, the conversations that reveal nothing, the look of innocence, the eyes of compassion for a friend.

I felt different now being with Peter. I *was* different. Before, I enjoyed his company, now I wished I was somewhere else. Before, I used to come and go without a feeling of obligation. Now, after sharing his wife, I was aware of everything around me, plus other feelings that I couldn't put my finger on, feelings I couldn't identify in order to give them a name, but I knew that they were feelings close to my animal instincts.

A small twinge of guilt kept circulating inside me, but I reasoned it away with the following. If Sissy did this with me, she must have done it with others. One doesn't learn one's tricks overnite. You learn them bit by bit as you go along. Others had been here

before me. Someone was waiting for me to leave. But for Peter it was business as usual. He watched them all come and go.
I had developed, in the months that I had been plundering Peter's sanctuary, a feeling of genuine pity for him and I hoped it didn't show on my face. This situation was worse than the banker's wife. I was helping Sissy create the possibility of two friends becoming total enemies.

The dinner as a test
This dinner was the test of whether my friend had detected anything. I had been very careful not to leave suspicious marks on Sissy's body. She would caution me, in the weeks that we spent together, not to bite or kiss her too hard or suck on her nipples too long. I had to be careful how I pissed and not leave piss marks on the bathroom floor. I had to be careful to empty my pockets before coming into the house. Sissy would warn me that the smallest thing could fall out of a pocket and not be missed until it was found by Peter. Sissy must have been an expert in what she was doing. She always assured me that Peter would never find out. I can still hear her voice saying that, "He'll never find out." Was she telling me that Peter was stupid or that she had done it so many times before that the outcome was predictable?

On the way over to his house that nite, I kept telling myself to keep the conversation low-key. Peter had a way of making the smallest element into a universal problem. The table conversation could become difficult to deal with because I didn't know what Peter knew or suspected. I could look at his wife a certain way and disclose the whole affair. A certain look on my face could be the look of a man who's been laying up in another man's bed with the other man's wife.

The look on the face
One never knows if guilt creates a certain look on the face, like other pains do. The look on the face when you have to piss. The look of fear, horror, happiness. One never knows when his face is betraying him. There are empathic people…born with the talent to read the deepest secrets in the face. Peter wasn't stupid. I had the feeling that he could see through me and now that I had

something to hide, it made me feel uncomfortable. I didn't know how empathic he might be.

The husband catering to the lover

I showed up at Peter's house without my wife. She said she wasn't feeling well, which was just a piece of luck for me. I'd have felt strange, being in the same room with two women that I'd been laying, my heaving chest banging on their bare tits. Peter opened the door.

"How you doing Pal?" he yelled out, giving me a big hug. "Come in, it's been so long since I've seen you, I forgot what you looked like. We've become voices on the phone, faces only in the imagination. What you been up to? Where's your wife?"

"She's sick."

"Oh that's too bad."

Just then Sissy came walking in, dressed like a lovely housewife. The type of wife that doesn't want to cause a guest a hardon during dinner, making the guest feel that he'd like to see the husband leave.

My eyes hit on her and wouldn't move off. I kept moving my eyes around trying not to look at Sissy too long. She knew her husband loved her modesty and when she sat down she crossed her legs so the guest wouldn't try to look up her dress for that lost coin. A quick look, as if nothing was going on. A look of innocence...hopefully a look of stupidity.

My opportunity had finally arrived but I had to be brave enough to accept it. This was the opportunity I waited for...to view the wife with the husband and me, the innocent lover, in the same room. The husband catering to my wishes, serving me, talking to me about old times.

He asked me in a very giving voice, "Beer, Whiskey, Vodka, Scotch, name it, I got it."

On the surface she was like any wife would be, with a dinner ready to serve. She went through the movements without a flaw. She paid no attention to me, her lover, other than to tell me, "Too bad your wife couldn't make it. I was looking forward to meeting her."

Sissy's face looked sincere, honest, and clear. There was no doubt in her voice, she really wanted to meet Nomi, but I felt it was to throw Peter off the trail if he happened to be on to us.

Concern is part of duplicity

Both me and Sissy were concerned. Sissy was filled with polite concern. She was asking me how my musical career was going along and if I had been performing. She was asking me questions as if she hadn't seen me in a long time. The questions she asked placed me somewhere in the dim past. I was so preoccupied with my own fears of discovery, I can't even remember what I ate, but I do remember the sense of tranquility that came over me when Sissy showed the ignorance she had, as to what I had been doing with my life. Sissy had mastered the art of deception like a card-conjuror's patter that leads you by the nose to realities you never knew existed.

Friendship

After dinner we sat around and Peter raised the conversation of friendship. The years that we had known each other...it really was a long time and Sissy sat there with a smile on her face, happy that two old friends could share the happiness and the thoughts of friendship. Peter said a true friend was an important part of a family. I tried not to put too much into the conversation, since I would have had to go deeper into the unknown regions of hypocrisy which were starting to surface in me. Could I be called a friend? Could I use the word friend to describe myself? This was something I would have to think about for a long time to come. Peter was providing me, even though he would not understand it, with the ability to study the face of a duplicitous woman which, in this case, was his wife. This could be considered a great gesture of friendship on his part, but I had no way to repay him, in order to keep it equal, other than by ferreting out the deviousness of his wife and telling him who she really was.

Somehow nature had to make sure that the male would be attracted to the female, and Sissy knew all there was to know about that subject. She sat on the couch quiet as a cat, and let me undress her with my eyes. I was afraid that Peter would see me gawking at his wife with that look of hunger on my face, but he missed it. He was intent on the conversation of friendship. I stared at Sissy as her dress crawled past the halfway mark of her thigh.

She pulled her dress back down past her knees, like a woman in church who felt her decency was at stake. I had to take my eyes off her and look at the vase on the wall, or let them fall on the floor in a look of pensive reflection...like a priest performing the Eucharist. A hardened bulge in my pants would blow the cover off the whole operation. It wouldn't take an alert husband long to figure out, that a bulge in my pants was a close enough sign that I wanted to screw his wife, or maybe him, whatever the case. I had something on my mind other than what Peter was talking about, and if Peter was as sharp as I thought he was, he could figure out that I had been there already.

I had to disguise my desires with a look on my face of extreme and intense concentration on what Peter was saying. At first I felt that he was directing the conversation of friendship towards me because he knew something, or suspected something, but if this was so, Sissy would have said something, at least warning me that the hound had ahold of the scent of the bedbug.

I calmed my nerves by telling myself that he just wanted to air out his feelings on friendship, and he really thought of me as a close friend. There was no way I could stop him, nor did I have my guitar with me to move the subject into the sounds of love and the depth of friendship. I looked at Sissy, and she just sat there looking bored as if Peter had been snoring.

The ingredients of friendship

Peter poured himself another drink and washed it down, like it was cool water on a hot day. "A friend is part of the family," Peter said, looking at me with such confidence that he must have felt like a minister in a church. Sissy's face was now blank. A look of total indifference had crept over her face like fog over darkened streets. Her blue eyes were wide open, bored and waiting for something to happen. "When you have problems at home," and he paused and looked at me, "you feel free to talk to your friend, knowing your friend has real concern for you."

You wonder what the ingredients of friendship are, and one day you finally know...it's concern and generosity. "Concern," Peter said, reaching for the glass. "Concern is marked with waiting to serve a friend. It's not as if your friend came, ate at your table, got up and left. He tells the children stories, they call him uncle. He's not the friends you've made while commuting to work or the ones you meet at the store every week or your neighbors or your workers. Many times you come home and find the friend there, waiting for you. Your wife has made him coffee. You hear his warm voice say,
'How you doing old buddy?' And how happy you are to see him and know that he's concerned. The children call him Uncle Bob."

He took another big drink and continued the painful and embarrassing conversation on friendship. "A friend's concern is beyond the definition of the word. What makes him a friend is the thought that for the sake of friendship, for the honor of a friend, nothing is or can be too great of a sacrifice."

I couldn't stand to listen to him talk about friendship and concern. I knew Sissy's concern was merely to misdirect Peter's attention, and my concern was to study duplicity without being caught by the duped husband. I had a feeling he knew about us or by accident he had hit on the central nerve. The more he drank the more his empathic fiber grew, like it was registering my fears and transmitting them to his whiskey-laden brain which in turn sent the information digested to his swollen tongue.

Just to keep the conversation off me, I told Peter, "I read that friendship is a very involved emotional-intellectual-social phenomenon." He paused for a moment, as if he was turning a page in his thoughts, poured another drink, took a gulp of it, then slowly ever-so-slowly he continued with his thoughts on friendship.

The forces that created friendship in man

"Who knows what the forces that created friendship in man were," he told me, "It's pure speculation. Maybe when man was a hunter, the feeling of closeness to another male was important. Survival required the closeness of friendship."

As he talked to me a thought crossed my mind like a leaf crosses a busy street. I had never been so close to Peter as when I shared his wife's love with him. We stuck our tongues into the same mouth, our hardened tools into the same hole. There were days I found him there and days when, if he was looking, he would have found me. Peter finished his vodka and what I thought was the end of the conversation on friendship, but it was merely the preparation for the final assault.

The frightened dinner guest

Peter must have given friendship a great deal of thought, its history and how it came to be. He had accumulated these arguments on friendship like one collects stamps or coins, to show them to a frightened dinner guest whom he suspects has had his wife. It might be a game that Peter had developed with rules I knew nothing of. He attached himself closer and closer to the sacredness of friendship, honor, fidelity, respect, sacrifice, as he unraveled the mystery of the swollen gland that his friend had for his wife.

Playing the word friendship down

It felt safer to play the word friendship down. I didn't want to raise the feeling of hypocrisy in me. One never knows how far that feeling of hypocrisy will take him...till everything has lost its value other than the manipulation of the moment. My mouth would trip me up, a look on my face would tell him the whole story.

Everyone is a Friend

I told Peter that the word friendship had changed in the last few years. "You have work friends, commute friends, old school friends, neighbors as friends, your friend's friends, shopping friends, and for the lack of a better word, people you barely know you call your friends. Everyone is called friend, lovers refer to each other as friend, till no one is really distinguishable. Finally you realize, and I quote an old Greek gambler, 'The best friend you have is your pocket. When it's there, it's there, and when it's not, it's not.'"

I was throwing any thought that came into my head into the conversation of friendship and without taking one side or the other, trying to be funny, adding humor to defuse a very dangerous subject. "You have to admit Peter," I said, "that in the last 30 years the word friendship has changed." But Peter was a romantic and the thought of dying for your friend was a noble cause.

"I know that the word is almost empty now," he told me, "but amongst men in war, there are stories of friendships that end in sacrifice to save a friend," and he throws down his mouth another piss pot of vodka. He tells me with tears in his eyes of his buddy who died in his arms at the burning of Tejon, in the Korean war. Of the hardships of the great retreat from the battle of the Chosen Reservoir. "It was so cold you didn't dare cry, because the tears would freeze in your eyeballs. To stay alive during the freezing nites, we hugged each other."

Peter grunts, he farts, he burps, he wipes his mouth, takes another swallow of vodka and says, "Homer in the Iliad speaks of the love between the two friends, Achilles and Patroclus. Patroclus dies protecting Achilles' honor." I heard Peter's voice crack, a tonal vibrato, a falsetimo before a sob, a sigh, a tear, a whimper. "Sailors have hugged each other," he whispers in a voice that is cracking with emotion, "they've hugged each other in the last rites of friendship as the ship went to the depths. Men have died for the sake and honor of friendship. Monuments and statues have been built to commemorate it."

Another glass comes up to Peter's lips, and his eyes close and his lips hold on to the crystal as the moon-glow sparkles his passion. Sissy winks at me. She must have heard it before, maybe many times before.

He wanted to show me he was my friend, that he had a need for a friend, that he valued friendship above all other possessions a man can have. But like the mystic who listens to his own heart beat in order to understand the weather, so does Peter want to hear what his heart wants him to hear. "One shows in the depth of friendship," and his voice cracked again, as if a hidden tear inside his soul had burst out, "certain qualities of humanity, that normally aren't present in our everyday life. Somehow you know you have been given one of the greatest gifts man can have...a friend."

The day I almost got caught

I remember one day when I nearly got caught in the bedroom with Sissy. The good husband Peter had walked into the house, and I didn't hear the door. I almost passed out from fear as I heard him yell out, "Sissy are you home, honey-dear?" I felt a twinge of terror come over me. Sissy was calm, composed. Her voice was as natural as a voice can be with another man's prick in her. "I've been waiting for you dear, I'm getting dressed, I'll be right out."

There sitting on the couch in the next room was my dear friend, waiting for his wife to come out of the bedroom with me still in her. "I'm coming love," she yelled out. The sound of her lovely voice coming from the rear bedroom as she dug her fingernails deep into my back! "I'm coming love," she yelled, as we both reached that state of bliss together.

"Hurry dear," he says.

"I'm coming as fast as I can."

Then she whispers in my ear, "Don't you pull it out you bastard until you come with me."

I lacked the nerve to welcome Peter home with an *"I've been...waiting...for you...old buddy."* I felt caught, but Sissy looked so cool, she just put her finger to her lips telling me to be quiet and not to make any noise. She put her pants on and told me in a hushed voice to make it out the back deck. "He won't hear anything," she said, "believe me."

The next day when I saw her, she said that Peter was so glad to see her, he didn't have a clue, and he wanted to make love to her.

"Did you let him?" I asked her.

"What else could I do? He didn't even give me time to get you out of me."

Friends sharing wives

As I sit and think about it now, I wonder what the hell friendship really means. I know it's not as clear in my mind as I once thought it was, but if he was my friend and I was making it with his wife, I should, as a good friend, have let him have my wife. But how could I do that? She wasn't mine like a pair of shoes would be. What part of her belonged to me so I could give her to Peter? As a matter of fact I was having Peter's wife because mine had turned off.

Trying to keep a secret

I had reached an impasse in my thoughts. If secrecy was to be maintained, it would require that I play a cruel joke on my friend, not just for now, but for as long as we knew each other. It wasn't so much the having of his wife, but the manipulation required to have her, and the imagination to cover up my acts with her. There was too much deceit involved, and the ingredient that makes up friendship was gone. I was the man with the secret. I was trying to keep a secret. I became the man who always has to listen so he can add more to his secret. Moulding my secret like a clay bowl, sending it deeper into my hidden world, afraid that it will be discovered by a look, by the slip of a word, by chance, by the confessions of a guilt-ridden wife. A feeling hit me, it just seeped up from the cauldron of fears that a guilty person has. I had a feeling that all of it was staged for my benefit, as if I was in a play of multiple dimensions, and I was just an actor that was given his lines as the play progressed through the nite.

Peter took another big drink of vodka. He was near the passage of the river Lethe, where one forgets everything with the taking of the waters. Peter was drunk, and as the feelings passed through the vapors, he remembered little things that made friendship possible. "Remember when we did this, and remember when you did that."

Old terms like, "you son-of-a-gun partner, you old bastard you," phrases like this were geared to drown my mind with the comfort of familiarity, putting my mind at ease, making my eyes dull and my ears deaf. Sissy's face was in a state of what seemed to be total indifference. Maybe she was happy that we were enjoying our friendship. A few more thoughts from Peter, and he put his head back on the couch and was gone. The lites had gone out of the old warrior, the advocater of friendship. The dog guarding the gate was asleep.

Sissy looked at me with a look of wanting. My face must have shown the same expression because she came over to where I was sitting and sat next to me. Her dress was up past her thighs. The flag of surrender was flying from the mizzen mast. Peter was right in front of us, his head laid back on the couch, his eyes were half-open. "He's looking at us," I said.

"Don't be silly." She lifted her dress up and took her panties off without a moment's hesitation. "Here," she said, and she took my hand and placed it on her cunt. "Let him look, if he's awake." She bent over and unzippered my pants and unbuttoned my belt. She took my limp prick and held it in her hand, then gently she ran her tongue up one side and down the other of my prick until it started to throb and jerk itself in repetitive spasms. She stopped, raised her head and told me...

"No one can say that we do things behind his back," and she laughed, bent her head and got right down to the business she seemed to know best. "Would it make you feel better," she said, "if we went into the bedroom and did it or shall we be brave and do it right here with Peter just a few feet away?"

A feeling of utter delirium came over me. I actually felt as if I was going to shit on the couch. It felt as if I was falling off a great height. I don't know what words to use to describe such an enormous feeling. I've never felt it before or since. What I was doing was profound in its cruelty and savagery. My total indifference to danger and the abandonment of all common sense and caution seemed to ignite my passion. I never knew such feelings existed in me. I realized there is no such thought or feeling as friendship when the tunnel is heated. "Put it in a little," she said, "right here in front of Peter so he can't say we done it behind his back."

Attraction toward a female

It was like crossing over a hidden line, that once you crossed it, there was no turning back. A world of frenzy and delirium. A world of hidden desires exploding in front of me. The attraction a man feels towards a female must be stronger than the feeling of friendship towards a man.…far more powerful in its attachment and need. I was feeling the awesome power of the female. I was looking at the bare feelings pouring out of Sissy and now me. If I went with her I'd be free, once and for all, of the shame, guilt and hypocrisy, of making it with the wife of a friend. I wouldn't care anymore what obligation existed between me and whomever.

The pleasure of deceit

There seems to be a great pleasure in deceit, like there is sweetness in the prickly cactus fruit. I asked Sissy if she loved Peter now that she was deceiving him. She must have had the answer all memorized because she answered me without a flash of hesitation. "To know I've deceived him allows me to love him even more. I can afford to love him, I'm ahead of him. I fooled him and he never felt a thing, because I loved him. Had I hated him, I would have fried him in suspicion and jealousy. Does that answer your question?"

Sissy must have really loved Peter. This wasn't duplicity I was looking at, it was love composed of thorns rather than petals, vinegar instead of water, pain composed of aloneness...like notes without a melody. She took me by the hand and we went and sat next to Peter. She bent down and kissed him. "Doesn't he look silly," she said, "the way his mouth turns at the corners." She started to unbutton Peter's pants. "There," she said, "you'll be more comfortable that way." She unbuttoned his shirt. She made him look as if he had tried taking his clothes off, but never made it. Then she spread herself at the other end of the couch…

"Look at me," she said and opened her legs. I stood there looking at her, wondering if all women looked the same. If you turned the lites off, would you really know what woman you were putting it into?

"Put it in," she said, "a little bit at a time...not all at once...I want to really feel it."

We did this for the next 4 nites. I would come over to Peter's house. Peter would get loaded, talk about friendship then pass out on the couch, Sissy would then get herself ready, stretch herself out at the other end of the couch and we'd screwed each other like 2 dogs, oblivious and indifferent of the whole world and everyone in it. We screwed each other in front of him, next to him, or so close that I could hear his breathing.

Uniting friendship
One nite she decided to add another element to her lovemaking and unite the friendship into some cosmic joke that she had concocted. She took Peter's prick out of his pants and hardened it up with her hand and tongue, while he snored in a drunkard's sleep. I looked at her doing it. She had a perfect right to include her husband. What could I say? I was just part of this nocturnal skit and I was there watching as she gave her husband a dream. "He can dream about it while we do it next to him."

At one time she had me do it to her while she held on to Peter's prick, jacking him off. Then one nite she must have overexcited Peter with her hand pumping and a few slurps of the mouth, because he woke up and grabbed her. She waved her hand at me, telling me to go hide while she crawled on to the couch and Peter got on top of her. I got up and hid behind the couch that Sissy and Peter were lying on, terrified that he would look and see me crawling with my pants off while he was trying to screw his wife. The couch that Peter was sleeping on had now become the central altar of this play. All that playing around with Peter, while he was asleep, must have done something to him, it must have released a gallon of endorphins in his dreaming brain that turned him from a sleeping drunk into a raving fuck-monster. I watched Sissy's face as it grimaced from Peter's swollen rod in her. She yelled, I watched his ass rear up, his huge balls swinging as he lunged and rammed her with the force of a 250-pound monster. She knew if she resisted he could hurt her and open her up like an over-ripe melon. I could hear loud farts as she spread her legs farther and farther apart to allow that monster a clear track. Then I watched her face become tranquil and serene. She opened her eyes and looked at me, then closed them again, as if I didn't exist. She had reached that moment of bliss when the gates of heaven open for the infidel. I went and sat down in the chair and looked at them. Then I got up and went into the kitchen and got a beer, came back and they had disappeared.

Instinctively I went to the bedroom and there they were. This time Sissy was on top of Peter like she was riding a horse going through the various gaits. First a slow walk, then a trot, then a canter and into a full gallop. Then a slow deliberate sound escalating into a scream of total frenzy. A passion that is difficult to look at without feeling it yourself. All these months of being with her, I had never seen her so liberated, so alive. I felt myself being drawn to the bed. Maybe this was their intent from the beginning. She gets me ready, then gets Peter lit up and all of us spend our nites in bed together taking turns on the darling little Sissy. I wasn't here to become part of their game. I had come to study the face of a duplicitous wife and the face of a duped husband, and by the looks of it I had been set up. I had wasted all my time. She wasn't duplicitous to her husband, they were both duplicitous to me. I was sure of it now. He would talk to me about friendship while his wife fed me her favors…then drag a guilt-ridden hulk on to their bed for the fuck of the depraved. I put my pants on, picked up my jacket and hat, looked in the hall mirror to see if I was ready for the outside world. I opened the door and left. I could hear her groaning and the bed banging as I shut the door behind me and ran for my car.

The Mask of Duplicity

The world runs on duplicity

The thought of being had

Man's spiritual need to be betrayed

Sexual rage

The hypocrisy of a smile

Duplicity and betrayal, the stimulators of passions

The limits of imagination

I left Peter and Sissy banging away on the bed. I got into my car and aimlessly drove around for an hour or so. I was in a daze. I was exhausted. I felt cold and depressed from too much of Sissy and Peter. I decided to go home and drove there in a deep trance. Nomi left the nite lite on over the entrance door. It was 5 A.M. and the sun was starting to come up over the East Bay hills. In an hour Nomi would be getting up and getting ready to go to work.

The world runs on duplicity

The apartment was dark and I could hear the darkness being broken open by Nomi's snoring. I had a feeling of uneasiness come over me like something was waiting to happen. I didn't want to be here anymore, and yet I found myself being drawn back here again and again, because I was fascinated with the thought of betrayal and duplicity. I was starting to feel like the whole world was totally duplicitous. It ran on duplicity like cars run on gas. The art of life was to choose the right mask to wear in order to hide the duplicity.

I took my clothes off for the second time that nite, got into bed and crawled up next to Nomi. Her body was warm next to my cold skin. I felt her body do a little jerk, and a little shriek came out of her mouth as my cold skin rubbed against hers. I had been naked at Sissy's house just a few hours ago and here I was in bed again. I put my hand on my dear Nomi's bare ass and listened to her snoring and chirping away. My brain was lit up with the evening's activities. It wouldn't quiet down, it was agitated and confused. A thought kept coming to me, and the more it circulated in my head the more it yelled out to be looked at and noticed.

The thought came to me, as natural as if I was thinking of taking a piss. It seemed almost obvious that Sissy and Peter were in on it together, right from the beginning.

Thought of being had

The more I thought of it the more it made sense to me. I felt I had been had, that I had been duped. Instead of me duping them, they guided me like I was a blind man crossing a busy street.

I felt that awful feeling that comes when you feel you lost your wallet and you're afraid to put your hand in your pocket and prove that it's missing. The thought scared me. The worst fear was that they were laughing at me and my attempts in the art of duplicity.

When Peter was talking to me about friendship, he knew what I had been up to and was looking at my face, studying my amateurism at duplicity. Maybe his house was a school where

Peter studied the faces of his lying friends?
It made me feel like I had been used in their plan, which was far more complicated than mine. Sissy was selecting friends for him, showing him that there never was such a thing as a friend amongst men when a woman was in the way. Or she was showing herself the power of being a woman in heat. The power of a woman over a man, over friendship, over truth and fiction. Nothing was safe from the wake of a turned-on woman.

Man's spiritual need to be betrayed
For some reason Peter felt the same need Christ must have felt…the spiritual need to be betrayed by his friends, and Sissy knew which ones to select for the job as easily as she would select a pair of pants or a tie for him to wear at the opera. All these possibilities depressed me even more.

At the beginning, in the fashion of an incompetent, it was important to me, if all my activities were to have any meaning or justification, that she deceive her husband. If he knew about her moteling and back-seating in my car, and approved of it, she was hiding the truth from me, and instead of duping her husband she was training me like a circus dog to jump in and out of the lion's cage, while Peter played the role of the ringmaster.

Sexual rage
The last 4 nites had been spent in sexual rages by Peter and Sissy. There were moments that I was engulfed in the fire of lust but it was only a brief flash. Nothing was mine. I had invested nothing, not even friendship. I had lost nothing other than the time I spent looking for the mask of duplicity. The fear of losing it all wasn't there. One feels the passion when the ground is giving way beneath you. When you lose that which you love. Nomi was providing me with nothing and Sissy was providing Peter with a built-in protected world of secrets, lies, hypocrisy, duplicity, betrayal, cruelty, pain, suspicion. Then a moment of truth like a great explosion had taken place...El Momento de Verdad...and the truth was apparent...another friend had fucked his wife.

The hypocrisy of a smile
While I felt the betrayal of my friend Peter was an essential part of my plan, it was now more probable that I along with Sissy was part of Peter's world. A world destined to show us that we were all no good. No deeper thought was necessary to explain what the words...No Good...conveyed.
Not only did I have the original sin, like Cain, blazed on my forehead, but also the hypocrisy of my smile when I sat and talked to Peter on friendship. Even after he told me of the virtues of friendship, the need for a friend, I went and screwed his wife right next to him.

If it was his plan to prove that I was no good then why did I have to help him prove it so quickly? Because I was his friend? I knew all of this was pure conjecture on my part. To me, Sissy looked like the average bored housewife who wanted to have a little fun on the side and got overly involved with me. But then again there were indications that she was deeper in it than what it looked like on the surface.

I stroked Nomi's ass, and for a moment my mind felt a sense of pleasure. A small figment of hope crept over me...that Nomi wasn't as deceitful as Sissy. For some reason Sissy represented the fear all men held that they could or would someday end up, if they didn't offer the right prayers to the gods above, with a woman like Sissy. (Con la gran puta.)
While all this was floating through my head I felt Nomi grab my hand and push it off her soft warm ass.

As I snuggled up to Nomi's warm body in the early morning darkness I started to see a very complex pattern.

One nite I was supposed to meet Sissy. She didn't show up, she wasn't at home, and she was gone for 4 hours.
"Where were you?" I asked her. She told me that Peter needed her and she just couldn't leave him. She didn't want him getting a feeling that she had someone else more important than him. It sounded so considerate, but I knew she was lying. I had called

Peter up that nite on a pretext that I wanted to get his advice on a legal matter concerning an upcoming performance. He told me he was worrying, Sissy was late coming home.

"How late is she?" I asked Peter.

"Four hours," he said, his voice sounding very upset.

"She's alright brother," I said, trying to sound as if I was attempting to relieve the poor bastard's stress, but it was me that I was concerned about.

At the time my thoughts were that Sissy was working on me, the same as she worked on Peter. But with this new realization I was having, it might have been that Peter was teasing me while they had another person over for dinner, and were doing the same with him as they did with me. Peter could have been talking to me on the phone while looking at Sissy banging away with the other friend on the couch. The thought of it gave me an empty feeling, a feeling of hopelessness, as if everything was ready to come down over me like a building in an earthquake and I couldn't get out.

At first I had a feeling that there were more than just me. How many more were involved in Peter's and Sissy's world was hard to estimate, but there was one nite that I called Peter to see how he was and to find out about Sissy. "Glad you called," he said. "Having a clam bake Friday nite, why don't you come over?"

"You going to have a lot of people there?" I asked.

"A few old friends, you know most of them, big Mike, Steve, Teddy, Alexandro, Art, more of a guys' nite. We'll drink and be merry."

"How about the wives?" I asked.

"Sissy is going out with a girlfriend. I think it'll just be old friends' nite."

Now I wondered if Peter would periodically have all the old friends over for a little ceremonial clam bake where I, as the new member, would be ushered into the inner sanctum along with the rest of the old friends that had something in common…we'd all screwed Sissy.

Duplicity and betrayal, the stimulators of passions

Detection became my main concern. I wanted to catch the look of duplicity on Sissy's face and yet I was concerned that Peter would catch the look of duplicity on my face, but I never thought of looking for duplicity on Peter's face.

Did they always wait for the phone to ring?

Did Sissy always say, "He'll be right back"?

Another dog for the lion's cage?

Was it always, "He'll never know"?

Was it my fucken bad luck to fall into a game where pain was the only pleasure? No wonder she was so easy. I did nothing. She took me by the hand to the couch. The thought just kept coming to me...I was used. Now it seemed so real, so explainable, it all made sense. It gave everything an explanation.

The limits of imagination

I had never been in such a complex situation before. My limits of understanding were the limits of my own imagination. I didn't know all the possibilities. My imagination had very little to work with. I felt I was from another world, another period in history, when duplicity and betrayal had another meaning. The meaning had changed, duplicity and betrayal now were the stimulators of passions. An emotion so strong, a fear so great as to be able to resurrect the dead feelings in Peter and Sissy.

That day when she stood at the door with her body on the alert, like a rent-a-cop in front of O'Kays Jewelers. Not only was she Peter's falcon, but she was also Peter's partner. What had Peter told her? How did he ask her to prepare such an elaborate mental dinner? Did he actually go away and tell her to have something ready for him by the time he got back? Or was he lurking outside, like the banker Larry looking in through the windows, or taking photographs and videos of me and his wife from some hidden wall?

Sissy duped me into believing she was duping her husband, and I couldn't see it. I didn't want to believe that Peter and Sissy had planned out this fucken scenario, because if this was true, everything I had thought of, every move I had made, was really planned out by Peter and Sissy.

I had no need to see Sissy and Peter anymore. She had dangled me in front of Peter like one dangles an amulet in front of danger to show that the power of the amulet comes from heaven. Maybe she dangled me like one would hang a piece of meat before a hungry lion, to hear it growl and see it salivate. Or maybe Sissy was like a matador, bringing the horns of the bull as close to her chest as her daring allowed her, ready to drive the sword deep into the heart of the charging bull. One wrong move and it's death for the brave matador, but a thrill of any value is determined by how close you can come to ultimate failure.

Hypnagogic Sex

The ecology of love

I had taken the wrong road and I knew it. I had gotten involved in a world I had very little understanding of. I had married a woman who for some reason had turned off so goddamn completely that it propelled me into the world of betrayal, suspicion, deceit, duplicity. A world that had its own reasons, its own logic, and its own peculiar pains and pleasures.

In the darkness of my own ignorance, I felt I was suffocating in a state of total futility. Like a man drowning, my hands reached out to grab any hope that might have been left behind by those more fortunate. Those that intelligence, hard work and luck gave the necessary parts to, to make life livable.

It was late Fall. The early dark nites, the low sun on the horizon, the coldness in the air, the shadowless days. It seemed the right time of the year to ask myself questions as they appeared from the void. I felt a sense of loss. I didn't have to ask myself if I had picked the right profession in life. My guitar was my inner voice, my emotional release, my canvas that allowed me to paint pictures in sounds, landscapes that were made of chords, harmonies, melodies, where one note could roam over a meadow like a hummingbird.

What was my error? Why did I feel so bad? A pain that never leaves. I had to accept the inevitable, that the end was rapidly approaching. I felt the immortality of the myths and the mortality of my own life. Not even my guitar could help me now. It stood on its stand waiting for me to pick it up and touch it, but I couldn't. I just felt so exhausted that the tuning of the guitar would be a task of heavy labor.

My error was love. I was so in love with love, I wanted someone to share it with me. I wanted love which was filled with passion, the same passion I played my guitar with, the same passion I ate with, saw the flowers bloom with. Love, I knew the feeling of love, I had no reason not to love, no one had ever treated me bad. I was like a dog that was loved from the time it was born, petted, stroked, held in its master's hands until all of life was just a dream that followed the sun around the clock, and now I felt the pangs of amputation. Love was taken from me by the same hand that gave it to me.

Miserable wreaths thrown on a white coffin. A lace of fine brocade matted in the soggy earth. At nite I hear the sobbing of a lonely creature mingling with the sounds of snoring. I had reached the end of my endurance, there was no more life left to my love...she was gone...forever gone.

Sleep makes all things equal

The only person I knew who, I felt, had any real understanding of the mysterious mechanisms of love and sex was Edgar, the ex-priest. He said he knew the spiritual part of sex. Being a priest he had to learn how to synthesize the most basic instinct of all creatures, and to bring it up to the highest metaphysical level of human existence. I guess he meant that he figured out how to make the woman, god, holiness, duplicity, scheming, and holy scripture unite into one exhilarating chord...one cataclysmic orgasm...one symphonic scream...pointed directly to the heavens.

He had advised me to marry Nomi with the thought in mind that if she didn't wake up, then I would by necessity learn to sleep with her, and in sleep we would find our equality. Sleep made all creatures equal and therefore in sleep we would find the beginning of our love rather than in the sensual world of awakeness...where nothing is equal. But the trail through the maze of possibilities wasn't laid out clear enough for me to follow. I felt like Odysseus going from dream to dream, with the horror of soft-voiced sirens dragging me deeper and deeper into my doom, and the only protection from them was to become deaf.

I had a woman, and it felt like I had found an oasis off the caravan trail. That place in the middle of a scorching desert...a watering hole hidden with shady trees from the deadly sun. A place on earth where the phone doesn't ring at nite with someone wanting in. But something was seriously wrong, deadly wrong, and if I didn't correct it soon, all of it would come to an abrupt end.

There must be more to the story than just sleeping and snoring together or hoping to see each other in some dream. The sleep part didn't work. I needed more. It was as simple as that. Either out of greed, insensitivity, selfishness, male hormones, too many daydreams, lust, self-love, I had a hardon that wanted Nomi.

Sleep didn't satisfy me. I tried to convince myself that I could adapt to my loveless, sexless, speechless existence. I couldn't. I decided that it was time to visit this ex-holy man whose advice I took when I got married. Now I needed the thoughts that keep you married.

I gave Edgar a call and made it sound like I was going down that way and would like to stop by to see him. "Fantastic!" he yells at me on the phone. "Bring your guitar and come down."

He lived in a beautiful beachfront house near the small town of Gaviota, just a few miles north of Santa Barbara. I drove down and left my wife behind to sleep, by herself or with her lover.

Etidorpha

I hadn't seen Edgar in ten years, and he had grown a big red beard and had put on at least 50 pounds. "It's being away from the church and its discipline that's put weight on me. Too much eating and lying around with this woman of mine."

He introduced me to his wife...Eti. "It's short for Etidorpha." She was beautiful in a strange sort of way. Her expressions made her beautiful. Her beauty was her plainness. The color of her skin was ivory, and across her cheek she had a small scar that added to the imperfections that made up her beauty. She was tall and lithe. She walked as if no blade of grass would break under her foot. She had a liteness about her that one associates with innocence. The soft breeze would move her silken hair across her face. Her long white fingers lifted the strands of golden silk to show a face of gentle beauty.

I thought she was perfect for the position of an ex-priest's wife. She looked as if she herself had made a pact with god, that if she was allowed to serve Edgar, she would promise to obey all of god's laws the way Edgar interpreted them.

Edgar was a great host. He brought out a big bowl filled with green resin-laden buds. We sat on pillows like we were in a Moroccan cabila waiting for the arguila and the roasted lamb to appear. Eti brought out the food...it was good. She brought out bottles of white wine, and we drank, ate and blew dope.

"Would you like to play us some of your beautiful Gypsy guitar?" Edgar asked me.

I felt like playing, even though there were only two people in front of me. I felt the urge to share my feelings with them, more so than if it had been an auditorium filled with a paying crowd of unknowns.

I had brought my favorite guitar with me, my Reyes. It was created out of Spanish cypress by the master guitarmaker, Manuel Reyes of Cordoba, Spain. It was a guitar that was suited to my personal temperament. It responded to a variety of my moods. In my lite moods I played the dance pieces of the Sevillanas, Alegrias, the Fandangos of Jerez. For my medium moods it was Granadinas, Tarrantas, Tientos, and for my deep moods I played the *canto hondo*, the deep songs of the Soleares, the Seguirias, the Serranas. The music that inspired the poet Garcia Lorca to write that the Seguirias needed a cathedral to be played in.

I took my guitar out from its case and folded the soft cloth that covered it over my knee. I placed the guitar on my lap and held its neck with the same tenderness that I would hold a beautiful woman. My fingers rested on the black ebony fingerboard, waiting for the command to begin playing.

Around 10 o'clock I was moving into my deep moods. I felt it was time to put the guitar down before I expended all my emotions. I had come here to talk to Edgar about my married life and the depression it put me in. I placed the guitar on the seat next to me, picked up the pipe and started to take another hit when Edgar stopped me.

"Save that," he said, "I have something much better." I took it for granted that he meant he had a finer grade of cannabis to smoke. I put the pipe down and started to tell him of my torturous relationship with my wife. I didn't care if Edgar's wife was listening. It would be good for me to have a woman listen to my tale like Dr. Boyle the sex therapist did. Since I wasn't paying Eti, she might, out of a desire to explain the female attitude, tell me what she thought.

The dominant force behind all of creation

"Edgar, I've run into a brick wall with my marriage. My wife is so out of it I can't make love with her at all." I assured him that I realized in certain circles this conversation would be trivia, but then again, sex was the dominant force behind all of creation, and 99% percent of all motivation, conversation and adulation.

"She has made sleep her pastime. She talks to me as little as possible. She's indifferent to me, and I can't break the walls that have grown between us. I know it sounds stupid, but out of desperation I have gone to a sex counselor and was made an ass out of, to the tune of $4,000. I was asked to buy a robotic doll to practice my lovemaking on." I told Edgar the minute details of my sessions with Dr. Boyle but I omitted, for obvious reasons, the story of Peter and Sissy.

"Is there someone else in the picture?" Edgar asked me. "There might be."

A blank face

I wanted to tell Edgar about my suspicions that her sleep was her retreat from me. I had developed the desire, like Larry the banker, to accuse her of the foulest betrayal and duplicity. To point my finger at her and victimize myself to the fullest. To rid myself of all doubt about her and free myself of the pain forever.

At this point I envied the banker. At least he knew, even if his wife had denied it, that it was her in the film. Her denials never severed the cord that connects the reality of images to the reality of acceptance. In a way I envied Peter also, these guys had accepted their wives.

"I don't know," I told Edgar in a voice that trumpeted my pain, "If there is someone else, I doubt if I'll ever know. I can't spend my time trying to find out. I would have to devote weeks of my life trying to catch her. My life, in any event, would take on the fulltime occupation of an investigator. I've tried to unearth some evidence of her activities, but no luck. Her face is a blank, her eyes are vacuous, she looks at me with such coldness that I feel the chill freeze my whole existence. I hardly play my guitar, and when I do it's merely cold, impersonal studies. There are no marks of guilt or fear or any telltale signs of outside activity on her face or body. She has developed, for my personal viewing, a death mask of white plaster that she wears in the house all the time."

The ayahuasca vine

Edgar's face was intense as he listened to me. He had that look of oceanic love a priest develops for the express purpose of listening to the confessions of the sinner. There was an answer waiting for me the moment I stopped talking. Eti was lying on the pillow, not saying a word. Her head resting on her arm, looking at me slobbering out my woes. I stopped talking. I was tired of hearing the same thought come out of my mouth for over a year. But on the other hand I had so memorized it that I was starting to edit the story and clarify the issue.

"All pains of the soul should be told and repeated at least a thousand times," Edgar told me, "until one can hear his own story."

I must have sounded like a child trying to wet his eyes on a painful tale of himself as the poor unsuspecting victim. "I have a most wonderful concoction," Edgar tells me, "from the Amazonian world." He motioned Eti and she got up, left the room and came back in a few moments, carrying a wooden carved tray with a flask and three little cups. She laid the tray down in front of Edgar, and then she lay down next to him, her head resting on the pillow.

The ceremony of dreams

A ceremony was about to begin. I stared at Edgar pouring the green liquid out of the flask into the little cups. "This is ayahuasca," he told me. "It's the divine vine of the Amazonian jungle. I learned about it when I did missionary work in the Xanada area of Bolivia, where the Rio Las Pedras and the Rio Madre de Dios meet. I spent five years there with the Amahuaca Indians in the attempt to missionize them to Catholicism. It was a futile attempt. Attempts to convert them had been going on for the best part of this century, but had always failed because of the ayahuasca vine and the elixir that was extracted from it. It took me a long time to realize that they probably were the most religious people on earth. They had lived a life closer to the other world than I could have ever imagined."

Edgar continued to enter into the vision world of the Indians. "They had a vision world all worked out where they made contact with their gods daily. Our communion was meaningless to them...where we sang hymns and prayers to God and concentrated on the holiness of the event, they painted portraits in their heads of their god with chants. They could, with the help of the ayahuasca, convert sounds into images. To me that was the most fascinating part of the ceremony. They could move images through a time continuum of past, present, and future with a language that could be seen, as opposed to just being heard."

He stopped for a moment to collect his thoughts, then, slowly, with a voice of pious correctness, he tells me...
"I became convinced of the meagerness of our religion, which was built on reason trying to bring you to the holiness of faith through philosophical debates of what truth is and what God wears. It wasn't just what God wears, but the size of his hat, pants and shoes, the cut of his shirt, the color of his tie. I realized that my god was a store-bought mannequin that came into my life for only a short joyful moment, like a bowel movement. It ended up that I was converted to the Amahuaca way of life and to the secrets of the vine. Now with that little introduction I offer you the elixir of the gods."

He handed me the cup with the ayahuasca drink in it. The thought of drinking it scared me. I didn't know how far the freak juice would take me. "Don't be scared of it," Edgar said, "There's a reason I'm introducing you to it," and his voice faltered for a moment. Then he began talking softly and slowly like he was reading out of a book. "The desire to share another person's consciousness is a universal desire. The high mark of all interaction is the sharing of this collective consciousness through love, sex, friendship. Visions are a collective event, my dear friend, so drink it slow and let yourself drift to the Other Side."

To resist now would show Edgar that I didn't want to go any further, and like the frog in the well, I would never know the ocean existed. I took a sip of the green liquid. There was a slight bitter taste that left immediately, leaving my mouth feeling dry. I took another sip, and the bitter taste disappeared as my mouth became accustomed to it. I kept looking at Edgar and Eti who both had finished their drinks and had put their cups down. "When you feel like it, please play something beautiful for my darling Eti." She was lying on one of the pillows with her head resting on her arm and her eyes looking at me.

My feelings were ready to explode. My fingers became very rigid and the muscles of my back and arms became stiff. I knew I was going through some muscle spasms. I heard Edgar tell me that the muscular feeling would soon leave, and I would experience a calmness. I felt my heartbeat increase, and my breathing become heavy and irregular. For a few moments I had trouble breathing, then that feeling left me. A feeling of nausea came over me. I wanted to vomit. A fear possessed me like I was going to die any moment. My feet became cold, and I had a strange tingling on the left side of my tongue. I heard Edgar tell me not to worry about these sensations, that they would soon leave. Whether it was his voice that soothed me or the transition of the ayahuasca, the physical part left me. I started to have feelings of exhilaration and a need to walk out of my world and into another world that I had no idea of...but merely felt.

I became aware of Eti's feelings trying to enter me. Was it the way she was looking at me? Was it me she was looking at, or was it some dream world long ago gone, something that passed into the rippling rings of yesterday?

I picked up my guitar and started to play. The tones were coming from some long-ago forgotten landscape. I lost myself in the sounds of Granados' La Maja de Goya. I knew the piece well. I had interpreted it faithfully many times, but this time its organization was being developed differently, as if someone else was playing it. I found simple meanings to passages which, at one time, I found difficult to explain. I found myself changing the sequences of the musical phrases, as if the Muses were in control of my fingers, moulding the sounds into a visual order that belonged to a totally different logical system. My guitar was humming or chanting on a single string. The complexities of the chord structures were now reduced to a single note, with the time durations drawn out like a human voice calling me from the past to enter into a universe that had a rhythmical pulsating structure.

I had just met Eti a few hours before, and the magic that exists only between man and woman had taken over. I could feel her, and the more I felt her the more I played. Edgar had fallen asleep on the pillows, leaving us both alone on this earth to search each other out. It reminded me of the nite I was at Peter's house for dinner and he fell asleep on the couch, and Sissy took her clothes off and screwed me like a cunning animal in heat.

I don't know how or when I fell asleep, all I can remember is that I put my guitar down and was looking at Eti as she lay on the pillows with her eyes closed. I drifted like a piece of wood does down a river, each breath of air moving it, sometimes to the left, other times to the right, but the current taking it deeper into the expanses of the open sea.

She came to me in deep colors of blue and magenta, wearing a diaphanous silken material that my eyes could penetrate. I could make out her beautiful form beneath it. A feeling of pure pleasure overcame me. It was beyond description. It was beyond any feeling I had ever experienced in my life.

The silence of the nite needed no words. She lay next to me, and without saying a word she pressed her lips to mine. So passionate were her kisses that I thought she was going to smother me. She took her hand and held my throbbing serf, then took her warm lips and kissed him, covering his bare head with the sweetness of her tongue. My hand held her long white neck as she made me tremble, like the earth was coming undone.

Then she held me in her arms till my breathing quieted down. I kissed her, and my fingers passed through her hair like a comb passing through silk. I felt I had, in the silence of the nite, and hidden from her husband, slid my throbbing cock into her with one gliding motion.
I was straddled on a tonal eclipse. I could hear his snores in one ear and her sighs in the other. Her lips opened, and I could feel her warm breath on me like the breezes of the tropics. Her wet

tongue searching for mine, to devour it, to swallow it, to turn me inside out like a velvet glove taken off the hand of the magnificent pontiff.

I had entered the totality of ecstatic madness. My whole body turned into a molten white foam destined to enter her in the same explosion that created the heavens.

The laws of hospitality

I woke up that morning and my body felt like a limp rag that had fallen on the floor. My clothes were wet as if I had been drenched by a heavy rain. My guitar was lying next to me. Edgar and Eti were gone. I had a nauseating feeling of being alone in an empty universe. I went outside. The sun was just coming up, and the white waves were disgorging themselves from the black ocean.

I felt a strange feeling of emptiness, sadness, love, all mixed together in the cauldron of my very existence. I didn't know if it really had happened or I had dreamt that it did. If it had really happened...with Edgar right there next to me...sleeping on the pillows...I had again, within a month, perpetrated the unthinkable. I had broken the laws of hospitality. I had entered a friend's house and fucked his wife while the husband was lying next to us asleep. Maybe he wasn't asleep. He might have been awake and said nothing, waiting to see who I really was. But surely his wife was the instigator in this, the same as Sissy was that nite with Peter sleeping next to us.

Why should ecstasy have any guilt? Pleasure of such magnitude should have no remorse. To lament pleasure and how it came to me would only tell me that I have lived a life of small expectations, oblivious to all that was beautiful. I had entered and now nothing should allow me to regret it. I had felt it, in all its reality, in all its force, in all its splendor and beauty. I had known Eti and all her beauty in just a few hours.

My introduction to hypnagogic sex and the book of Dr. Panukla

As I walked down the beach I thought of how beautiful a woman is in the silence of the nite with moonbeams breaking the darkness, like knives darting across a black canvas. Words would have destroyed that which happened, like an avalanche of rocks falling on a meadow.

I walked down the beach for a mile or so, and on my way back I saw Edgar walking toward me alone. For a moment I wondered where Eti was and why he was alone. Did he have something he wanted to tell me? Something he had seen? Again the childish fear came to me that I would be accused of wrongdoing. I had violated the etiquette of a guest. But was there any witness to what had happened during the nite?

"How did you sleep last nite?" he asked me. I looked him in the eye like an honest man would, trying to read his face as to his real intent for asking me.

"It was the best sleep I've had in months."

"Good!" he said, like a man who was satisfied to hear that his guest had enjoyed the comforts of his hospitality. For some reason none of us mentioned the ayahuasca that we had drunk.

"I've been thinking of what you told me last nite," he said. Then silence, a long period of silence as we walked down the beach for a half a mile or so together. All of a sudden Edgar said to me, "I have a book in my possession." Not waiting for me to ask him about it, he began to tell me about the author and the book. "It's the work of an Englishman who had studied in India...the philosophy of Tantra and its application. He also studied entheogenics, Eastern and Mideastern thoughts on ecstasy and euphoria. His studies included lucid dreaming, mutual hypnosis, mutual dreaming and hypnagogic sex.

Dr. Panukla

"The book was written by a Doctor Panukla, more than likely a pseudonym to protect him from the despite of the Victorians. His work speaks quite frankly and openly on how to enter the dreams of one who is asleep (man or woman). How to be able to stimulate and direct your dreams and reap the pleasures of nocturnal lovemaking. It's a treatise on making love without the inhibitions and the debilitating mumbo jumbo of conscious existence. He was a contemporary of Freud, and speculation has it that Freud was influenced by the work but for fear of shocking the scientific community of the time, backed off from taking Panukla's discoveries to their logical conclusion.

As we walked down the beach front, Edgar continued to lay out the subject matter of the book. "I feel the real intention of the book was to allow sex to overcome the restrictions placed on it. Its intent was to fully explore the possibilities of having sex while asleep with your partner, and both enjoying each other in total abandonment."

"I've never heard of such a thing," I told Edgar. "It sounds like a fairy tale made up to suit the dreamers of the world."

"No," Edgar said, "I first came upon the thought when I was studying in Rome and had access to the Vatican library. In my readings I came upon the existence of a religious cult, the Cathari that flourished from the 5th Century A.D. till they were eradicated in the Middle Ages. They had practiced hypnagogic sex. They never called it that, but it was the same thing. They had, by the study and belief in Isis, the Egyptian goddess of love, discovered the purity of union in the innocence of sleep. Unfortunately for humanity the Cathari were almost totally exterminated in the Albigensian Crusade of 1230, and their name exists only in the records of the Inquisition or so it had been thought. It seems that during the period of the Arab invasion of Sicily, a group of Cathari had been captured and transported back to Damascus to the court of the Caliph al-Walid, where they revealed their secrets on hypnagogic sex to the Caliph in return for their freedom to practice their religion.

"It was in the Caliph's writings that Dr. Panukla read that the Caliph's observations of his wives in sleep coincided with the revelations of the Cathari on hypnagogic sex.

Dr. Panukla felt that the women of the harem had discovered hypnagogic sex by the usage of the Tabernanthe iboga tea, a beta-carboline plant that had been in use in Africa for millenniums for dream stimulation and visionary direction, similar to the ayahuasca."

I spent the rest of the morning talking with Edgar on the subject of hypnagogic sex and the possibility of introducing my wife to it.

There was a great difference between Edgar and Peter, Eti and Sissy. Eti and Sissy were both modern women, but Sissy was so brutal in her sex, it was loaded with hatred, with a sense of getting even. Eti's love was soft, tender, sensitive, composed in a dream world, possibly allowing her a greater variety of males without the complications of consciousness and a psychology filled with guilt, moral indignation and fear of detection. If Eti knew the way to come to me in a dream state, the second greatest revolution in sex since the discovery of sex face-to-face had taken place. It seemed that no other period in history would have such shocking consequences as to how man and woman would see themselves.

How envious one could become of Edgar! He had it all put together, a person in command of his world and a woman who was part of it. He looked satisfied and content. He had everything to the last detail. A location next to the ever-moody ocean, a woman the gods would envy him for, secrets that expanded his life beyond the clock and the hum of the daily drum beating in his ears. I realized how shallow my existence was, how much I needed another way of life. It wasn't just sex I was deprived of, I needed ecstasy to engulf me, to transport me, to elevate me to beauty I had never thought possible.

After lunch Edgar brought out Dr. Panukla's leather-bound mysterious-looking book. He carried it with the tenderness of a knight carrying the Holy Grail, ready to share with another member of the Knights' Templar, the ultimate truth. "Here," Edgar told me, "spend the rest of the afternoon enjoying it or for that matter take as long as you want." He handed me the book and left for an afternoon walk on the beach.

For the next three days I read and took notes on the work of Dr. Panukla. I had no other visits from Eti in my dreams. What was interesting, the ayahuasca drink did not appear again nor did anyone mention it, but I knew that her appearance in my dream was facilitated by the secrets that somehow survived the religious inquisitions of the medieval period and the scientific inquisitions of modern times. I knew that the secrets of hypnagogic sex were now in the hands of Edgar and Eti. Edgar knew I had no time to waste. I threw myself into the study of the book and he left me alone to do it.

I would stay in my room and come out only to use the toilet and eat. Eti would prepare lunch and dinner and I would eat with her and Edgar, then excuse myself and enter into the world of Dr. Panukla's work. The next nite I went to sleep hoping that I would have a visit from Edgar's dear wife. Desire has no guilt, it has need. Eti had come to me…how she did it, I really didn't understand, but I wanted it to happen again, and again, but nothing happened. Was it that my desires weren't strong enough to conjure her? Was it merely a one-shot deal by Edgar, letting me know that he had mastered the secret that Doctor Panukla talked about? Was it that my guitar didn't lead the way with tones and rhythms that turned into visual symbols and physical sensations? Was it all a waste of time, even thinking of it? Were dreams desires from some hidden world that somehow manifested as a theatrical presentation with the taking of the ayahuasca?

The next day Edgar gave me one more piece of advice before I left. "You have to have a willing partner," he said, "By yourself nothing can happen. Both wills must be for the purpose of one event."
This I felt was impossible. Nomi had fallen prey to sleep. I was eradicated from the scene by sleep. As far as I knew or could understand, I had no sexual existence for her anymore. There was no willing partner, there was only a reluctant wife.

I was determined to break that barrier. I could stimulate her while she was asleep and evoke, in her dream world, a lover who would be me. Oh what a glorious feeling, I thought, to be able to go to bed at nite knowing that this was the nite that the gates of heaven would open, and I would be ushered by the goddess Aphrodite herself into the ecstatic domain of the gods.

I never dreamt that trying to make love to my wife while she slept would lead me to being charged with rape. I no more felt like a rapist than Genghiz Khan felt like a saint. To be truthful, I knew that my life would change, but as to how it would change one never knows. I was in possession of information that wasn't merely facts that you forget, it was a view of life that precedes great revolutionary changes. For me life could never be the same again, knowing that a flicker away existed a world that made what I had ever known before, pure absurdity.

The Nite I Was Arrested

A woman who will not love up her husband
creates a monster

My disappointment was quick

A hollowed-out human

The reality of a shared dream consciousness

Oneirogenesis through bioprogramming

The ethics of hypnagogic sex

The sexual organ at sleep

Ayahuasca

The nite before my arrest is the hardest to talk about, because I'm not really sure what took place from Saturday nite into Sunday morning when the police arrested me on the charge of raping my wife.

It was a densely confused world I had entered into. A world where reality hinged on dreams, dark shadows, phantasies and the invocation of pleasure. What is real and what isn't depends merely on the explanations one gives to reality. The event I'm trying to describe fits perfectly into this philosophical problem that has confused not only philosophers, but clergymen, lawyers, and poor bastards like me since the beginning of time. I don't know now, at the present, if what took place actually took place in the world we call the world of consciousness or was totally manifested in the "Other World" of the dream. If I attempt to tell the arresting authorities that the event actually took place in a mutual dream, I might escape the charges of rape by being sent to the madhouse.

The laws of reality dictate that if two people share an event, the event can be looked at objectively.

In the dream world that I claim we had entered, and where the event took place, we shared a mutual dream together, a collective event that was purely subjective and yet both of us experienced it as an objective reality.

We shared our passions in a dream. It was what Edgar said, the world of hypnagogic sex. But something went wrong under the influence of chemical alteration, she was for some reason startled from her dream sex. She came out of the warmth of her dream into the cold consciousness of our bedroom. The enormity of the situation must have blown her over. Something had happened, the symbols must have changed, the images weren't the same. I might have given her a larger potion of the ayahuasca than she could handle. The darkness of the Amazon was re-created in her imaginative existence through the ayahuasca plant genetics while I was making love to her. It might be that she found herself in the jungles being confronted by a huge python or maybe a killer cat stalking her. I really don't know, but I will make an attempt to describe what took place from the day I arrived from Gaviota till I was arrested a week later.

A woman who will not love up her husband creates a monster
It was 6:30 P.M. on a foggy Saturday afternoon. I had just arrived from my trip to Edgar's house in Gaviota. I had misplaced my house keys and had to ring the doorbell. Nomi opened up the door. She just stood there like a piece of sculptured ice. Two sounds grated out of her mouth like 2 chunks of ice falling on my head.
"Oh...hi." Nothing more came out of her mouth for at least another hour, while I unpacked my traveling bag, lit up a bowlful and put my guitar away. She stood silently at the kitchen counter and slowly prepared dinner. Two cans of tuna, a can of precooked macaroni and cheese, and slowly mixed it all in the bowl like one would prepare the dinner for the dog or the goddamn cat. She placed that gruel in front of me and we sat down to eat that shit in a state of togetherness.

The silence became a thunder in my ears. Through the whole dinner not once did she ask me what I did, or who I saw, while I was visiting Edgar at Gaviota. This wasn't anger I was looking at, it was total indifference. She stared at the gruel in front of her, and now and then she'd throw a look of empty recognition towards me, as if I had just gone in the shithouse and came out a week later to sit down for dinner.

I tried to make conversation with her. When I asked her about her job, she mumbled semicoherent sentences about her work and about her boss, the hooked-nose, beady-eyed insurance peddler. She pushed her plate of dog food to the side, yawned a few times and got up, walked over to the big bay window and stood there staring out at the glowing city beneath us. She stood there in silence, her hands stuffed in the pockets of her nitegown, her shoulders drooped in misery. Then she turned around, walked over to the couch and sat down again. I wanted to pray to the powers-that-be that some heavenly force would intervene and break the coldness that was freezing my soul.

She started yawning, over and over her mouth opened and shut, then finally the long-awaited string of words came out of her mouth.

"I'm tired. I think I'll go to bed early tonite." She got up and was gone before I could tell her good nite.

I stood staring out the bay window at the city below me, glowing in the electric soup that once I found so beautiful, and now the same view was so depressing.

I had returned home with a feeling of excitement as if I had discovered another law that lay hidden in the universe. I felt like the alchemist did when he first discovered the properties of getting high off distilled alcohol. I felt excited. I wanted to share my discoveries of hypnagogic sex with my wife…but sharing has to begin in the form of sharing something. Begins somewhere but where?

My disappointment was quick

Her face was a blank. Her voice was cold. Her eyes were empty. How did I find this woman so attractive, so beautiful, so desirable, so pleasurable when I first met her in the Glen that day? How my thoughts on pleasure changed since I began living with her! Was marriage such a painful state of familiarity that one ends up, by necessity, developing a mental condition to soothe the agony of existence? I had developed, in the year that I lived with her, a painful addiction to her silent rejection. It had become the fuel to my imagination. Not only the painful exhilaration of rejection but also the immediate suspicion that it gives birth to. I had developed a perfect system for emotional destruction. I had, by some strange mixture of thought, somehow united inside of me a bizarre emotional ecosystem of desperate feelings that interfed each other.

Three distinct feelings converged on me daily. Their duration merely depended on how much time I spent on each one of them.

My day would begin with a long, studied, detailed coverage of her rejection. This included the study of her face, body, what she said or didn't say, the intonation of the words. This would occupy most of my morning. The afternoon was spent going over all the information that had fed my curiosity that morning. Every rejection found a corresponding suspicion. Every suspicious detail became just one more excruciating step up Mount Ararat in search of the Lost Ark.

The evening I usually spent with the terrifying chimera of my own imagination. Seeing her getting screwed by this anonymous lover, this faceless motherfucker who was hiding in the fabric of my life. He had settled permanently in my brain as my wife's lover, and now out of habit I entertained him faithfully every day.

Some days my suspicions demanded such concentration that I thought I would drown in the dung heap of my misery. In the depths of my soul I feared that I had become a cunt lackey, a slave to the woman's favors, a flunky to her moods, a peasant in the bedroom of hope. Like an indignant beggar I searched for a mysterious lover who I felt was plundering the cave of gold that belonged to me.

A hollowed-out human

A world of anger, rejection, disappointment, kept filling the well of my imagination. I knew that indifference was the only antidote to this situation, but how could I become indifferent?

The purpose to my life with Nomi was impassioned concern and the desire I had for her love. Though this might sound like a contradiction, she visually stimulated my desire to have her. But all desire has a corresponding flaw...her personality and her indifference frustrated me and gave me emotional pains. These 2 contradictory conditions existed side by side, and I could find no tool of logic to separate them. I was being driven to seek out the only solution possible...indifference.

I wondered as to how I could become indifferent when my eyes enjoyed looking at her body.

The way she moved her body made me want to grab her. The shape of her calves, the smoothness of her thighs, her curved hips, the small waist. She visually reminded me of spring, of fresh winds blowing through the leaves, of ponds filling with running water. The promise of a hot summer coming as each day turned into a warm nite.

I wanted to lift her dress and look at her, touch her, kiss her. The minute I became indifferent it would all end, the desire would end, the pleasure my eyes gave me would end, the touch of my fingers which guided me to the softness of her breast, the pliability of her ass…these were pleasures that only the female could give me, and they would cease to exist.
I didn't want to lose those pleasures.

The fact that I didn't find someone else in our laundry or in between the bedsheets inflated my frustration even more. I felt my own stupidity. Either I was too stupid to catch them or too stupid to see that daily existence had sapped the life out of her, leaving her as a hollowed-out human with no desire other than to sleep. No matter what the reasons for her rejection were, I still received the same punishment from a hollowed-out human, a creature emptied of desire, love, instincts, passion…a hollowed-out human whose only salvation is to enter the dream world of Dr. Panukla and to seek her pleasure in hypnagogic lovemaking.

The reality of a shared dream consciousness
I would have to relearn, along with Nomi, how to give less attention and credibility to the world of our senses, and deal more with the possibilities and pleasures of our dreams. I could see that there was no other alternative, either I united somewhere with Nomi or Nomi would become history. She would be carted off to the memory dump where discarded romances end up.

I was ready to enter into the world of hypnagogic sex. The little bottle of the ayahuasca elixir that Edgar gave me was in the top drawer of my dresser, like holy water, waiting to transform the most vulgar into the realm of sanctity. But like all beginners I made the fatal error, I didn't know the sequence of events. Edgar had given me the ayahuasca with the advice that if I did use it, to make sure it was in a ceremonious setting. But what was a ceremonious setting? Was there a ritual that went along with the elixir? Was there a story that was necessary to create a reality?

The nite I was with Edgar's wife Eti…the nite that I had her in my dream…did I unknowingly participate in some sort of a ceremony before entering the dream? I played the same scene out in my head over and over, trying to understand the exact movements that took place that nite.

Oneirogenesis through bioprogramming
I remember Edgar telling me that reality was a shared consciousness, that visions could be shared, that the participants had to prepare themselves in order to enter the dream world. Both man and woman would have to bioprogram themselves through meditation, the taking of entheogenic plants, mutual hypnosis, chants, sensory touching, and other activities that help to find the way through *mindfulness* to the "Other World" where ecstasy and euphoria exist.

I had asked Edgar if I had entered the Other World. He didn't answer me. He avoided the question purposely. It would have been so much easier for me had he just said yes or no, but he must have withheld his answer in fear that I might consider him a third party involved in having his wife debauched by his guest, the way Peter did with Sissy. This could raise ethical issues as to the responsibility for one's conduct in a dream.

The ethics of hypnagogic sex
It was evident that Edgar and his wife had studied the dream world or the Other World and had become participants in the art of hypnagogic sex.

It was in a dream that Eti came to me and took command. But did we both enter into each other's dream world? I dreamt of her, but did she dream of me? Did I enter her dream world as a mutual dreamer or did she stay in this world and enter my Other World by manually stimulating me, by rubbing the kundalini gland in my rectum or masturbating me as I slept? Did she touch, poke, lick, and squeeze the proper erogenous zones peculiar to a man's anatomy, while Edgar sat in a chair, directing and instructing her in the techniques and the mysteries of the nocturnal dream world? I wanted to ask Edgar these questions but I didn't know how. What if I was wrong in my assessments? Nevertheless the important question on my mind now was centered on one issue. Could I enter and get involved in the Other World's sex with my own woman?

To the faithful, not only is the dream world a place of prophecy but it's also the world where great decisions are made, great inventions created, hidden laws discovered, where women appear to hold you, love you, and offer themselves. Edgar told me that "One's own psychic sense will govern the amount of ecstasy that can be attained from a mutual dream." I felt like pleasure was going to be born not merely from my Nomi, but from within me, from the experience of experiencing myself.

At times Nomi looked dead to me as she slept. She must have been within that part of sleep that was connected with the Other World. It was devoid of snores and slurps, teeth snarling and an occasional fart...a whiff...a move. She was in that part of sleep where the face took on the tranquility of a doll's face. A perfect stillness. This might be The Sacred Moment...when Nomi was dreaming of her lover who appeared to her, disguised as a lowly shoe salesman or maybe as a shepherd, a staff in his hand, a look of need on his face.

There have been many women in the past that have been had while they slept. Christ was conceived in a dream, so were Leda's two daughters, Helen of Troy and her sister Clytemnestra, the wife of Agamemnon. Zeus came to Leda's dream disguised as a swan, and impregnated her with the fluids of a god. Evidently the gods knew a way to enter into the dream world of humans, and also found a way to impregnate them in that world of dreams. "We know that gods can do it, and men and gods," Edgar says, "are of the same family...we owe the breath of life to the same mother."

I sat on the couch and looked out the bay window at San Francisco beneath me. The apartment was dark and I waited, like a burglar, till she had fallen asleep. When the snoring stopped I knew she was deep into the Other World. Then I took my clothes off, crawled into the bed and lay, like a trained dog, next to her naked body. I wasn't in any hurry. I would take my time and develop the conditions necessary to make love to her while she was asleep.

I let my hand softly touch her knee, then very tenderly, like a butterfly nestled amongst the petals, I fluttered up her thigh and onto her nest, resting my hand on her ever-vigilant cunt, hoping that it would become familiar to my hand like a dog does the hand of a stranger. I remembered an old saying, "He who hesitates is lost, and he who hurries stumbles." I would be persistent but patient. I would leave my hand on her body until it felt as comfortable to her as the nipples on her breasts.

I fell asleep next to her with my engine throbbing at a fast idle, or as the Bible would say, with a fire in my loins, hoping that I would open up the oneiritic channels in our dream world.
I did this routine nitely for a period of seven days. I would get into bed and lie quietly next to her. I would follow the same path to the *cueva de oro,* and then rest my hand on her divine mat of silken golden hair, letting it tickle the palm of my hand. I let my middle finger rest gently near her sensitive clitoris. What a wonderful feeling. I was doing it the way Dr. Panukla's illustrations demonstrated in his chapter "How to begin the stimulation of the ever-vigilant vagina." How could I fail? It was chiseled in stone, written in the book of *The Sleeping Woman…the secrets of making love while mutually dreaming.*

I was as gentle as a leaf falling in an autumn breeze. Everything seemed to be going fine. During the day I would spend time going over the oncoming evening's performance and procedures.

I rubbed her clitoris as was suggested with a very lite pressure, which I increased ever so softly.
I developed a circular clockwise motion ever so delicately, then reversing to counter clockwise, stopping every few seconds so as not to irritate the organ and to allow it to become self-generating, to come alive, to vibrate, to vulvate, to lubricate, to do what it is that a cunt does when it comes to life and wants a hard object to enter it and become one with it.

The sexual organ at sleep

I heard many men say that they fingered their women while they were asleep, making them hotter than the fires of hell. I heard men say that they had awakened and found their pricks as hard as shovel handles in the mouths of their beloved wives. Maybe these were exaggerations, because Nomi didn't respond to the A's, B's and C's of Dr. Panukla's book, nor to what Dr. Boyle had taught me, nor to what Edgar had told me.

I waited for the magic to happen, and like the believer who patiently waits for the miracle to take place soon, I waited on the walkway to the holy shrine. I read and reread the works of Dr. Panukla. Over and over I heard the experienced words of Edgar come into focus. Contrary to Dr. Panukla's argument that the sexual organ of a woman is ever-vigilant, Nomi's sexual organ was asleep.

The great divine opening showed no evident response. It might be that she needed the tongue to bless it with words, warm exhalations, and vibrant aspirations. To salivate it back into the world of need and desire.

Maybe it was my misfortune that Nomi was the exception to the general law. With all the fingering I had given her, the snoring was still going on and her sleep was very deep. I must be patient, I thought, the next few days would be crucial.

I felt that the nitely masturbations I had given her had prepared Nomi's body for the ayahuasca. Either the oneiritic channels would be opened or I had wasted 7 nites in preparation to enter her.

Ayahuasca

On the Great Nite, the nite that the great event was to take place, I gave her 5 mg of ayahuasca in a cup of strong espresso coffee that I made for both of us. I didn't know if the coffee would alter the mixture, the potency, or add to the elevation of the vision. There was no way I could know unless I took the same amount in a cup with her. The coffee disguised the bitter flavor…and I hoped it prepared us for the evening to come.

"I feel funny," she told me. I waited, with my breath locked in a canister deep inside my stomach, for something to happen. It was like trying to sneak into a vault that had an alarm installed to prevent a nite crawler from entering.

I tried to reproduce the same events that took place at Edgar's house a week before. I had played the guitar for Edgar and Eti with a feeling of passion. The tones were constructed from some inner need that made it possible to turn words into tonal visions. But tonite the events weren't going right. I could feel it. I was thinking about things. I was planning, scheming, constructing. In the world of dreams nothing goes right if you have to think.

"I feel funny," she told me again, and got up and headed for the couch. I remember when I first took the ayahuasca, I felt like I was going to vomit and my muscles became rigid for a few moments, but it passed as I drifted into the Other World.

I should have stopped and not gone any further. I should have told her that I was giving her ayahuasca. I should have been up front with her, but mistakes take place when the details are overlooked. I wanted an easy way to have my wife and there was no easy way.

"It's the strong coffee," I told her. Every explanation I gave made the scheme more desperate.

"I have to go to bed," she said, "God I feel funny." She got up from the couch and headed for the bedroom. I followed her and watched her hit the bed. In a few moments she was in a dead sleep. I was starting to feel the effects of the ayahuasca. A peculiar feeling in my stomach, a dryness in my mouth. A feeling of dizziness...lite-headedness and a tightness in my muscles. It didn't feel the way it felt at Edgar's place, something was different. I felt alone and the feelings were merely physical.

I lay on the bed next to her, hoping that the dream world would consume both of us like a blaze in the middle of the nite.

I stared at the ceiling. The nitelite from the bathroom made patterns on the wall. I could hear the wind blowing outside. I could see leaves, trees, visual mumbo jumbo.

I must have fallen asleep, but I hadn't passed into the dream world because I awoke in the middle of the nite trembling. Nothing had happened, no visions appeared. I hadn't dreamt of her nor did I feel she had dreamt of me...she had crawled inside the covers of the bed and was in a deep snoring binge.

The next nite I decided to try again. This time I would try to copy everything that had happened at Edgar's house. I prepared the same dinner Eti had made, roasted lamb along with the green sensimillan indica, wine, and the ayahuasca elixir waiting in its little flask. I don't know why I never told Nomi about the ayahuasca. I probably felt that she would say no and kill the possibilities. The longer you hide something, the harder it is to reveal it. Maybe I didn't want to reveal to her the emotional plight she had driven me to.

We ate, drank and for the first time in months we started to talk. The conversation was really about odds and ends, but better than nothing. We talked about what most people talk about. Car needing tires, getting a laundry-washer and dryer, when was my next recital coming up. Having a conversation is really a work of art. Unless you're willing to go to the depths of your existence, a conversation can be a ride in a car with all the tires flat.

After dinner and a bottle of Chianti wine, I loaded the pipe and took a long pull on it and handed to her. "Maybe I shouldn't," she said, "I have to go to work tomorrow."
"Just a little toke to polish out the nite."

I handed her the pipe and she took one little hit and handed it back to me.
"You want more wine?" I asked her, "Or do you want me to make coffee for you?"
"I had enough, anymore wine will give me a headache, coffee will keep me awake." I couldn't think of anything that I could pass the elixir in without spilling the plot. Goddamn her, even when she didn't know it, the bastard was a killjoy.

Just as I was ready to give up, she changed her mind and asked me to make a cup of espresso for her. "I might as well go all the way," she told me in a voice loaded with resignation, apathy, indifference. For a moment I felt like telling her to go fuck herself, but I had come this far, I might as well go to the end of the line. I was obsessed with her, and I'd let myself get involved in some cheap plot that really didn't make sense. I was drugging up my own wife so I could screw her. I should have followed my instinct and got as far away from her as my money could take me. I was betting on a dead horse. I was trying to revive a dead feeling. Everything was decaying around me. It really didn't make any difference why she was the way she was…she was what I didn't want anymore.

It was some great mind that said it, and I'm sure that it could be found in some fortune cookie:

What one second can bring, a life time can't undo.

I poured the ayahuasca in her coffee. I added a little bit more than what Edgar had poured for me. I watched her take it down. I waited and really I didn't know what I was waiting for. I didn't know what would happen other than her yawning, stretching her arms, telling me she should get to bed, or that she felt funny. My only hope was like that of someone who had spent all week working on an engine now puts the key in the ignition and prays it will start.

A few moments went by and she said nothing. I watched her like a child watching snowflakes fall outside his window, with a curiosity as to how long will it be before Santa brings the toys. Her eyes were glazed but that was from the divine sensimillan. The god of the vine was yet to make his appearance.

I watched her face begin twitching, her lower lip kept moving without saying a word. "Let's go lie down," I told her. She looked at me as if she was looking at a stranger. Maybe if she saw me as a stranger she would become excited...most sex dreams are about strangers, people we don't know who come into our Other World for a few moments then leave.

We both headed for the bedroom. I lay on the bed and watched her take her clothes off. She didn't utter a sound nor did she look at me. She took her clothes off slowly and lay on the bed next to me. If we were going to do it in our dreams, clothes had no meaning. She was naked and I was dressed. I had taken the elixir and I felt as if I was ready to enter a dream state with a hardon tempered by Hephaestus in the fires of hell.

I didn't know if I had lain on the bed for a minute or an hour or half the nite. Time and the events that are regulated by time had become meaningless. I didn't know if I was in a dream. Everything seemed so real. I felt the soft naked flesh of a woman roll over on top of me. I felt the warmth of her naked breast on my lips. Her flesh vibrated with every beat of her heart. She took her hand and unzippered my pants. I could see her doing it in the glow of the nite. I put my arm over her naked body as she pulled my engine out of its stall. I rolled her over and started kissing her, my heart beating in my chest like an army of addicts wanting to grab the opiate of life. The dam had broken from a trickle of piss to a roaring cascade of white foam.

A soft nitelite cast a glow over the bed. My dream had the perfection of the nite. I could see her in front of me like a shadow lying on the bed waiting, her legs spread apart like the wings of a swallow, a silent beckoning to mount her while her wings wrapped around my shoulders, and like Icarus, I ascended to the heavens to find my love.

She grabbed me by my balls. The pain made me scream. No sooner had the last breath of agony escaped from my mouth when I felt a warm sense of pleasure overcome me. The thought of her wanting me made me feel as if I wanted to be devoured...to be eaten up alive. She scratched me and bit me. Every painful bite gave me a pleasure beyond what I had ever experienced. She squeezed harder and I trembled with agony. She started to scream. My dream had become an orgy of utter abandonment.

"You bastard," she screamed. I was on fire.
Only in a dream can one feel such excitement.

My tool was in her. I rammed it with the force of an earthquake. I felt her hand reach down. I left my swollen rod in her divine altar as she gulped for air. In a dream, time is so distorted and insignificant, the sequences from one event to another don't follow the rules of logic. One minute I was in her wet cunt, the next moment I was in her wet mouth. How I got from one place to another belongs to the logic of dreams. There were no poetic words, no words of love exchanged. Only grunts and the action that one only dreams about.

She pushed me and shoved me as if she was trying to unsaddle me. I grabbed her tits and tried to hold on. She took my hand and pushed it away. The thought of her struggling to avoid my lovemaking wasn't even a possibility in my dream world. She was on fire, the elixir had worked. She was like the mysterious Jaguar of the Amazonian jungle. The ayahuasca had genetical properties that re-created the wonders of the forest. I could feel her hand strike me. Her nails dug deep into my flesh. In a few moments I would be torn apart and left in a heap of unrecognizable flesh. This was the woman I had fallen in love with, this is what it was like at the beginning…passion at the outer limits of human capabilities.

I was in a state of a high fascination. Love in the dream world, a world that had no bounds, no parameters, no conceivable limitations other than the limit of the imagination. All one had to do was to enter it. How beautiful. What freedom, what an escape from the inhibitions of rejection. In my mind the dream existed outside the elements of time, the logic of daily life and the need for correctness.

I felt that I had connected our 2 dream worlds together. I was having Nomi while she was asleep, and with a little effort on both our parts, she would always be ready for me when I wanted her. We both could have what we wanted...life to its fullest. We could with some effort overcome our meager existence, which depended so much on our energy. We could enjoy a blissful sexual world, where the only limits would be imposed by our feeble imaginations.

I awoke, and the police had me in handcuffs. I was drug out of the house and put in a black and white patrol car. Her screams transformed bliss into horror, beauty into disgust. I was a character in some tragic play written by a demented mind. I was arrested for raping my wife while both of us were asleep. I was fingerprinted, mug shot and thrown into the lockup.

How strange the workings of fate. What began on a beautiful morning, that day in the park, has transformed itself into a horror show of which I cannot even see or imagine the end.